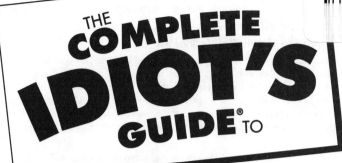

THE **COMPLETE IDIOT'S GUIDE**® TO

Computer Basics

Third Edition

by Joe Kraynak

ALPHA

A member of Penguin Group (USA) Inc.

To my kids, Nick and Ali, who constantly inspire me to keep up with the latest technology.

Copyright © 2003 by Kraynak Enterprises, Incorporated

THE COMPLETE IDIOT'S GUIDE TO and Design are registered trademarks of Penguin Group (USA) Inc.

International Standard Book Number: 1-59257-168-9
Library of Congress Catalog Card Number: 2003112979

06   05   04   8   7   6   5   4   3

Interpretation of the printing code: The rightmost number of the first series of numbers is the year of the book's printing; the rightmost number of the second series of numbers is the number of the book's printing. For example, a printing code of 03-1 shows that the first printing occurred in 2003.

Printed in the United States of America

Note: This publication contains the opinions and ideas of its author. It is intended to provide helpful and informative material on the subject matter covered. It is sold with the understanding that the author and publisher are not engaged in rendering professional services in the book. If the reader requires personal assistance or advice, a competent professional should be consulted.

Most Alpha books are available at special quantity discounts for bulk purchases for sales promotions, premiums, fund-raising, or educational use. Special books, or book excerpts, can also be created to fit specific needs.

For details, write: Special Markets, Alpha Books, 375 Hudson Street, New York, NY 10014.

Publisher: *Marie Butler-Knight*
Product Manager: *Phil Kitchel*
Senior Managing Editor: *Jennifer Chisholm*
Acquisitions Editor: *Mikal E. Belicove*
Development Editor: *Ginny Bess Munroe*
Senior Production Editor: *Christy Wagner*
Copy Editor: *Drew Patty*
Illustrator: *Chris Eliopoulos*
Cover/Book Designer: *Trina Wurst*
Indexer: *Heather McNeil*
Layout/Proofreading: *John Etchison, Ayanna Lacey*

Contents at a Glance

Contents

Introduction

A funny thing happened on the way to the twenty-first century. Computers became more human. By "human," I don't mean "humanoid." I only mean that the computer has evolved from being a stodgy office tool to a revolutionary home appliance, a device designed to help us manage and enjoy our lives more fully.

Sure, you can still use a computer to type and print a letter, but the latest computer technology can completely revolutionize your professional and personal life. Here's just a glimpse of what you can do with a computer, an Internet connection, and some additional equipment:

- Compose letters, create custom publications, and print envelopes and labels for mass mailings.

- Decorate your documents with professional clip art and other graphics.

- Shop at mega-malls and specialty shops without leaving your home, and save money, too!

- Send and receive mail electronically—no postage, and same-day delivery.

- Carry on conversations with friends, relatives, and complete strangers anywhere in the world—without paying long-distance charges.

- Plan your vacation, get medical advice, and find maps to nearly any location.

- Copy music clips from the Internet and from your CD collection and burn your own custom CDs.

- Take photos with a digital camera, transfer them to your computer, make prints, or e-mail photos to your friends and family.

- Create your own websites or blogs (web logs) to express your views, communicate with family and friends, or market your products and services.

- Edit your home videos and copy your video clips to CDs, DVDs, or VHS tapes.

- Find a mate. (I do recommend meeting in person before you make any commitments.)

Sounds pretty cool, huh? Well, it is—assuming, of course, that you know what you're doing. In order to master the high-tech world of computers and electronic gadgets, you must first master the basics. You need to know your way around a computer, how to point and click with a mouse, how to run programs in Windows, and how to enter commands. Once you've mastered a few basics, as explained in the first few chapters of this book, you will be well prepared to explore and exploit the full power of your computer and the Internet as you proceed through later chapters.

Welcome to *The Complete Idiot's Guide to Computer Basics, Third Edition*

Most computer documentation is based on the assumption that you, the user, are the computer's servant. The documentation lists the parts of the computer and explains how each part works, as if you purchased a computer to impress your friends and neighbors rather than to perform a particular job.

The Complete Idiot's Guide to Computer Basics, Third Edition, is different. Instead of installing the computer as your master, this book places *you* in charge of the computer. This book assumes that you want to do something practical with your computer, and it shows you how to use your computer as you would use any appliance in your home to perform practical, hands-on tasks. You'll learn how to do everything from typing and printing letters to editing videotapes.

What You Will Learn in This Book

You don't have to read this book from cover to cover (although you might miss some savvy tidbits if you skip around). If you just purchased a computer, start with Chapter 1 to learn how to get your computer up and running. If you need a quick lesson on using Windows, skip ahead to Chapter 3. If you need to get wired to the Internet, check out Chapter 16. To provide some structure for this hodgepodge of computer skills and techniques, I've divided this book into the following six parts:

Part 1, "Firing Up Your Computer: Bare-Bones Basics," covers the bare minimum: setting up and turning on your computer, dealing with Microsoft Windows, running programs, and managing the folders and files that are stored on your computer.

Part 2, "Personalizing Your Work Space," shows you how to take control of the Windows desktop (a virtual desktop on which you create documents and play games). Here, you learn how to pick a theme for your desktop, change the background, turn on a screen saver, configure the audio clips, install programs, and give yourself more room to work.

Part 3, "Creating Letters, Greeting Cards, and Other Documents," teaches you everything you need to know to type a letter, change the type size and style, center text, add clip art and other graphics, and print your letter. You also learn how to print envelopes and mailing labels and how to use a spreadsheet program to create accounting sheets that do your math for you.

Part 4, "Getting Wired to the Internet," launches you into the world of telecommunications. In this part, you find out how to select and install a modem, connect to an online service, surf the Internet, send and receive electronic mail, surf the World Wide Web, and much more.

Part 5, "Going Digital with Music, Photos, and Video," takes you on a tour of the wonderful world of digital audio, imaging, and video. Here you learn how to copy music clips from CDs and from the Internet to burn your own custom CDs and transfer music clips to a portable MP3 player; buy a digital camera and use it to snap and print photos and e-mail them to your friends and family; and use video-editing software to splice your home movie clips into a full-length motion picture.

Part 6, "Maintaining Your Investment," acts as your computer maintenance guide. Here, you learn how and when to clean your computer, how to give it regular tune-ups to keep it running like new, and how to upgrade your computer with more powerful components and useful accessories.

Conventions Used in This Book

I use several conventions in this book to make it easier to understand. For example, when you need to type something, here's how it appears:

```
type this
```

Just type what it says. It's as simple as that.

Likewise, if I tell you to select or click a command, the command appears in **bold.** This allows you to quickly scan a series of steps without having to reread all the text.

A plethora of margin notes and sidebars offer additional information about what you've just read. These boxes are distinguished by special icons that appear next to them:

Tech Term

In the computer industry, jargon and cryptic acronyms rule. When a computer term baffles you or an acronym annoys you, look to the Tech Term icon for a plain English definition.

Whoa!

Before you press that button, check out the Whoa! icons for precautionary notes. Chances are that I've made the same mistake myself. Let me tell you how to avoid the same blunder.

Inside Tip

When you've been in the computer business for as long as I have, you learn better ways to perform the same tasks and pick up information that helps you avoid common pitfalls. To share in my wealth of knowledge, check out my Inside Tips.

Computer Cheat

Do the steps required to perform a simple computer task seem convoluted? Then they probably are. Software programs commonly have hidden shortcuts that help you perform a task more efficiently. Check out the Computer Cheat icon for tips from the masters.

Panic Attack

You did everything right, but the same error message keeps popping up on your screen or, worse yet, nothing happens. When your computer or program does the unexpected, look to the panic attack icon for an explanation and a fix.

Acknowledgments

Several people had to don hard hats and get their hands dirty to build a better book. I owe special thanks to Mikal Belicove for choosing me to author this book and for handling the assorted details to get this book in gear. Thanks to Ginny Bess Munroe and Drew Patty for guiding the content of this book, keeping it focused on new users, ferreting out all my typos, and fine-tuning my sentences. Christy Wagner deserves a free trip to Aruba for shepherding the manuscript (and art) through production. The Alpha Books production team merits a round of applause for transforming a collection of electronic files into such an attractive book. I also owe special thanks to my agent, Neil Salkind, and the rest of the staff at Studio B for expertly managing my career.

Trademarks

All terms mentioned in this book that are known to be or are suspected of being trademarks or service marks have been appropriately capitalized. Alpha Books and Penguin Group (USA) Inc. cannot attest to the accuracy of this information. Use of a term in this book should not be regarded as affecting the validity of any trademark or service mark.

Part 1

Firing Up Your Computer: Bare-Bones Basics

Right after you purchase a car, the salesperson sits you down behind the wheel and shows you how to work the controls. You learn the essentials, such as how to tune the radio, activate cruise control, adjust the seat, and work the headlights and windshield wipers.

When you purchase a computer—a much more complicated piece of machinery—you're on your own. You get several boxes containing various gadgets and cables, and it's up to you to figure out how to connect everything, turn it on, and start using it.

To make up for this lack of guidance, this part acts as your personal tutor, leading you step by step through the process of setting up and starting your computer and using the controls (the keyboard and mouse) to run programs and enter commands.

Up and Running with Your Computer

In This Chapter

- Preparing a home for your computer
- Unpacking your computer's fragile components
- Plugging stuff in
- Turning everything on in the correct sequence
- Following the startup instructions (if there are any)

Bringing home your first computer is nearly as exhilarating and worrisome as adopting a puppy. You're excited, but you really don't know what to expect or how to get started. Where should you set up your computer? How do you connect everything? What's the proper sequence for turning on the parts? How do you respond to your computer the first time you start it?

This chapter shows you what to expect. Here, you learn how to prepare a space for your computer, set it up, and turn on everything in the correct sequence. This chapter also provides plenty of tips and tricks to help you be sure that you received everything you ordered, to test your computer, and to deal with the unexpected the first time you start your computer.

Finding a Comfortable Home for Your Computer

Your home seems spacious until you take delivery of a new sofa or entertainment center. Then you just can't figure out how you'll wedge that new piece of furniture into your existing collection. Likewise, few people spend much time considering where they're going to place their computer until they bring it into their home or office. In their haste to get the computer up and running, they might place the computer on a rickety card table in a dank room, where it teeters precariously until they get the time and money to set it up properly.

This is a risky strategy. Perching your computer on unstable furniture in a damp or dusty room can significantly reduce its life expectancy—not to mention your enjoyment of your computer. Think ahead and prepare your computer area *before* you start connecting components:

◆ Think about how you'll use your computer. If you intend to use it as a tool for the family, don't stick it in the basement next to that treadmill you never use. Place it in a room that's convenient for everyone and where you can supervise your kids.

Inside Tip

If you're in an old house and you're not sure if the outlet is grounded, go to the hardware store and buy an *outlet tester;* it has indicator lights that show if the outlet is properly wired.

◆ House the computer next to a grounded outlet that's *not* on the same circuit as a clothes dryer, air conditioner, or other power-hungry appliance. Power fluctuations can damage your computer and destroy files.

◆ Keep the computer away from magnetic fields created by fans, radios, large speakers, air conditioners, microwave ovens, and other appliances. Magnetic fields can mess up the display and erase data from your disks.

◆ Choose an area near a phone jack, or install an additional jack for your modem. (If you purchased the computer mainly for working on the Internet, consider installing a separate phone line for your modem.) If you plan on connecting to the Internet through your cable company, contact the cable company to install a cable connection near the computer.

◆ Place your computer in an environment that is clean, dry, cool, and out of direct sunlight. If you have no choice, cover the computer after turning it off to keep it clean. (Don't cover it when the power's on; it needs to breathe.)

◆ To reduce glare on the monitor, be sure it doesn't directly face a window or other source of bright light. Otherwise, the glare will make it difficult for you to see the screen.

◆ Give the computer room to breathe. The computer has fans and vents to keep it cool. If you block the vents, the computer might overheat.

Whoa! _____

To prevent lightning damage to your computer (which is usually excluded from manufacturer warranties), plug all your computer components into a high-quality *surge suppressor*. The surge suppressor should have a UL rating of 400 or less, an energy-absorption rating of 400 or more, and a warranty that covers damage to the surge suppressor *and* to your computer. If possible, use an outlet located on an inside wall to further reduce the likelihood that lightning will strike your computer.

Unpacking Your New Toys

When you bring your computer home (or when it's delivered), you will be tempted to tear open the boxes and unpack everything. Before you do, read the following list of precautions for unpacking and connecting your equipment:

◆ Take your time. It's easy to get flustered and make mistakes when you're in a hurry.

◆ Clear all drinks from the work area. You don't want to spill anything on your new computer.

◆ When unpacking your equipment, keep the boxes on the floor to avoid dropping any equipment from up high.

◆ If your computer arrives on a cold day, give the components two to three hours to adjust to the temperature and humidity in the room. Any condensation needs to dissipate before you turn on the power.

◆ Don't cut the boxes. Carefully peel off the packing tape. This serves two purposes: It reduces the risk of your hacking through a cable or scratching a device, and it keeps the boxes in good condition in case you need to return a device to the manufacturer.

◆ If you have trouble pulling a device, such as a monitor, out of the box, turn the box on its side and slide the device out onto the floor. Don't flip over the box and try to pull the box off the device.

◆ Save all the packing material, including the Styrofoam and bubble wrap. Many manufacturers accept returns only if you return the device as it was originally packed. The packing material is also useful if you need to move your computer to a different home or office later.

♦ Read the packing list(s) thoroughly to be sure you received everything you ordered. If something is missing, contact the manufacturer or dealer *immediately*.

♦ Find all the cables. The cables are often stored in a separate compartment at the bottom of the box. They're easy to overlook. (Some cables, including the all-important printer cable, might not be included.)

♦ Inspect the cables. Look for cuts in the cables, and check for bent pins on the connectors. Although you can straighten the pins using tweezers or needle-nose pliers, you can easily snap off a pin, voiding the warranty. If you find a bent or damaged pin, call the manufacturer. The manufacturer probably will instruct you to straighten the pin, but then if it breaks, it's the manufacturer's fault.

♦ Remove any spacers or packing materials from the disk drives and printer. Cardboard or plastic spacers are commonly used to keep parts from shifting during shipping. To avoid damaging your new equipment, remove these spacers before you turn on your computer.

Inside Tip

As you dig through the boxes, find the warranty forms, fill them out, and mail them in. This ensures that if a device goes belly-up within the warranty period, the company will fix or replace the device. Taking time now to complete the forms could save you hundreds of dollars down the road.

♦ Unlock any devices that might have been locked for shipping. Some scanners, for instance, have a switch that locks the scanner's carriage in place. That switch might be at the back or bottom of the scanner.

♦ Don't force anything. Plugs should slide easily into outlets. If you have to force something, the prongs are probably not aligned with the holes they're supposed to go in. Forcing the plug will break the prongs.

♦ Don't turn on *anything* until *everything* is connected. On some computers, you can safely plug in devices when the power is on, but check the manual to be sure.

Identifying Your Computer's Parts and Appendages

A computer is not a single entity, like a refrigerator or a TV set. A typical computer consists of several components that contribute to its operation and performance. As you work through this chapter to connect the components, you must be able to identify each component and know its common name. Figure 1.1 points out the key parts.

The central component of all computers is the *system unit*, which contains the brains and memory of the computer and the disk drives where data is stored. All other components are considered *peripheral devices*, and they plug directly or indirectly into the system unit. These include the keyboard and mouse that you use to enter commands and data; the monitor, which enables you to see what you're doing; the speakers that provide audio feedback; the printer, which enables you to make paper copies of the documents you create; and the modem, which connects the computer to the Internet. (The modem may be built right into the system unit.) Peripheral devices also include joysticks for playing games, digital cameras, scanners, and a host of other electronic gadgets.

System unit   Monitor   Printer

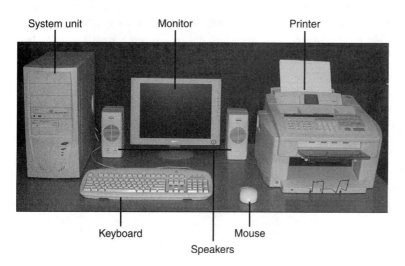

Keyboard   Mouse

Speakers

Figure 1.1

A computer consists of several parts.

Making the Right Connections

When everything is unpacked, arrange all the devices on your desk. If you connect the devices before arranging them, you'll tangle the cables. If you have a standard desktop unit (rare these days), you can place the monitor on top of it. If you have a mini-tower or full tower system unit, you can set it on the floor to conserve desk space. (If the floor is carpeted, set the unit on an anti-static pad to prevent static buildup that could damage the sensitive components inside the system unit.)

After everything is properly positioned, you can connect the devices. This is where life gets a bit complicated. Connections differ depending on the computer's design and the types of components you're connecting. For example, although most computers include a central system unit into which you plug the monitor, keyboard, mouse, and printer, some newer computers combine the system unit, monitor, and speakers as a single device into which you plug other devices. In addition, newer computers make greater use of USB (Universal Serial Bus) ports, special receptacles that allow you to connect a string of up to 127 devices to a single receptacle. If your computer comes with a USB mouse and keyboard, you need to plug them into the USB ports instead of into the standard PS/2 mouse or keyboard ports.

If you have a USB keyboard, chances are that the keyboard itself has USB ports; you plug the keyboard into a USB port on the system unit and then plug your mouse into the USB port on the keyboard. If your keyboard has an extra USB port, you can plug an additional device, such as a USB joystick into the keyboard as well. This frees up additional USB ports on the system unit.

To figure out where to plug things in, look for words or pictures on the back (and front) of the central unit (the system unit or combination system unit/monitor). Most receptacles (ports) are marked, and some newer systems even have color-coded cables. If you don't see any pictures next to the receptacles, try to match the plugs with their outlets, as shown in Figure 1.2. Look at the overall shape of the outlet to see if it has pins or holes. Count the pins and holes and be sure there are at least as many holes as there are pins. As a last resort, look for the documentation that came with your computer.

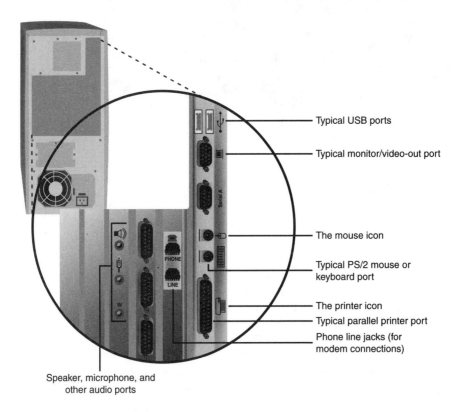

Typical USB ports

Typical monitor/video-out port

The mouse icon

Typical PS/2 mouse or keyboard port

The printer icon

Typical parallel printer port

Phone line jacks (for modem connections)

Speaker, microphone, and other audio ports

Figure 1.2

Look for clues on the system unit to figure out where to plug in devices.

Panic Attack

If your mouse or keyboard has no cable, don't panic. A relatively new technology, called *Bluetooth,* is used in many new keyboards, mice, printers, and other peripheral devices to enable them to connect to the system unit via radio-frequency signals. Devices typically connect automatically when they are within 30 feet of the system unit. Wireless keyboards and mice require batteries. Wireless printers typically plug into an electrical outlet, just like standard printers.

Bringing the Beast to Life

Dr. Frankenstein must have had a real rush just before he flipped the switch and sent that mega-volts jolt through his monster's patch-worked body. You get a similar thrill just before you turn on your new computer. What will the screen look like? What sounds will it make? How fast will things pop up on the monitor?

Well, you're about to have all your questions answered as you perform the following steps to start your computer:

1. Press the button on the monitor or flip its switch to turn it on. Computer manufacturers recommend that you turn on the monitor *first*. This allows you to see the startup messages, and it prevents the monitor's power surge from passing through the system unit's components. (On many newer computers, the monitor turns on automatically when you turn on the system unit.)

2. Turn on the printer if it has a power button or switch (many new printers have no power switch). Be sure the online light is lit (not blinking). If the light is blinking, be sure the printer has paper, and then press the online button (if the printer has an online button).

Panic Attack

If this is the first time you're turning on your printer, you must install the ink or toner cartridge. Check the printer manual for instructions.

3. If you have speakers or other devices connected to your computer, turn them on.

4. Be sure the floppy disk drive is empty. If it has a floppy disk in it, press the eject button on the drive and then gently remove the disk. (Don't worry about removing any CDs from the CD-ROM drive.)

5. Press the power button or flip the switch on the system unit. (On notebooks and some newer desktop models, you must hold the button for one or two seconds before releasing it.)

What happens next varies from one computer to another. Most computers perform a series of startup tests, load a set of basic instructions, and display text messages (white text on a black background) on the monitor. These messages typically disappear before you have time to read them, so don't worry if things seem to rush by too quickly. Your computer then runs its *operating system*, typically Windows XP, which welcomes you and prompts you to log on by clicking your user name, as shown in Figure 1.3. (The operating system provides the basic instructions your computer needs in order to function.) If this screen does not appear, your computer is set up for a single user and does not require a password to log on. If this screen does appear, click your user name and then, if requested, enter the password that has been assigned to this *user account*.

Tech Term

A **user account** is an identification badge that enables each user to log on to Windows XP and set it up to suit his or her own tastes. It also provides some low-level security by requiring each user to sign on using a unique password (if a user chooses to do so). Skip to Chapter 4 for details.

Figure 1.3

Click your user name.

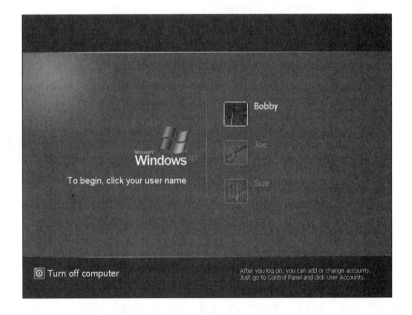

After you log on, your monitor should display the Windows desktop. Figure 1.4 shows the Windows XP desktop. If you have a different version of Windows, such as Windows 2000 (commonly used in business settings), Windows Me (Millennium edition), or Windows 98, the log on screens and desktop look different but function in much the same way. You might also encounter different displays on startup if your copy of Windows is set up to run additional software when it starts.

Figure 1.4

When your computer finally settles down, it should display the Windows desktop.

Installing the Software That Runs Your Hardware

You're not the first person to have turned on your computer. The manufacturer or dealer turned it on right after it came off the assembly line to test the computer before shipping it. However, the manufacturer typically tests the computer without the printer and other accessories connected, so the first time you run your computer with everything connected, Windows runs the Add New Hardware Wizard. (A *wizard* is a series of screens that lead you step by step through the process of performing a task.)

The Add New Hardware Wizard steps you through the process of installing the software (called a *device driver*) that tells Windows how to communicate with a particular device. If a device came with its own device driver (on a floppy disk or CD), use that driver instead of the driver included with Windows. The Add New Hardware dialog box displays a **Have Disk** button, which you can click to install a driver from a disk or CD. Otherwise, you must install the driver from the Windows CD, which should be included with your system. Follow the onscreen instructions, as shown in Figure 1.5, and use your mouse as described here:

◆ To point to an option or button, slide your mouse across the desktop until the tip of the arrow is over the desired button or option.

Panic Attack
If you have trouble installing a device, refer to Chapters 29 and 30 for some helpful guidance.

◆ To select an option or "press" a button, point to the option or button and then press and release the left mouse button without moving the mouse. (This is called a *click*.)

Chapter 2 provides additional instructions on how to use your mouse and keyboard to "drive" your computer.

Figure 1.5

The Add New Hardware Wizard or Add Printer Wizard leads you through the process of installing a device driver.

Now What?

You've arranged everything to your liking, turned everything on, and responded to any startup messages. Now what?

At this point, you're ready to start working (or playing). If the Windows desktop is displayed, as shown in Figure 1.3, you can click the **Start** button in the lower-left corner and point to **All Programs** to check out which games and programs are installed on your computer. Chapter 3, teaches you how to move around in Windows and navigate the Windows desktop.

Shutting It Down or Leaving It On?

You might be wondering if it's better to leave your computer on or turn it off when you're not using it. In most cases, leaving the computer on is a good idea. Newer system units and monitors have built-in power-saving features that automatically shut down the devices that use the most power (disk drives and monitors) or place them in standby mode.

Turning your computer on and off places additional strain on the power switches and sensitive electrical components. Each time you turn the computer off and back on, the components cool down and heat up, which, over a long period of time, can cause components or solder joints to crack.

When your computer goes into power-saving mode, the screen might go blank. Don't panic. Your computer is just taking a snooze. The best way to wake it up is to press and release the **Shift** key. Sometimes you can wake your computer by rolling the mouse around, but the **Shift** key is more reliable—and because the **Shift** key doesn't type any characters or enter any commands, it's a safe way to snap your computer out of hibernation.

> **Inside Tip**
>
> If you decide to leave your computer on all the time, consider purchasing an uninterruptible power supply to keep a steady flow of current running to your computer during short power outages or brownouts (those fluctuations that cause your lights to flicker and that might force your computer to restart).

If you decide to leave your computer on, be sure you save any documents you're working on before you step away from your computer. (You'll learn how to save documents in Chapter 11.) Saving a document records the document to the hard drive so that if the power goes out, you don't lose your work.

The Least You Need to Know

- Place your computer in an environment that is clean, dry, and cool.

- Plug all your computer components into a high-quality surge suppressor or uninterruptible power supply to prevent damage from lightning and power fluctuations.

- When inserting a connector into a port, be sure the pins align with the holes, and never force the connection.

- Turn on all the components that are connected to the central unit before you turn on the central unit so that your computer can identify the components during startup and you can view the startup messages.

- The first time you run your computer, you might need to install hardware drivers (software that tells Windows how to use specific devices).

- It's okay to leave your computer on when you're not using it, but be sure you save your work before you step away from the computer.

2

Behind the Wheel with Your Keyboard and Mouse

In This Chapter

- ◆ Ctrl, Alt, F1, and other bizarre keys
- ◆ Go beyond typing with a programmable keyboard
- ◆ Pointing, clicking, dragging, and other manic mouse moves
- ◆ Pointing devices for alternative types

If you're brave (and extremely patient), you can strap on a headset and microphone and train your computer to interpret commands and take dictation. However, most people still prefer using the more traditional, low-tech input devices—the mouse and keyboard. But even these tools require a little bit of technological know-how and manual dexterity to master. In this chapter you learn how to use these standard input devices along with a few other technologies to "talk" to your computer and enter text and other data.

Pecking Away at the Keyboard

The old, manual typewriter keyboard was fairly basic. It had letter keys, number keys, a shift key, a backspace key, and a spacebar. When you needed to start a new paragraph, you reached up and took a swipe at the carriage return. Newfangled computer keyboards are much more complex, as you can see in Figure 2.1. They still have the letter and number keys, but they also have several keys that you might not recognize:

- **Function keys.** The 10 or 12 F keys at the top or left side of the keyboard (F1, F2, F3, and so on) were frequently used in older programs to quickly enter commands. F1 is still used to display help in Windows and most Windows programs, and you can assign function keys to perform specialized tasks in most programs.

- **Arrow keys, Page Up, Page Down, Home, and End.** Also known as cursor-movement keys, these keys move the cursor (the blinking line or box) around onscreen. Wherever the cursor (also known as the insertion point) ends up is where your text will appear as you type.

- **Numeric keypad.** A group of number keys positioned like the keys on an adding machine. You use these keys to type numbers or to move around on-screen. Press the NumLock key to use the keys for entering numbers. With NumLock off, the keys act as arrow or cursor-movement keys. Most computers turn on NumLock on startup.

- **Ctrl and Alt keys.** The Ctrl (Control) and Alt (Alternate) keys make the other keys on the keyboard act differently from the way they normally act. For example, in Windows you can press Ctrl+A (hold down the Ctrl key while pressing A) to select all of the text or objects displayed in the current document.

- **Esc key.** You can use the Esc (Escape) key in most programs to back out of or quit whatever you are currently doing.

- **Print Screen/SysRq.** This sends the screen image to the Windows Clipboard, a temporary storage area for data. To learn more about the Clipboard, see Chapter 11.

- **Scroll Lock.** Another fairly useless key, in some programs Scroll Lock makes the arrow keys push text up and down on the screen one line at a time instead of moving the insertion point.

- **Pause/Break.** The king of all useless keys, Pause/Break is used to stop your computer from performing the same task over and over again—something that old programs seemed to enjoy doing. I have pressed this key only a few times, usually by mistake.

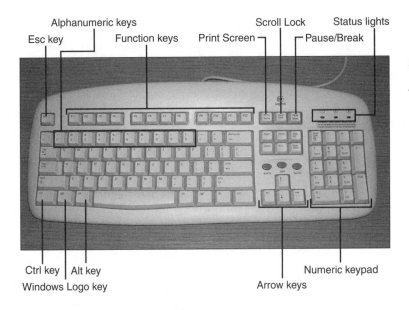

Alphanumeric keys

Esc key   Function keys   Print Screen   Scroll Lock   Status lights   Pause/Break

Figure 2.1

A typical keyboard.

Ctrl key | Alt key

Windows Logo key

Arrow keys

Numeric keypad

Cutting Corners with the Windows Logo Key

Inspect your keyboard carefully to see if it has a Windows Logo key. This key has a picture of a four-paned window that looks as though it is flying through the sky. The key is typically located near the lower left corner of the keyboard—to the left of the spacebar. If your keyboard has this key, you have a "Windows keyboard," which was probably manufactured after 1995. Besides acting as a decorative addition to your keyboard, the Windows Logo key provides quick access to commonly entered Windows commands, as explained in the Table 2.1.

Table 2.1   Windows Logo Key Shortcuts

Press	To
Windows	Open the Start menu.
Windows+Tab	Cycle through running programs in the taskbar.
Windows+F	Find a file.
Ctrl+Windows+F	Find a computer on a network.
Windows+F1	Display the Windows Help window.
Windows+R	Display the Run dialog box (for running programs).
Windows+Break	Display the System Properties dialog box.
Windows+E	Run Windows Explorer for managing folders and files.
Windows+D	Minimize or restore all program windows.
Shift+Windows+M	Undo minimize all program windows.

Dual-Function Keys on Notebook PCs

Portable computers, including notebook and laptop PCs, typically lack the space for a full set of keys plus buttons to turn on the computer, adjust the display, and move the mouse pointer. To fit all the keys and buttons in this limited amount of space, many keys are assigned double duty. For example, some of the keys can be used to adjust the brightness and contrast of the display.

In most cases, the keyboard includes a key labeled Fn that is a different color (typically blue). Keys that perform double-duty have their primary functions displayed in black or white, and their secondary functions displayed in the same color used for the Fn key. To take advantage of the secondary function of the key, hold down the Fn key while pressing the key that is labeled with the desired secondary function.

Keyboards with Buttons (Programmable Keyboards)

In the last few years, keyboards have begun to expand to include special buttons that enable you to quickly open your Internet home page, navigate the Internet, check e-mail, and put your computer in sleep mode. In addition, if you don't use one of the buttons for its designated function, you can reprogram it to perform some other time-saving shortcut. Figure 2.2 shows one of the more popular programmable keyboard models from Logitech.

Figure 2.2

An Internet keyboard contains keys you can assign to your favorite web pages and programs.

(Photo courtesy of Logitech, Inc.)

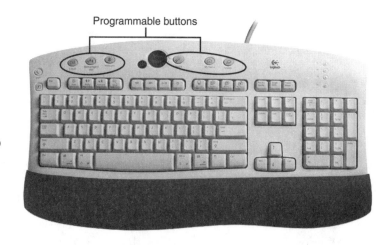

Programmable buttons

Mastering Basic Mouse Moves

If you're the type of person who orders from the menu by pointing at the item of your choice rather than speaking to the waiter, you're going to love your computer's mouse. The mouse provides a more intuitive way for you to enter commands—you simply slide the mouse across your desk until the mouse pointer (on the monitor) is over the desired menu or object, and then you click (press and release) the left mouse button. Figure 2.3 shows a typical mouse. To use a mouse you must master the following basic moves:

- **Point.** Slide the mouse around till the tip of the onscreen arrow is over the item you want. Easy stuff.

- **Click.** Point to something (usually an icon or menu command), then press and release the left mouse button. When you click, be careful not to move the mouse when you click, or you might click the wrong thing or move an object unintentionally.

- **Right-click.** Same as click but use the right mouse button. A couple years ago, the right mouse button was pretty useless. Now it is used mainly to display context menus, which contain commands that apply only to the currently selected object.

- **Double-click.** Same as click but you press and release the mouse button twice real fast without moving the mouse. Mastering this move takes some practice.

- **Drag.** Point to an object and then hold down the left mouse button while moving the mouse. You typically drag to move an object, draw (in a drawing or paint program), or select text (in a word processing program). In some cases, you can drag with the right mouse button; when you release the mouse button, a context menu typically appears asking what you want to do.

> **Inside Tip**
>
> A typical mouse has a ball inside it that turns rollers inside the mouse to move the mouse pointer on screen. The ball typically picks up a lot of dust and hair, which eventually makes the mouse pointer move erratically. The newer, optical mouse, uses laser technology to sense the mouse movement, making the mouse much more reliable.

Figure 2.3

A typical mouse.

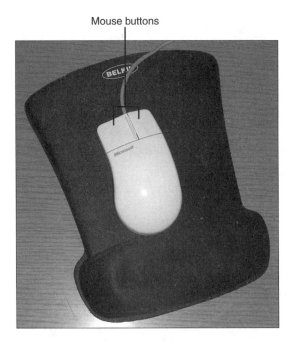

Mouse buttons

Mouse on Wheels

Computer designers have never been satisfied with the standard, two-button mouse. They've tried adding a third button, adding shortcut buttons (like those on a programmable keyboard), and modifying the shape of the mouse. I have even seen a new mouse that includes an FM radio tuner, so you can listen to the radio while you work! Finally, designers have come up with a relatively stable design called the IntelliMouse. Similar in shape to the standard two-button Microsoft mouse, the IntelliMouse has a small, gray wheel between the left and right buttons. Although it feels like a growth on an otherwise smooth mouse, the wheel gives you more control over scrolling and entering commands and is fairly easy to use.

The left and right mouse buttons work as they always have; however, in applications that support the IntelliMouse (including most new Microsoft applications) you can do two things with the wheel: Spin it and click it. What spinning and clicking do depends on the application. For example, in Microsoft Word you can use the wheel to scroll more accurately, as described here:

♦ Rotate the wheel away from yourself to scroll text down; rotate toward yourself to scroll up.

♦ To pan up or down, click and hold the wheel while moving the mouse pointer in the direction of the text you want to bring into view. (Panning is sort of like scrolling, but it's smoother.)

♦ To autoscroll up or down, click the wheel and then move the mouse pointer up (to scroll up) or down (to scroll down). Autoscrolling remains on until you click the wheel again.

♦ To zoom in or out, hold down the **Ctrl** key and rotate the wheel. Rotate away from yourself to zoom in or toward yourself to zoom out.

Wheel

Figure 2.4

The IntelliMouse sports a wheel between its two buttons.

Customizing Your Mouse

If you're a lefty or if you have trouble clicking fast enough to execute a double-click, you will be happy to know that you can customize your mouse to accommodate the way you work. In Windows XP, click the **Start** button (in the lower left corner of the screen) and click **Control Panel.** Click or double-click **Printers and Other Hardware** and then click or double-click **Mouse.** This opens the Mouse Properties dialog box, shown in Figure 2.5. You can use this dialog box to specify the function of each mouse button and the appearance of the mouse pointers.

Figure 2.5

The Mouse Properties dialog box enables you to customize the mouse and mouse pointer.

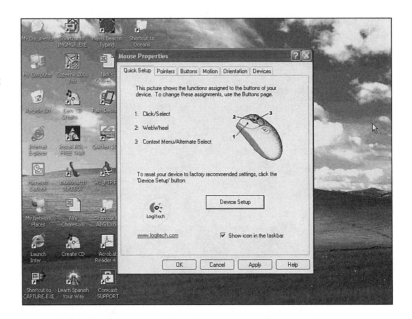

If you have a different version of Windows, such as Windows Me or Windows 98, display the Control Panel by clicking the **Start** button, pointing to **Settings,** and clicking **Control Panel.** When the Control Panel appears, double-click the Mouse button and use the resulting dialog box to enter your settings. Part 2 provides additional instructions on how to customize Windows for the way you work.

Panic Attack

Click or double-click? Your version of Windows may enable you to click the Mouse icon once in order to open the Mouse Properties dialog box or it may require you to double-click the icon. In Chapter 3, you learn how to adjust the setting in Windows that controls this option. For now, you should know that if the icon's name appears underlined when the mouse pointer is resting on it, then you can single-click; otherwise, you must double-click.

Pointing Devices for the Alternative Crowd

In search of the perfect pointing device, computer manufacturers have toyed with other ideas: trackballs, joysticks, touchpads, light-sensitive pens, and little gear shifts stuck in the middle of keyboards. I've even seen two-foot pedals set up to act like a mouse! The following list describes the more standard fare:

♦ **Trackball.** A trackball is an upside-down mouse (sort of). Instead of sliding the mouse to roll the ball inside the mouse, you roll the ball itself. The good thing about a trackball is that it doesn't require much desk space and it doesn't get gunked up from dust and hair on your desk. The bad thing about trackballs is that manufacturers haven't figured out a good place to put the buttons. You almost need two hands to drag with a trackball: one to hold down the button and the other to roll the ball. Stick with a mouse.

♦ **Touchpad.** A touchpad is a pressure-sensitive square that you slide your finger across to move the pointer. A typical touchpad has two buttons next to it that act like mouse buttons: You click or double-click the buttons or hold down a button to drag. With most touchpads you also can tap the touchpad itself to click or double-click. Touchpads are the pointing devices of choice on most notebook computers, but they can be a little temperamental, especially if your fingers are a little sweaty.

♦ **TrackPoint or AccuPoint Pointers.** You've probably seen portable computers with a little red lever smack dab in the middle of the keyboard. The lever acts sort of like a joystick; you push the lever in the direction you want to move the mouse pointer. You use buttons next to the keyboard to click and drag.

♦ **Joystick.** A joystick is a must-have for most computer games. A standard joystick looks like a flight stick or one of those controls you've seen on video arcade games. It has a base with a lever sticking out of it, which you push or pull in the direction you want to move. The lever usually has a few buttons for blasting away at opponents and making a speedy getaway.

♦ **Voice activation.** For no-hands control over your computer, you can purchase voice activation software and bark commands into a microphone. With speech recognition software, such as IBM's Via Voice, you can even type without touching your keyboard. Microsoft Office XP and later versions include voice activation features that enable you to enter commands and text in the Office applications: Microsoft Word, Excel, Access, Outlook, and PowerPoint.

The Least You Need to Know

♦ The 12 function keys on your keyboard are positioned across the top or along one edge of your keyboard.

♦ The Ctrl and Alt keys augment the standard keyboard keys to provide extra functions.

♦ The cursor keys move the cursor or insertion point around onscreen.

♦ The five basic mouse moves are point, click, right-click, double-click, and drag.

♦ The center wheel on an IntelliMouse can be used to make scrolling through documents and web pages easier.

♦ Other devices for poking around on your computer include a trackball, touchpad, TrackPoint or AccuPoint pointer, joystick, and voice recognition software.

Meeting Windows:
Up Close and Personal

In This Chapter

- ◆ First encounters with your new electronic desktop
- ◆ Conversing with menus and dialog boxes
- ◆ Checking out a few choice Windows programs
- ◆ Moving, resizing, and hiding windows on your desktop
- ◆ Dumping stuff in the Recycle Bin and digging it out later

When you start a PC-compatible computer, it automatically runs some version of Windows: Windows XP, Windows Me (Millennium Edition), Windows 98, Windows 95, or Windows 2000 (or Windows NT for networked computers). But what is Windows?

If you pry off the top of your desk and hang it on the wall, you have Windows … well, sort of. Although its initial appearance might be deceiving, Windows is little more than an electronic desktop that's displayed on a two-dimensional vertical surface—your computer's monitor. It even comes complete with its own *desktop utilities*, including a calculator, a notepad, and a blank canvas that you can doodle on during your breaks.

This chapter teaches you the basics of how to work on your new computerized desktop.

The Windows Nickel Tour

When you first start your computer, your new desktop appears, very neat and tidy. Several *icons* (small pictures) dot the surface of the Windows desktop, and a gray or blue strip called the *taskbar* appears at the bottom of the screen, as shown in Figure 3.1 (unless you or someone else moved it). On the left end of the taskbar is the all-important **Start** button, which opens a menu containing the names of all the programs installed on your computer.

Figure 3.1

Initially, the Windows desktop is sparsely populated.

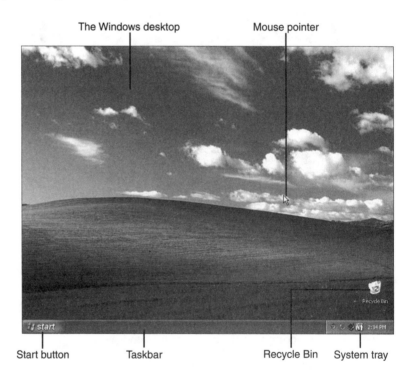

The Windows desktop   Mouse pointer

Start button   Taskbar   Recycle Bin   System tray

Panic Attack

The icons you see on your desktop might differ depending on how you or the manufacturer installed Windows and on whether you have additional programs.

Before we start exploring the Windows desktop, find out which version of Windows you have. This book assumes you are using a relatively new computer that is running Windows 95, 98, Windows NT, Windows 2000, Windows Me, or Windows XP. Because Windows XP is the latest, greatest version for both home and business users, this book focuses on Windows XP. For performing basic tasks, these versions of Windows are nearly identical. To find out which version of Windows you're running, right-click **My Computer** (on the desktop or click the **Start** button and right-click **My Computer,** and then click **Properties**). The System Properties dialog box appears, as shown in Figure 3.2, displaying the version of Windows that's installed on your computer along with some additional interesting tidbits about your computer.

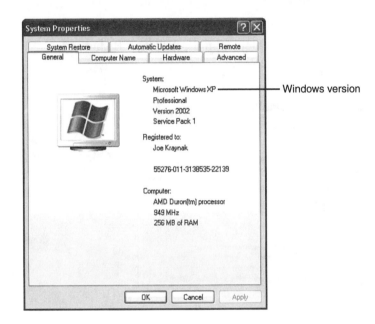

Figure 3.2

The System Properties dialog box.

If the icon names are underlined, you have a version of Windows that's more recent than the original Windows 95, and Web Style is turned on; you click an icon once to run its corresponding program. If the icon names are not underlined, you must double-click the icon to run the program. To turn *Web Style* on (in versions of Windows newer than Windows 95), take the following steps:

1. Double-click the **My Computer** icon on the Windows desktop, or click the **Start** button and click **My Computer.**

2. Click **Tools** in the menu bar near the top of the window and click **Folder Options.** (If **Folder Options** is not on your **Tools** menu, open the **View** menu by clicking it, and then click **Folder Options.**)

Tech Term

Web Style makes your Windows desktop look and act like an Internet web page. On a web page, you click icons, buttons, or underlined text (called *links*) to jump from one page to another. See Chapter 20 for more information. Web Style is a key feature of the post–Windows 95's "Active Desktop," a design that integrates Windows with the web.

3. Take one of the following steps depending on which version of Windows you
   have:

   ◆ For **Windows XP** or **Windows 2000:** Click **Single-click to Open Item
   (Point to Select)** and then click **OK,** as shown in Figure 3.3.

   ◆ For **Windows Me:** Click **Enable Web Content on My Desktop** and
   Enable Web Content in Folders to turn on both options, and then
   click **OK.**

   ◆ **Windows 98:** Click **Web Style,** and then click the **OK** button.

4. Click **File** in the menu bar, and click **Close.**

Figure 3.3

*In Windows XP, turn on the
Single-Click to Open Item
option.*

With Web Style on, you simply point to icons to select them and single-click icons to
activate them. With Web Style off, you click to select and double-click to activate.

Ordering from Menus and Dialog Boxes

Computer technology hasn't quite reached the point of *2001: A Space Odyssey* (you
know, that 1968 Stanley Kubrick flick in which the astronauts actually converse with
Hal, the computer that runs the spaceship). However, Windows provides several ways
for you to "talk" to your computer by clicking buttons, selecting menu commands,
and responding to *dialog boxes* (onscreen fill-in-the-blank forms).

Clicking Menu Options

The Windows interactive tool of preference is the *menu*. You'll find menus everywhere: on the left end of the taskbar (the Windows **Start** menu), in menu bars near the top of most program windows, in toolbars, and even hidden inside objects. To open a menu, you simply click its name, and it drops down or pops up on the screen, as shown in Figure 3.4. Then you click the desired menu option. (To display a hidden—*context*—menu, right-click the desired object or the selected text or image.)

Click the menu's name to open it

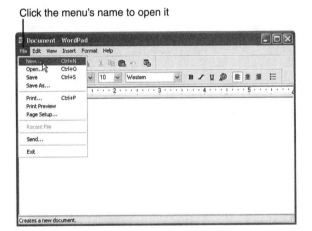

Figure 3.4

Menus are available in the menu bar at the top of most program windows.

Computer Cheat

To quickly open a menu without lifting your fingers from the keyboard, hold down the **Alt** key and press the key that corresponds to the underlined letter in the menu's name. For example, press **Alt+F** to open the **File** menu. Press **Shift+F10** to display a context menu for the currently selected text or object. To open the Windows Start menu, press **Ctrl+Esc**. Use the arrow keys to highlight the desired command and then press **Enter**.

As you flip through any menu system, you might notice that some of the menu options look a little strange. One option might appear pale. Another might be followed by a series of dots. And still others have arrows next to them. Their appearances tell all:

♦ Light gray options are unavailable for what you are currently doing. For example, if you want to copy a chunk of text but you have not yet selected the text, the **Copy** command is not available; it appears light gray.

♦ An option with an arrow next to it opens a submenu that requires you to select another option. Point to the option to open the submenu.

♦ An option with a check mark indicates that an option is currently active. To turn the option off, click it. This removes the check mark; however, you won't know it, because selecting the option also closes the menu.

♦ An option followed by a series of dots (...) opens a dialog box that requests additional information. You learn how to talk to dialog boxes in the next section.

CAUTION

Whoa! _____

To further confuse new users, Microsoft has come up with something called the "smart" menu, featured in its Office applications, which lists only the most commonly selected options. To view additional options, you must point to a double-headed arrow at the bottom of the menu. In addition, the menu is designed to customize itself, so options automatically move up on the menu the more often you use them. In other words, you never know where they'll be. In case you can't tell, I think smart menus are pretty dumb.

Talking with a Dialog Box

If you choose a menu command that's followed by a series of dots (...), the program displays a *dialog box*, as shown in Figure 3.5, requesting additional information. You must then navigate the dialog box, select the desired options, type any required text entries, and give your okay—all using the following controls:

♦ **Tabs.** If a dialog box has two or more "pages" of options, tabs appear near the top of the pages. Click the tab for the desired options.

♦ **Text boxes.** A text box is a "fill in the blank"; it allows you to type text, such as the name of a file.

♦ **Option buttons.** Option buttons (also known as *radio buttons*) allow you to select only one option in a group. Click the desired option to turn it on and to turn any other selected option in the group off.

♦ **Check boxes.** Check boxes allow you to turn an option on or off. Click in a check box to turn it on if it's off or off if it's on. You can select more than one check box in a group.

◆ **List box.** A list box presents two or more options. Click the desired option. If the list is long, you'll see a *scrollbar*. Click the *scrollbar* arrows to move up or down in the list.

◆ **Drop-down list box.** You will see only one item when you first view this kind of list box. The rest of the items are hidden initially. Click the arrow to the right of the box to display the rest of the list, and then click the desired item.

◆ **Spin box.** A spin box is a text box with controls. You can usually type a setting in the text box or click the up or down arrow to change the setting in predetermined increments. For example, you might click the up arrow to increase a margin setting by .1 inch.

◆ **Slider.** A slider is a control you can drag up, down, or from side to side to increase or decrease a setting. Sliders are commonly used to adjust speaker volume, hardware performance, and similar settings.

◆ **Command buttons.** Most dialog boxes have at least three buttons: **OK** to confirm your selections, **Cancel** to quit, and **Help** to get help.

Inside Tip _____

In the upper-right corner of most dialog boxes is a button with a question mark on it. Click the button, and a question mark attaches itself to the mouse pointer. Then you can click an option in the dialog box to display information about it. You can also right-click the option and choose **What's This?**

Figure 3.5

A dialog box asks you to enter additional information and settings.

Bypassing Menus by Using Toolbar Buttons

Although menus contain a comprehensive list of available options, they are a bit clunky. To perform a task using a menu, you must click the menu name, hunt for the desired command, and then select it. To help you bypass the menu system, most programs include *toolbars* that contain buttons for the most frequently used commands. To perform a task, you simply click the desired button, as shown in Figure 3.6.

Figure 3.6

Toolbars provide quick access to commonly used commands.

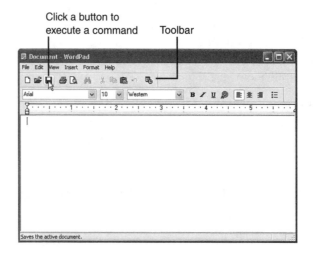

Checking Out Some Windows Programs

Chances are your computer came loaded with all sorts of software. If you purchased a home PC, it probably came with Microsoft Works or some other program suite (package) and a couple computer games. But even if your computer wasn't garnished with additional programs, Windows has several programs you can use to write letters, draw pictures, play games, and perform other tasks.

To run any of these programs, click **Start,** point to **Programs** or **All Programs,** point to **Accessories,** and then click the program you want to run:

- **Games** is a group of simple computer games, including Solitaire. (You might find the Games submenu on the Programs or All Programs menu, rather than on the Accessories submenu.)

- **Entertainment** is a group of programs enabling you to play audio CDs and video clips, and adjust the speaker volume.

- **System Tools** is a collection of programs that help you maintain your system. These tools include a backup program, a program for fixing your hard disk, and a hard disk *defragmenter*, which can increase the speed of your disk. See Chapter 28 for details.

- **Calculator** displays an onscreen calculator to perform addition, subtraction, division, and multiplication.

- **Notepad** is a text editing program useful for typing notes and other brief documents.

- **Paint** is a graphics program for creating and printing pictures.

- **WordPad** is a more advanced word processing program that enables you to create fancier, longer documents.

Rearranging the Windows Inside Windows

Each time you run a program or open a document in Windows, a new window opens on your desktop. After several hours of work, your desktop can become as cluttered as a real desktop, making it difficult to locate your desktop utilities and documents. To switch to a window or reorganize the windows on the desktop, use any of the following tricks:

- To quickly change to a window, click its button in the taskbar. (To hide the window later, click its taskbar button again, or click the Minimize button in the upper-right corner of the window; it's the button with the small horizontal line on it.)

- If you can see any part of a window, click it to move it to the front of the stack.

- To quickly arrange the windows, right-click a blank area of the taskbar and, from the shortcut menu that appears, choose one of the following options: **Tile Horizontally, Tile Vertically,** or **Cascade.**

- To close a window (and exit the program), click the **Close** button (the one with the X on it) that's located in the upper-right corner of the window, as shown in Figure 3.7.

◆ To increase the size of a window so that it takes up the whole screen, click the **Maximize** button (just to the left of the **Close** button). The **Maximize** button then turns into a **Restore** button, which you can click to return the window to its previous size.

◆ To shrink a window, click the **Minimize** button (two buttons to the left of the **Close** button). The minimized window appears as a button on the taskbar. Click the button on the taskbar to reopen the window.

◆ To resize or reshape a window that is not at its maximum size, place your mouse pointer in the lower-right corner of the window and, when the pointer turns to a double-headed arrow, drag the corner of the window.

◆ To move a window, drag its title bar. (You can't move a maximized window, because it takes up the whole screen.)

Figure 3.7

You can close, maximize, and resize windows.

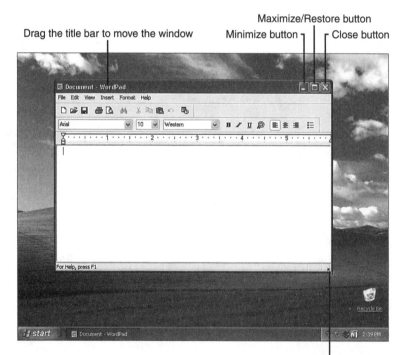

Drag the title bar to move the window

Maximize/Restore button
Minimize button
Close button

Drag a border to change the window size and shape

You can also control your windows from the taskbar. Whenever you run a program, a button for it appears in the taskbar. The button acts like a toggle switch; click the program's button to open the program's window, and click again to hide the program's window. Right-click a program's button to display options for minimizing, maximizing, restoring, moving, resizing, or closing the program's window.

Try this trick: Click a program's button in the taskbar, and then **Ctrl+click** all other program buttons. Right-click one of the buttons and click **Minimize.** All program windows are minimized, returning you to the Windows desktop. Pretty cool, huh? Well, there's actually an easier way in Windows 98 and later. To the right of the **Start** button is a tiny toolbar called the Quick Launch toolbar, which contains buttons for Internet Explorer (Microsoft's Web browser), Outlook Express (an e-mail program), Windows Media Player, and the desktop. Click the **Show Desktop** button to quickly return to the Windows desktop. Click the button again to return to your programs.

Seeing More with Scrollbars

If a window cannot display everything it contains, a scrollbar appears along the right side or bottom of the window. The scrollbar on the right enables you to scroll up and down; the scrollbar at the bottom lets you scroll left and right. You can use the scrollbar to bring the hidden contents of the window into view, as follows (see Figure 3.8):

♦ **Scrollbar.** Click once inside the scrollbar, on either side of the scroll box, to move the view one windowful at a time. For example, if you click once below the scroll box, you will see the next windowful of information.

♦ **Scroll box.** Move the mouse pointer over the scroll box, hold down the mouse button, and then drag the box to the area of the window you want to view. For example, to move to the middle of the window's contents, drag the scroll box to the middle of the bar.

♦ **Scroll arrow.** Hold down the mouse button to scroll continuously in that direction.

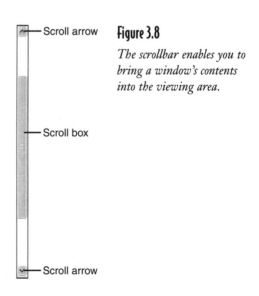

Scroll arrow

Scroll box

Scroll arrow

Figure 3.8

The scrollbar enables you to bring a window's contents into the viewing area.

Help Is on Its Way

If you plan to thrive in the world of computers, learn how to use the help system in Windows and your Windows programs. These online help systems might not provide the detailed hand-holding instructions you find in books, but they usually provide the basic information you need to get started.

If you get stuck in Windows, click the **Start** button, and then click **Help** or **Help and Support.** The Help window appears, which differs depending on which version of Windows you have. In Windows XP and 2000, the help window looks like the window shown in Figure 3.9, providing links to the most common help topics. Click a link and follow the trail of links until you find the answer you need. Or, click in the **Search** text box, near the top of the window, type your question or a brief description of the desired topic, and press **Enter.** Then select the desired topic from the list that appears.

Click here and type the desired help topic or question

Figure 3.9

Windows provides additional help for specific tasks.

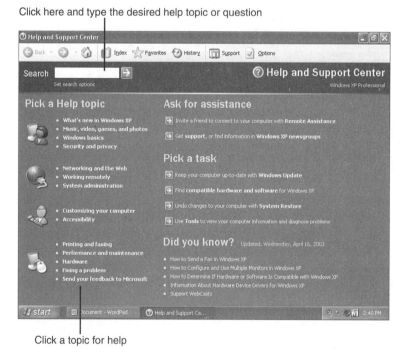

Click a topic for help

In earlier versions of Windows, the help system offers a table of contents and an index. Click the **Contents** tab or **Home** button if you're searching for general information about how to perform a task or use Windows. If you get a list of topics with little book icons next to them, double-click a book icon to view additional subtopics, and then double-click the desired topic. For specific help, click the **Index** tab or button. Click inside the text box at the top, and then start typing the name of the feature, command, or procedure for which you need help. As you type, the list scrolls to show the name of the topic that matches your entry. Double-click the desired topic. For a more thorough search, click the **Search** tab, if available, and perform your search. In Windows Me, a **Search** text box is located in the upper-right corner of the Help window; type your search phrase and press **Enter** or click **Go.**

The Least You Need to Know

- ◆ When you start your computer, Windows presents you with an electronic desktop on which you do all your work.

- ◆ When you choose an option that's followed by three dots, Windows displays a dialog box asking for additional information.

- ◆ Three buttons appear in the upper-right corner of every window. Use these buttons to open, close, or quickly hide (minimize) or restore the window.

- ◆ To manually resize a window, drag its lower-right corner.

- ◆ For more information about Windows, click the **Start** button and then click **Help** or **Help and Support.**

Sharing Your Computer Peacefully with Others

In This Chapter

◆ Creating a user account for each person who uses your computer

◆ Requiring a password to log on

◆ Logging off Windows so someone else can log on

◆ Acquiring a .Net passport to access valuable Microsoft services

◆ Keeping folders and files private when sharing a computer

Sharing a computer with other users is like sharing a car with other drivers. When you share a car, each driver adjusts the seat and steering wheel for his or her own comfort, adjusts the mirrors so the driver can see out the back, and hides the garage door opener in a unique hiding place. Likewise, some computer users prefer to clutter the Windows desktop with an assortment of icons, decorate their desktop with colorful images, and keep several programs running at the same time. Other users might prefer a cleaner, well-organized desktop with fewer bells and whistles.

Fortunately, the latest versions of Windows enable you to set up a separate user account for each person, so that each person can customize Windows

Whoa! _____

User accounts are available only in Windows XP. If you have an earlier version of Windows, including Windows Me, Windows 98, or Windows 95, skip this chapter. The figures in this chapter show how to set up user accounts in Windows XP.

without affecting the appearance and function of Windows for other users. In addition, user accounts enable each user to keep his or her e-mail account separate, so that the messages for all users do not get mixed up in the same mailbox. User account passwords also provide privacy in a shared environment.

This chapter shows you how to create a user account for each person who plans on sharing the computer, how to log on and log off Windows XP, how to add a password to the accounts, and how to perform some other tricks with user accounts.

Adding a New User to Your Computer

When you or your computer's manufacturer installed Windows, the setup program automatically created a user account, so Windows could greet you on startup. The user account that Windows created is an *administrator account*, which gives you the authority to create additional accounts, assign passwords to users, and limit other users' access to system settings and computer resources. To add a user account for another user, take the following steps:

1. Click the **Start** button, in the lower left corner of your screen, and then click **Control Panel.** The Control Panel appears, as shown in Figure 4.1.

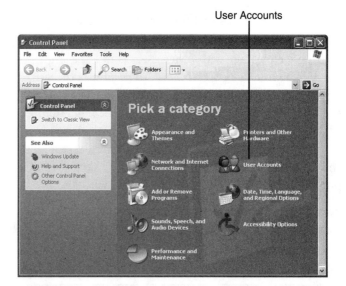

Figure 4.1

The Control Panel provides access to User Accounts.

2. Click the **User Accounts** icon shown in 4.1. The User Accounts window appears, as shown in Figure 4.2.

3. Under **Pick a task...** click **Create a New Account.** The User Accounts feature prompts you to type a name for the account.

Click Create a New Account

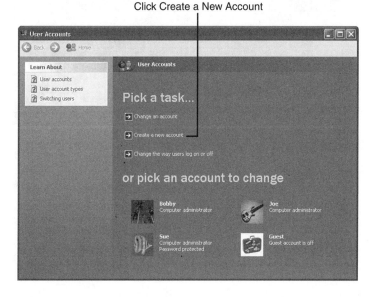

Figure 4.2

You can create a new user account.

4. Type the user's name as you want it to appear on the Windows Welcome screen and on the Start menu.

5. Click the **Next** button. The User Accounts feature prompts you to pick an account type.

6. Click the desired account type:

   ◆ **Computer Administrator** allows the user to create, edit, and delete accounts; change system settings; install programs; and access all folders and files on the computer.

   ◆ **Limited** allows the user to change his or her own password, change the picture used to identify the user, change Windows desktop settings, view files that the user created, and view any files in the Shared Documents folder.

Whoa!

If you're using a networked computer at your place of business, your business should have a network administrator who is in charge of adding user accounts. The process is much different for setting up user accounts on a corporation's network. Ask the network administrator for help.

7. Click the **Create Account** button. Windows returns to the User Accounts window and displays the icon and name of the new user account, as shown in Figure 4.3.

Figure 4.3

Windows displays the name of the new user account and its icon.

New user account

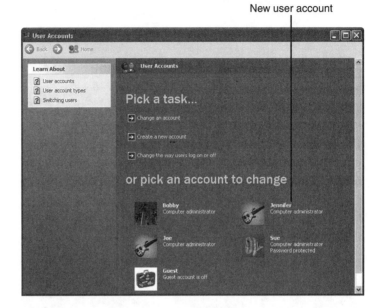

Requiring a Secret Password to Log On

When you first create a user account, the account has no password. When the Windows log on screen appears, the user can simply click the account icon to freely access that account. If you're looking for privacy, you need to lock the account by adding a password. Windows will then require the password before allowing the user to log on.

Whoa!

Choose a password that's easy for you to remember but difficult for anyone else to guess. In addition, write down your password and store it in a secure location, so that if you do forget it, you won't be locked out of your account permanently.

To add a password to an account, take the following steps:

1. Click the **Start** button, and then click **Control Panel.** The Control Panel appears.

2. Click the **User Accounts** icon. The User Accounts window appears.

3. Click the icon for the account you want to password-protect. The User Accounts feature prompts you to choose the aspect of the account you want to change.

4. Click **Create a Password.** The User Accounts feature prompts you to enter your password, as shown in Figure 4.4.

5. In the **Type a New Password** text box, type the desired password.

Type your password

Figure 4.4

A password deters other users from logging on in your name.

Enter a hint to help you remember your password

6. Click in the **Type the New Password Again to Confirm** text box, and type your password again, exactly the same way you typed it in Step 5.

7. *(Optional)* Click in the **Type a Word or Phrase to Use as a Password Hint** text box, and type a hint to help remind you of the password. (This hint will appear on the Windows log on screen, so don't use a hint that can help other users guess your password.)

8. Click the **Create Password** button.

You can change your password at any time or remove it. To remove a password, log on, repeat steps 1 to 4, and then click **Remove the Password.**

Giving Your Account Icon a Makeover

Every account has its own picture to help identify each account and add a little personality to the log on screen. To personalize your account, consider choosing a picture that represents your personality and interests. Following are the steps:

Inside Tip

You can use nearly any graphic image on your computer as your picture. When selecting a picture, click **Browse** and then use the resulting dialog box to locate the desired image. You can navigate drives and folders just as you do in My Computer. When you find the picture you want, click the picture and click the **Open** button.

1. Click the **Start** button, and then click **Control Panel.** The Control Panel appears.

2. Click the **User Accounts** icon. The User Accounts window appears.

3. Click the icon for the account whose picture you want to change. The User Accounts feature prompts you to choose the aspect of the account you want to change.

4. Click **Change the Picture.** The User Accounts feature displays a collection of available images, as shown in Figure 4.5.

5. Click the desired picture and click the **Change Picture** button.

Figure 4.5

Personalize your account with a unique image.

Click the picture

Wiping Out a User Account

In Part 2 of this book, you will learn how to customize the Windows desktop, the Start menu, and other Windows features. As you customize Windows, Windows saves your settings in your user account. In addition, Windows saves all files in your My Documents folder, your e-mail messages, any websites you add to your Favorites menu, and any passwords to websites that the user chose to save on the computer. Some of the settings and information Windows saves might be private, so if a person stops using the computer, that person might want to delete the user account.

To delete an account, open the **Start** menu and click **Control Panel.** Click the **User Accounts** icon, and the click the icon for the account you want to delete. Click **Delete the Account.** Windows asks if you want to save the desktop settings and the contents of the My Documents folder for this account. To save the desktop settings and the contents of My Documents, click the **Keep Files** button. To completely remove the account and any files and settings saved for this account, click the **Delete Files** button. The User Accounts feature asks you to confirm that you want to delete this user account. If you are absolutely sure you want to delete this account, click the **Delete Account** button; otherwise, click the **Cancel** button.

 Whoa!

Don't delete an account unless you're absolutely sure you will never again use it. Deleting an account permanently removes any passwords that the user has chosen to save and any e-mail messages.

Letting Guest Users Log On

If you have guests who occasionally use your computer to check their e-mail, browse the web, or play games, you can enable the Guest Accounts feature so others can log on as guests. With guest accounts, users can log on without having to enter a password. They can run programs, check their e-mail, browse the web, and perform other tasks, but they cannot install new software or change any account settings. In short, guest users can use your computer without messing it up.

To enable the guest account, click the **Start** button and click **Control Panel.** Click the **User Accounts** icon and then click the **Guest** icon. The User Accounts feature displays a message asking if you want to turn on the guest account. Click **Turn On the Guest Account.**

Logging On and Logging Off Windows

On weekends, when my kids and their friends are hanging out, they circle my computer like vultures, just waiting for me to step away from the keyboard. Then, they descend to play games, chat with friends, and do other things that don't require them

Inside Tip _____

To find out who's currently logged on to Windows, click the **Start** button and look at the top of the Start menu for the name of the current user.

to work or play outside. When I return to the computer, I usually find a couple new programs installed on "my" account and several changes to my desktop. The moral of the story is: Always log off when you step away from the computer. When you log off, Windows shuts down your desktop and user account and displays the log on screen, so another user can log on. This prevents other users from changing your settings, snooping in your e-mail account, and performing other sinister acts. The following sections show you how to log on, log off, and switch users when sharing your computer.

Logging On at Startup

When you turn on your computer, the Windows Welcome screen appears, as you saw in Chapter 1. To log on, click your user account icon. If your user account is password protected, Windows prompts you to type your password, as shown in Figure 4.6. Type your password and then click the green arrow button to log on to Windows. Windows displays the Windows desktop, and you can start working.

Figure 4.6

Enter your log on password if prompted.

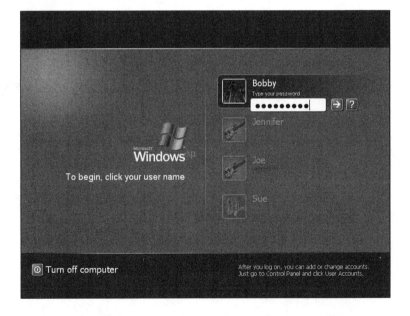

Inside Tip

To make it more difficult for unauthorized uses to log on, disable the Welcome screen. With the Welcome screen disabled, a log on dialog box appears on startup, requiring the user to type both a user name and password. Click **Start, Control Panel, User Accounts.** Click **Change the Way Users Log On or Off** and then click **Use the Welcome Screen** to remove the check mark from its check box. Click the **Apply Options** button.

Logging Off Windows

As explained earlier in this section, you should log off whenever you are done using your computer to prevent other users from accidentally changing your Windows settings. Before logging off, you should save any files you have been working on to avoid losing any of your work. When you're ready to log off, simply open the **Start** menu and click **Log Off.** The Log Off Windows dialog box appears.

At this point, you have two choices. You can click **Log Off** to log off completely, which shuts down any programs that might be running and returns you to the Windows Welcome screen. The other option is to use *fast user switching*, which keeps you logged on to your account but allows another user to log on as well. When the other user is done working, you can then quickly switch back to whatever you were in the process of doing. To remain logged on, click **Switch User.** Whichever option you choose, Windows displays its Welcome screen, so another user can log on.

Tech Term

Fast user switching allows a second user to log on without shutting down the first user's programs. For instance, if you're in the middle of writing the great American novel and your son wants to check his e-mail, he can use fast user switching to quickly log on, check his mail, and log off. When he logs off, your document remains onscreen, and you can immediately return to work.

If you have programs running and Windows locks up when the other user is working, you are at a greater risk of losing data. To ensure that Windows safely shuts down any running applications when you log off, you can disable fast user switching. Click **Start, Control Panel, User Accounts.** Click **Change the Way Users Log On or Off** and then click **Use Fast User Switching** to remove the check mark from its check box. Click the **Apply Options** button.

Setting Up Your Account to Use a .Net Passport

Microsoft encourages all users to register for a .Net passport, which acts as an online identification tag, providing access to any .Net-enabled sites and services on the Internet. .Net passports are designed to simplify your ability to access various Internet sites and services. Instead of having to use a different user name and password for each site, Microsoft wants you to be able to use your .Net passport as your universal ID badge, so you have only one user name and password to remember. (To register for a .Net passport, you must be connected to the Internet. See Chapter 16 for details.)

Tech Term

.Net (pronounced *dot-net*) is a new operating system technology designed to expand the capabilities of personal computers through the Internet. With .Net, your computer will be able to run *rented* programs from the Internet. .Net also provides a central storage location for your data, enabling you to access your work from any computer or computerized device that's connected to the Internet from anywhere in the world. The .Net initiative is also designed to integrate communications services, including phone, fax, and e-mail services. Most Microsoft sites and services require a .Net passport, including MSN Messenger for instant messaging.

To obtain a .Net passport and add it to your user account, take the following steps:

1. Log on to the Windows user account for which you want to obtain a .Net passport. See "Logging Off Windows," earlier in this chapter for instructions.

2. Click the **Start** button and then click **Control Panel.** The Control Panel appears.

3. Click the **User Accounts** icon. The User Accounts window appears.

4. Click the icon for the user account for which you want to obtain a .Net passport. The User Accounts feature prompts you to select the aspect of the account you want to change.

5. Click **Set Up My Account To Use a .Net Passport.** The .Net Passport Wizard appears, as shown in Figure 4.7, displaying a brief introduction.

6. Read and follow the Wizard's instructions to obtain your .Net passport and enter your preferences.

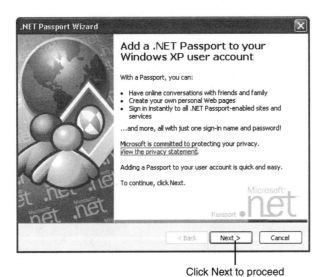

Click Next to proceed

Figure 4.7

The .Net Passport Wizard can lead you through the process of obtaining and setting up your passport.

Your passport initially contains your e-mail address and your geographical location (your country, state, and ZIP code). To make additional information available to other .Net Passport users whom you might bump into online, you can edit your Passport profile. You can, for instance, enter your real name, birthday, and occupation.

To edit your profile, first log on to Windows with the user account whose .Net Passport information you want to change. Choose **Start, Control Panel,** and click **User Accounts.** Click the icon for your user account, and then click **Change My .Net Passport.** Click the **Change Passport Attributes** button, enter or edit the passport details, and then click the **Update** button.

Whoa!

Don't enter your real last name, especially if it's unique. Anyone on the Internet could use your last name and other details in your profile to track you down.

Preventing Unauthorized Access to Your Documents

People can be quite snoopy, so if you have any sensitive documents on your computer, such as love letters, a diary, financial information, etc., you should consider hiding your My Documents folder to prevent other users who share your computer from looking at those documents without your permission.

Whoa! _____

You cannot hide your My Documents folder unless your account is set up to require a password when you log on, as explained earlier in this chapter.

Before we get into the step-by-step instructions for blocking access to a folder, you should understand a little about how Windows treats the My Documents folder. Each user has a My Documents folder, but it appears as My Documents only for that user. When Bob logs on to the computer, Bob's folder appears as My Documents, but Susan's folder appears to Bob as Susan's Documents. When Susan logs on, Bob's folder appears to her as Bob's Documents.

To lock your My Documents folder, you designate the folder to be a private folder. This keeps the folder hidden when other users log on to Windows. To make your My Documents folder private, take the following steps:

1. Run **My Computer** by selecting it on the desktop or on the Start menu. The My Computer window opens, displaying icons for the available drives.

2. Double-click the icon for the drive on which Windows is installed, typically drive C. My Computer displays the contents of drive C.

3. Double-click the **Documents and Settings** folder. My Computer displays the contents of the Documents and Settings folder, which consists of a folder for each user account.

4. Double-click the folder for your user account. My Computer displays the contents of your user account folder. You can block access to any and all folders in your account folder.

5. Right-click the **My Documents** folder and click **Sharing and Security.** The My Documents Properties dialog box pops up with the Sharing tab in front, as shown in Figure 4.8.

6. Click **Make This Folder Private** and click **OK.**

Whoa! _____

Do not convert a drive from FAT32 to NTFS format if you plan on ever running an older version of Windows on your computer or if you plan on reverting back to FAT32 for any reason.

Can't Make Your Folder Private?

If the Make This Folder Private option is grayed out, indicating it is unavailable, your computer's hard drive may be formatted as a FAT32 drive. FAT32, short for File Allocation Table 32, is a system that controls the way data is stored on the disk. In order to make a folder private, the disk must be converted to the NTFS (New Technology Filing System) format, which is the preferred format for computers running Windows XP.

Click Make this folder private

Figure 4.8

Make your My Documents folder private.

Windows XP comes with its own conversion utility that converts your hard drive to the NTFS format in a matter of minutes. To run the conversion utility, take the following steps:

1. Close all programs that are currently running.

2. Open the **Start** menu, point to **All Programs** and then **Accessories,** and click **Command Prompt.**

3. Type `convert c: /fs:ntfs` and press **Enter.** (If Windows is installed on a drive other than C, replace "c" with the drive's letter.)

4. Follow the onscreen instructions.

Sharing Your Documents with Other Users

Now that you locked your confidential files in a safe place, how do you provide access to those files you want to share with your fellow users? Simply copy or move the files you want to share to the Shared Documents folder. The Shared Documents folder also contains a Shared Pictures folder and a Shared Music folder, so you can share digital images and music clips with your fellow users. The Shared Documents folder is accessible to all users on the computer. See Chapter 6 to learn how to copy files from one folder to another.

The Least You Need to Know

- To access most user account settings, display the Control Panel and click the **User Accounts** icon.

- To prevent others from logging on to your Windows account, add a password to your account.

- To enable guest users to log on to Windows and prevent them from making any changes to Windows, enable guest accounts.

- Fast user switching enables two or more users to remain logged on at the same time and switch accounts without logging off.

- To gain access to some valuable Microsoft online services, register for a .Net passport and add it to your user account.

- To prevent other users from snooping around in your My Documents folder, make the folder private.

Launching Your First Program

In This Chapter

- ◆ Picking a program from the **Start, Programs** menu
- ◆ Running programs right from the Windows desktop
- ◆ Quickly launching programs from the taskbar
- ◆ Rearranging programs on the **Start** menu

An empty desktop might be a rare and beautiful sight, but it's useless. To get something done, have some fun, or at least make your boss think you're productive, you need a little clutter. You need to run a program or two.

The standard (albeit slow) method of running a program is to open the **Start** menu and click the name of the desired program. (The next section shows you just what to do.) However, Windows provides several more creative and much faster ways to run programs with a single click of the mouse. In this chapter, you get to try various techniques for running programs so that you can settle on the method you like best.

Computer Cheat

For some programs, the installation utility places a shortcut icon on the Windows desktop or at the top of the **Start** menu so you don't have to poke around on the **Start** menu to find the program.

Picking a Program from the Start Menu

Whenever you install a program, the installation utility places the program's name on the **Start, All Programs** menu (or **Start, Programs** menu in earlier versions of Windows) or one of the All Programs menu's submenus. To run the program, you simply click the **Start** button, point to **All Programs,** point to the desired program group (the name of the program's submenu), and click the program's name, as shown in Figure 5.1.

Figure 5.1

*You can find all installed programs on the **Start, All Programs** menu.*

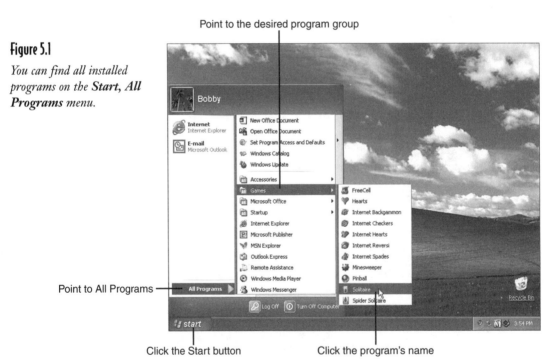

Point to the desired program group

Point to All Programs

Click the Start button

Click the program's name

More Creative Ways to Run Programs

Think of the **Start** menu as a storage cabinet in your basement. If you need something, you can always find it in the storage cabinet, but it's not the most convenient location. You might store your heavy-duty party-size cookware in the cellar, but you store the pots and pans you use daily right next to your stove.

The same is true in Windows. It's fine to run the programs you rarely use from the **Start** menu or one of its submenus, but if you use a program frequently, you should place it in a more convenient location and use the techniques described in the following sections to run the program.

Make Your Own Program Shortcut

The Windows desktop displays a few icons, called *shortcuts*, that let you run commonly used programs. Unlike bona fide icons that represent files, these "dummy" icons merely point to the original file. Windows displays a small arrow in the lower-left corner of each shortcut icon to indicate that it is not an icon for an actual file.

If you frequently run a program, you can create your own shortcut for that program and place it on the Windows desktop by performing the following steps:

1. Open the **Start** menu, point to **Programs,** and open the submenu that contains the desired program.

2. Right-click the name of the program you want to add to the desktop.

3. Point to **Send To,** and then click **Desktop (Create Shortcut).**

You can create desktop shortcuts for just about any object in Windows: a disk, folder, file, or program. Simply right-click the icon and choose **Create Shortcut.** This places the shortcut inside the same window or on the same menu as the original. You must then drag the icon to a blank area of the desktop.

To quickly arrange icons on the desktop, right-click a blank area of the desktop, point to **Arrange Icons,** and click **Auto Arrange,** (If you turn off the **Auto Arrange** feature, you can drag icons anywhere on the desktop.)

Is your desktop cluttered with shortcuts? Then consider storing your shortcuts in a folder on the desktop. Right-click a blank area on the desktop, point to **New,** and click **Folder.** Type a name for the folder and press **Enter.** Drag the desired program icons from the desktop over your new folder icon and release the mouse button; this moves the shortcuts to the folder, removing them from the desktop. You can click or double-click your folder icon to view its contents. Drag the folder to any edge of the Windows desktop to transform the folder into a toolbar; this gives you one-click access to the programs you use most frequently.

Inside Tip

Deleting a shortcut does not delete the original file it points to. However, deleting an actual file or program icon does delete the corresponding document or program file. Be careful whenever you choose to delete any icon.

Run Programs from Your Keyboard

You don't need a fancy programmable keyboard to have quick keyboard access to your programs. Windows lets you program any standard keyboard to run programs with a single key press. But first, you must assign a keystroke to the desired program. To do so, follow these steps:

1. Right-click the program's icon and choose **Properties.** (The icon might be on the **Start, All Programs** menu, on the Windows desktop, or in My Computer or Windows Explorer.)

2. Click in the **Shortcut Key** text box.

3. Press the key that you want to use to run this program. You can use any key except **Esc, Enter, Tab, Spacebar, Backspace, Print Screen,** or any function key or key combination used by Windows. If you press a number or character key, Windows automatically adds **Ctrl+Alt+** to create a *key combination.* For example, if you press **A,** Windows will create the **Ctrl+Alt+A** key combination, and you will press **Ctrl+Alt+A** (hold down **Ctrl** and **Alt,** and then press **A**) to run the program.

4. Click **OK.**

Run Programs When Windows Starts

Here's one last trick. If you always run a particular program right after starting your computer, you can make Windows run the program for you on startup. In Windows XP and Windows 2000, you can simply drag the icon for the desired program over the Start button, over All Programs, and over the Startup folder icon and drop it in place. The next time Windows starts, it automatically runs all programs in the Startup menu. If you have an earlier version of Windows, take the following steps to place a program in the Startup menu:

1. Right-click a blank area of the taskbar and click **Properties.**

2. Click the **Start Menu Programs** tab.

3. Click the **Advanced** button. This displays the entire **Start** menu and its submenus in Windows Explorer.

4. Click the plus sign next to **Programs.**

5. Change to the folder that contains the program you want Windows to run on startup, and then select the program icon by pointing to it (if its name is underlined) or clicking it (if the name is not underlined).

6. Scroll down the folder list on the left until you can see the Startup folder.

7. Drag the highlighted program icon from the file list on the right over the Startup folder on the left, and release the mouse button.

The next time you start your computer, Windows will start and then automatically run the program you just placed in the Startup folder.

Moving a Program to a More Convenient Location

If Windows buries your favorite program five levels down on the **Start** menu, you don't have to live with it. You can move your programs to place them right at your fingertips. Simply open the menu on which the program appears, and then drag the program to the desired location—to the **Programs** or **All Programs** submenu, the top of the **Start** menu, another submenu, a blank area on the desktop, or the programs folder you created a moment ago. If you drag the program to a different location on the **Start** menu, a horizontal bar appears as you drag the program, showing where it will be placed (see Figure 5.2). When the bar shows the desired location, release the mouse button.

Computer Cheat

To place a program at the top of the Start menu in Windows XP, open the **Start** menu, point to **All Programs**, right-click the desired program name or icon, and click **Pin to Start Menu**.

This bar shows where the program will be placed.

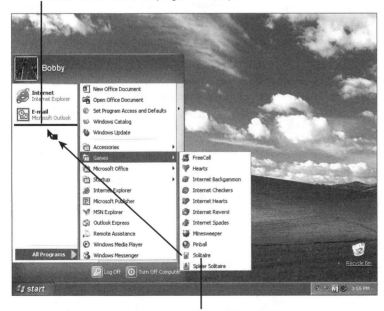

Figure 5.2

*You can rearrange items on the **Start** menu and its submenus.*

Drag the program to the desired location.

Running Programs with a Single Click

In late versions of Windows 95, Microsoft introduced a nifty little program launch pad called the Quick Launch toolbar. This toolbar roosts just to the right of the **Start** button and provides single-click access to commonly used programs. If the Quick Launch toolbar is not displayed, right-click the taskbar, point to **Toolbars,** and click **Quick Launch.** Initially, the Quick Launch toolbar contains the following four buttons:

Launch Internet Explorer Browser runs Microsoft's Internet Explorer, a program for navigating the World Wide Web.

Launch Outlook Express runs Microsoft's e-mail program to allow you to send and receive electronic mail over an Internet connection.

Show Desktop minimizes all open program windows to take you immediately to the Windows desktop.

Media Player runs the Windows Media Player, which allows you to listen to CDs and online radio stations, watch music videos and movie trailers, and experience other types of media. (If you have an older version of Windows, you might have the View Channels button instead, which displays a list of websites you can click to immediately "tune in to" the most commercialized sites on the web.)

Computer Cheat

Trick 1: Drag the top edge of the taskbar up to make the taskbar taller. Trick 2: Drag the taskbar to the top, left, or right side of the desktop and see what happens. Trick 3: Right-click a blank area of the taskbar and click **Properties** to view additional options.

To add your own buttons to the Quick Launch toolbar, simply drag the desired program icon to a blank spot on the toolbar and release the mouse button. If the new button does not immediately appear, drag the vertical bar just to the right of the Quick Launch toolbar to the right to make the toolbar bigger. You can also turn on other similar toolbars or create your own toolbar; right-click a blank area of the taskbar and point to **Toolbars** to check out your options.

Opening Documents with a Single Click

When you install a program, Windows associates that program with certain document types. For example, if you install Microsoft Word, Windows associates Word with all document files whose names end in .doc. Whenever you click or double-click a document icon that's associated with Word, Windows automatically runs Word and opens the document in Word.

Inside Tip

File names consist of two parts: the main file name and its extension (the last one to three characters that follow the period). Windows typically hides the file name extensions in My Computer and Windows Explorer. To view extensions, open My Computer, open the **View** or **Tools** menu, and click **Folder Options.** Click the **View** tab and click **Hide File Extensions for Known File Types** to remove the check mark. Click **OK.**

If you frequently open a particular document to edit it or refer to it, consider placing a shortcut icon for that document on the Windows desktop or in the Quick Launch toolbar. Use My Computer or Windows Explorer to change to the folder in which the document is stored, and then, using the right mouse button, drag the document's icon to the desired location. Release the mouse button and click **Create Shortcut(s) Here.**

The Least You Need to Know

- You can right-drag a program icon to a blank area on the desktop to create your own program shortcut.

- You can right-click an icon and click **Properties** to assign a key combination to a program.

- You can drag a program icon from a submenu to a more convenient location on the **Start** menu.

- For one-click access to a program or document, drag its icon to the Quick Launch toolbar.

- You can reconfigure the taskbar by dragging its top edge up to make it taller or by dragging it to a different location on the desktop.

Chapter 6

Managing Disks, CDs, Folders, and Files

In This Chapter

- ◆ Identify your computer's diskette drive (if it has one)
- ◆ Find drive A, C, D, and sometimes B
- ◆ Insert a diskette into a disk drive and pull it out
- ◆ Explore your computer's disks, folders, and files in Windows
- ◆ Cut, copy, move, and dump files and folders

Your computer comes complete with a well-stocked library of instructions and data that it uses to function, to help you do your job, and to play games. This library is stored on various disks inside the computer. The hard disk (or fixed disk), which you never see, is hidden inside the system unit. Other disks, called *removable disks*, reside outside the computer. These are the diskettes or "floppy disks," CDs (compact discs), DVDs (digital video discs), and other disks (and discs) that you load into your computer's disk drives to install programs or copy files to your computer.

In this chapter, you'll learn everything you need to know about disks and drives, including how to insert and remove various types of disks; recognize a drive by its letter; keep your disks, CDs, and DVDs in good condition; and explore and manipulate the files and folders stored on your disks.

Disk Drives: Easy as A-B-C

Most computers have three disk drives, as shown in Figure 6.1. Your computer refers to the drives as A, C, and D. If you're wondering what happened to B, it's used only if the computer has a second diskette drive.

Figure 6.1

Your computer uses letters from the alphabet to name its disk drives.

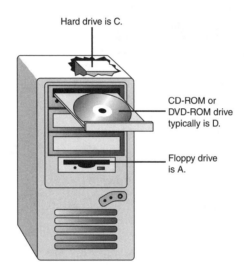

Hard drive is C.

CD-ROM or
DVD-ROM drive
typically is D.

Floppy drive
is A.

Panic Attack

If your computer has no diskette drive, don't panic—you might not need it. Many manufacturers are beginning to exclude diskette drives from their PCs, because most programs are distributed on CDs.

The Diskette Drives: A (and Sometimes B)

Your computer's system unit disk may have one or more slits or openings on the front, into which you can insert a diskette. The slit may be horizontal or vertical, depending on how your system is set up. This is your computer's diskette or "floppy disk" drive. Your computer typically refers to this drive as drive A. If your computer has two diskette drives, the computer refers to the second drive as drive B; otherwise, the letter B is not applied to any of your computer's drives.

The Hard Disk Drive: C

The drive inside the computer is the internal hard disk drive, usually called drive C. Some computers have an extra external hard drive that sits outside the computer and is connected to the system unit by a cable; the extra drive typically is assigned a letter that comes later in the alphabet, such as E or F. With hard drives you don't handle the disk; it's hermetically sealed inside the drive.

The CD-ROM, CD-RW, or DVD Drive: D

A CD-ROM (Compact Disc-Read Only Memory) is standard equipment on every new computer. It typically is located on the front of the system unit above or below the diskette drive, and the computer typically refers to it as drive D. A standard CD-ROM drive can only read data from discs—they cannot write data to discs. However, many computers, especially new computers, include disc drives that provide more powerful features. Following is a list of fairly common disc drives:

> **Tech Term**
>
> A hard disk drive can be **partitioned** (or divided) into one or more drives, which the computer refers to as drive C, drive D, drive E, and so on. The actual hard disk drive is called the **physical drive**; each partition is called a **logical drive**. If you encounter a computer that displays letters for more than one hard drive, the computer might have multiple hard drives or a single drive partitioned into several logical drives.

- **CD-R** drives can read data from CDs and can write data to special CD-R discs. These drives write data only once; they cannot erase data from a CD-R disc or record over it.

- **CD-RW** (CD-ReWritable) drives can read data from CDs and write data to CD-R or CD-RW discs. With CD-RW discs, the drive can record over data, erase data, and write data to the disc many times. This makes CD-RW drives an excellent choice for backing up the data files you create. Unfortunately, many audio CD players cannot play music clips stored on CD-RW disks.

- **DVD** (Digital Video Disc) drives can play DVD videos and read data from DVDs. DVDs can store more than 7 times as much data as can be stored on a CD, which is why they are used for full-length feature films.

- **CD/DVD, CD-R/DVD, or CD-RW/DVD** drives are combination drives that can read both CDs and DVDs. The CD-R/DVD and CD-RW/DVD drives can record data to CDs, but cannot record data to DVDs.

- **DVD-R** drives are relatively new disc drives that can record data to special DVD-R discs. These drives are excellent for storing home video clips (which take up a great deal of storage space).

◆ **DVD-RW or DVD+RW** are relatively new disc drives that can record data to special DVD-RW discs, erase or record data over existing data, and write to a disc several times.

Serving Information to the Computer on Diskettes

A diskette is like a skinny cassette. To get information that's stored on the diskette into your computer, you must load the diskette into your computer's diskette drive. Likewise, if there is something in your computer that you want to store for safekeeping or share with another user, you can copy the information from the computer to a diskette.

Two characteristics describe diskettes: *size* and *capacity*. You can measure size with a ruler. All new computers use 3½-inch diskettes. Capacity is the amount of information the diskette can hold; it's sort of like pints, quarts, and gallons. A 3½-inch high-density diskette (typically labeled HD) can store 1.44MB (megabytes). A 3½-inch, double-density diskette (typically labeled DD) can store 720KB (kilobytes).

Tech Term

Capacity is measured in **kilobytes** and **megabytes** (MB). Each *byte* consists of eight bits and is used to store a single character—A, B, C, 1, 2, 3, and so on. (For example, 01000001 is a byte that represents an uppercase A; each 1 or 0 is a bit.) A **kilobyte** is 1,024 bytes (1,024 characters). A **megabyte** is a little more than a million bytes. A **gigabyte** is just more than 1,000 megabytes.

Diskettes are fairly sturdy. You can fling a diskette across the room, and it probably will survive the flight. However, you should be somewhat gentle with your diskettes, especially if they contain data that you don't want to lose. To avoid damaging the sensitive magnetic media inside the diskette case, don't manually open the diskette, don't store it next to magnets or devices that generate strong magnetic fields (such as speakers or fans), don't carry the diskette around in your pocket or purse, don't eject the diskette when the drive light is on, and never use a diskette as a drink coaster. When you're not using a diskette, keep it in a pouch or envelop to prevent it from collecting dust.

To load a diskette in your computer's diskette drive, insert the disk, label side up, into the drive and push it all the way in. (If the disk slot is vertical, hold the disk so the label faces away from the eject button.) To eject a diskette, make sure the drive light is off and then press the eject button on the drive, and pull out the diskette.

Loading and Unloading CDs and DVDs

If you ever have loaded a compact disc into your audio CD player or a DVD into your DVD player, you have all the technical expertise required to load discs into your computer's CD or DVD drive. Just be sure to handle the disc only by its edges, so you don't scratch the surface or get any dirt or fingerprints on the disc. The technique for loading a disc in a CD or DVD drive differs depending on the drive. The following list covers the three most common ways to load a disc.

♦ If the drive has an open slot on the front, slide the disk, shiny side down, into the slot, just as you would insert a coin in a Coke machine.

♦ If the drive has a drive tray, press the Load/Eject button on the front of the drive to open it, and then lay the disc in the tray and press the Load/Eject button to load the disc.

♦ If the drive has a removable carriage, which is rare, press the Load/Eject button to eject the carriage, remove the carriage from the drive, place the disc inside the carriage, and insert the carriage into the drive.

Panic Attack
If you ever have trouble playing a CD or DVD, the disc might be dirty. To clean the disc, wipe it off with a soft, lint-free cloth from the center of the disc out to its edges. (Wipe the side without the picture or printing on it, because this is the side that the drive reads.) If something sticky gets on the disc, dampen the cloth with a little distilled water and wipe. Let the disc dry thoroughly before inserting it into the drive.

Can I Play My Music CDs?

CD-ROM drives can play audio CDs as well as computer CDs, so you can rock to your favorite tunes while balancing your budget. With Windows, you simply load the audio CD and Windows starts to play it. If your computer has a sound card, the audio will play through the speakers. If not, you must plug a set of headphones into the headphone jack on the CD-ROM drive. See Chapter 24 for details.

Can I Watch DVD Video Flicks on My PC?

The short answer is yes, if your PC has a DVD drive you can watch DVD videos on your PC. However, you probably won't want to watch DVD videos on your PC. I once watched *Apocalypse Now* on my 17-inch monitor and had a headache for two days. The picture was sharp and the sound was incredible—my computer has a better sound system than my TV—but the picture was so dinky I had to press my face to the screen to see anything.

Whoa!

Windows should start to play the audio CD as soon as you insert it. If you're using Windows 98, Me, or XP, and Windows does not start to play the CD, hold down the **Alt** key while double-clicking the **My Computer** icon and then click the **Device Manager** tab (Windows NT and 2000 do not display the Device Manager). Click the plus sign next to CD-ROM, and then double-click the name of your CD-ROM. Click the **Settings** tab and make sure there is a check mark in the **Auto Insert Notification** box. Click **OK** to save your changes and click **OK** again to close the System Settings dialog box.

At any rate, if your computer has a DVD drive, it probably has a DVD video player. Windows Me and later versions include a DVD player (on the Start, Programs, Accessories, Entertainment menu) but it might not appear unless you have a DVD decoder installed. As shown in Figure 6.2, the DVD player has its own onscreen controls for playing, stopping, pausing, fast-forwarding, and rewinding the video. You also can right-click the video as it is playing to access the video's built-in menu system.

Figure 6.2

The onscreen DVD player has controls comparable to a DVD player that's connected to a TV.

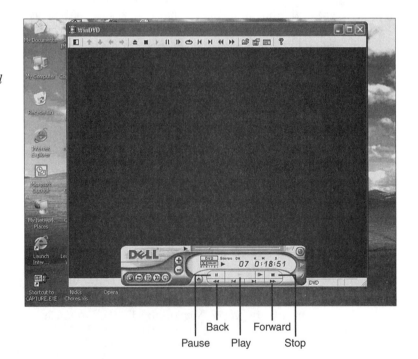

Back   Forward

Pause   Play   Stop

Inside the Belly of Your Computer: The Hard Disk

The hard disk drive is like a big diskette drive complete with a disk (you don't take the disk out; it stays in the drive forever). A small hard disk drive can store more than 20 gigabytes, the equivalent of about 15,000 3½-inch, high-density diskettes. Many new computers come with hard drives that can store more than 100 gigabytes! Sound excessive? Well, 100 gigabytes is excessive if you plan on using your computer to play games and do a little work, but if you plan on editing video clips and storing photo albums on your computer, your computer can gobble up a gigabyte in a hurry. A 20 to 30 gigabyte hard drive is plenty for most users.

To get information to the hard disk, you copy information to it from diskettes, CDs, DVDs, or Internet sites, or you save the files you create directly to the hard disk. The information stays on the hard disk until you erase the information. When the computer needs information it goes directly to the hard disk, reads the information into memory, and continues working.

Inside Tip

If your computer is part of a network, it might not have a disk drive. If that's the case, forget all this babble about diskettes, CDs, and hard drives. Your network probably has a central network server with a disk drive as big as a building that stores all the information and programs you and everyone else in the company will ever need.

The Outsiders: External Drives and Other Anomalies

Although the hard disk, CD-ROM, and diskette drives round out the team lineup for standard drives, other types of disk drives have been and continue to be popular additions to computer systems. Some of these drives are installed in the drive bays inside the system unit and appear next to the diskette and CD-ROM drives, whereas others sit outside the system unit, like your printer, and connect to the system unit with a USB cable or other type of cable. The following list describes some of these more popular add-on drives:

- **Iomega Zip drives** store data on 100MB, 250MB, or 750MB removable disks. These drives are excellent for doing small backups and for storing presentations that you need to take on the road.

- **Iomega Peerless drives** store data on 10GB removable cartridges. These drives are popular for backing up data and adding storage to a computer that's running out of hard disk space.

- **USB flash drives** are tiny cards that plug right into your computer's USB port. They typically store upwards of 64MB per card and are great for carrying around audio clips, digital images, and other files.

- **Imation SuperDisk drives** are super-diskettes capable of storing up to 120MB or 240MB per disk. These drives can also read and write to standard 1.44MB diskettes.

- **Tape drives** are more similar to audio cassettes than they are to disks. Tape drives are primarily used to back up data. They're too slow for most other purposes.

What's on a Disk? Files and Folders

Now you know that your computer has disk drives and disks/discs, but what's on these disks? Unless a disk is completely empty, the disk contains files. Your computer's hard disk, for example, at least has the files it needs to run Windows. It probably has many other files, as well, for any installed programs and any files you or someone else has created when using the computer. Your computer uses two types of files: *data files* and *program files*. Data files are the files you create and save—your business letters, reports, the pictures you draw, the results of any games you save. Program files are the files you get when you purchase a program. These files contain the instructions that tell your computer how to run the program. A program can consist of hundreds of interrelated files.

To manage all of these files, your computer stores the files in separate folders (also called *directories*). Whenever you install a program, the installation utility (which places the program on your hard disk) automatically creates a folder for the program.

Before you lay your fingers on any folders or files, you should understand how the folders are structured. Think of your disk as an oversized filing cabinet stuffed with manila folders. Each folder represents a directory that stores files or additional folders. The structure of the folders comprises what is called a *directory tree*, which looks a little like a family tree, as shown in Figure 6.3. The drive letter always sits atop the directory tree; the drive letter is considered to be the *root directory*. Folders then branch off from the root directory. Programs often display the location of a file as a *path* to the directory or folder in which the file is saved. For example, if Tom's My Documents folder contains a file named taxes.doc, the path to the file would be as follows:

```
c:\documents and settings\tom\my documents\taxes.doc
```

The path begins at the root (drive C), proceeds through the first folder to the second folder, through the third folder, and then specifies the filename. Paths can be much longer, of course.

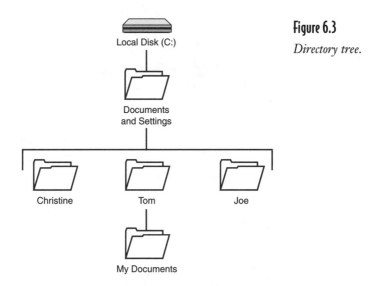

Figure 6.3

Directory tree.

Exploring Your Disks and Folders

Windows gives you two ways to poke around on your computer and find out what's on your disks and what's in your folders. You can double-click the **My Computer** icon on the Windows desktop (or click the **Start** menu and click **My Computer**), or you can run Windows Explorer by taking one of the following steps:

 ♦ In Windows 98, choose **Start, Programs, Windows Explorer.**

 ♦ In Windows Me, choose **Start, Programs, Accessories, Windows Explorer.**

 ♦ In Windows XP, choose **Start, All Programs, Accessories, Windows Explorer.**

If you open **My Computer** in Windows 95 or 98, Windows displays icons for all the disk drives on your computer, plus three folder icons: **Control Panel** (which allows you to change system settings), **Printers** (for setting up a printer), and **Dial-Up Networking** (for Internet access). To find out what's on a disk or in a folder, double-click its icon. (Remember, if your icons are underlined, click once; double-clicking these icons might perform the action twice.) In Windows Me, My Computer displays icons for all disks plus an icon for the Control Panel. The **Dial-Up Networking** and **Printers** icons are in the Control Panel. In Windows XP, My Computer displays icons for all disks plus a bar on the left that contains icons for system tasks, network resources, and other items, as shown in Figure 6.4.

Figure 6.4

My Computer enables you to explore the contents of your computer's disk drives.

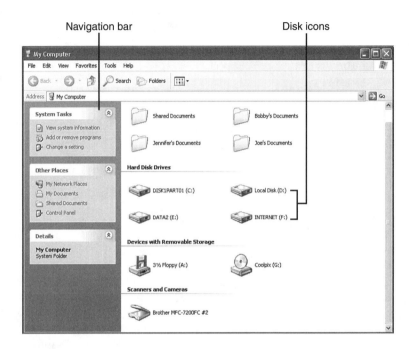

Navigation bar   Disk icons

Windows Explorer is My Computer's older, more capable sibling. It allows you to perform the same basic tasks you can perform in My Computer, but it provides a two-pane window that displays a folder list on the left and a file list on the right. This two-paned layout lets you easily copy and move files and folders from one disk or folder to another by dragging them from one pane to the other, as shown in Figure 6.5.

Computer Cheat

You can make Windows Explorer or any other program more accessible by placing an icon for it on the Windows desktop. Open the **Start** menu and display the icon for Windows Explorer or whichever program you want to add to the desktop. Right-click the icon, point to **Send To,** and click **Desktop (Create Shortcut).**

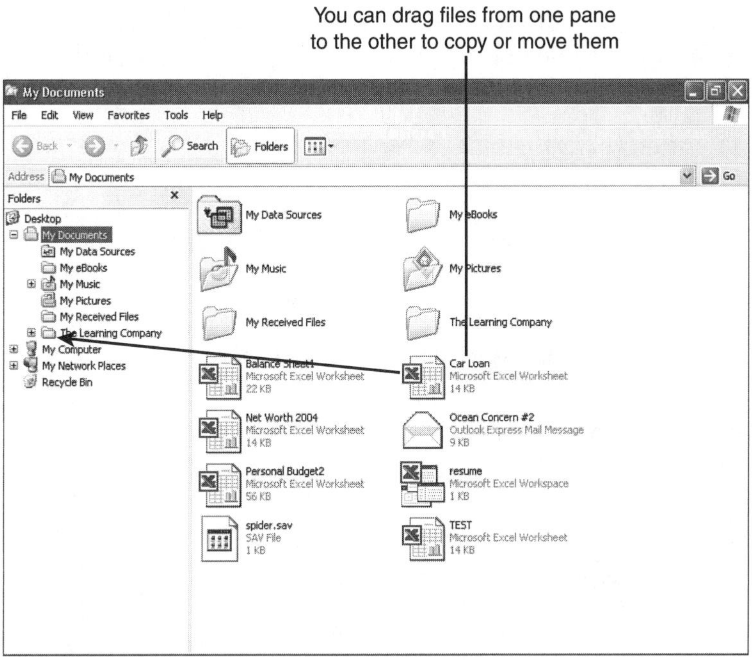

You can drag files from one pane
to the other to copy or move them

Figure 6.5

Windows Explorer is a use-ful tool for copying and mov-ing files.

Copying, Moving, and Dumping Files and Folders

Using My Computer or Windows Explorer, you can copy files from any disk. On hard disk drives, diskettes, and other rewriteable storage media, you have complete control over the folders and files on the disks. You can copy files, move files from one disk or folder to another, or even delete files or folders to completely remove them from a disk. The following sections show you how to perform these essential disk-management tasks.

Selecting Folders and Files

If you're copying, deleting, or moving a single file or folder, selecting it is about as easy as picking a lemon off a used car lot. If the file or folder name is underlined (Windows Web Style is on), simply rest the tip of the mouse pointer on the icon for the file or folder you want to select. If the file or folder name is not underlined, click the file or folder. You would think that if you clicked another file or folder you'd select that one, too, but it doesn't work that way. Selecting another file deselects the first one. This can be maddening to anyone who doesn't know the tricks for selecting multiple files or folders; here's how you do it:

◆ To select neighboring (*contiguous*) files and folders, click the first file or folder and hold down the **Shift** key while pointing to or clicking the last one in the group (see Figure 6.6).

◆ To select non-neighboring (*noncontiguous*) items, hold down the **Ctrl** key while pointing to or clicking the name of each item.

◆ To deselect an item, hold down the **Ctrl** key while pointing to or clicking its name.

◆ You also can select a group of items by dragging a box around them. When you release the mouse button, all the items within the box's borders are highlighted.

Keep in mind that if Web Style is on, you point to files or folders to select them and you click to open files or folders. With Web Style off, you click to select and double-click to open.

To select neighboring files, select the first file and then
hold down the Shift key while selecting the last file

Ctrl+click or Ctrl+point to select noncontiguous files

Figure 6.6

You can use the Shift and Control keys to select neighboring or non-neighboring files.

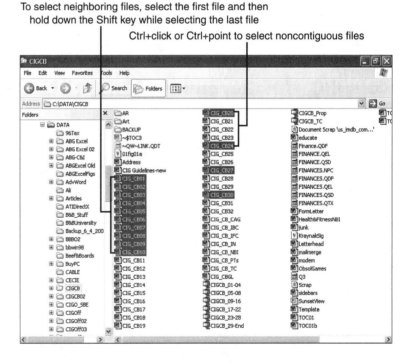

When you're selecting groups of files, it often helps to change the way the files are sorted or arranged. Open the **View** menu and choose to sort files by name, by type (using their filename extensions), by size, or by date. For example, you can sort files by type to list all the document files that end in .DOC. You also can arrange the icons by opening the **View** menu and selecting one of the following options:

- ◆ **Large Icons.** Good if you want to select only a few files or folders.

- ◆ **Small Icons.** Displays tiny icons. Folders appear at the top; files at the bottom. In this display you can drag a box around items down and to the right.

- ◆ **List.** Displays tiny icons (just like Small Icons view), but folders (directories) are listed on the left; files are listed on the right.

- ◆ **Details.** Displays additional information such as the date and time at which files were created. (This view makes it tough to manage large numbers of files.)

Inside Tip

In Small Icons view, if you click an item in one column and Shift+click an item in another column, you select a rectangular block of items, just as if you had dragged a box around them. In List view, items snake up and down a page like newspaper columns. If you click an item in one column and Shift+click an item in another column, you select the two items you clicked and all the items in between.

Making Your Own Folders

You rarely need to create your own folders. When you install a program it usually makes the folders it requires or uses existing folders. In addition, if your computer runs Windows Me or a later version, Windows creates a folder for you called My Documents, in which you can save all the files you create. However, if you want to store your files in a different folder or you want to store files in a subfolder inside the My Documents folder, you need to know how to create a folder. Give it a shot; create a new folder on drive C. You can always delete the folder later if you don't need it. Follow these steps:

1. Run **My Computer.**

2. Double-click the icon for drive **C.** A window opens showing all the folders on drive C.

3. Right-click a blank area inside the window to display a shortcut menu.

4. Rest the mouse pointer on **New** and then click **Folder.** Windows creates a folder on drive C, cleverly called New Folder.

5. Type a name for the folder (255 characters or fewer). As you start typing, the **New Folder** name is deleted and is replaced by what you type. You can use any character or number, but you cannot use any of the following characters: \ / : * ? " < > |.

6. Press **Enter.**

Long names (255 characters for folders and files) are great for programs that support them, but some older programs and DOS cannot display long names. In such cases the program displays a portion of the name, such as letter~1.doc. This does not affect the contents of the file, and you can still open it.

Inside Tip

If the Windows desktop becomes too crowded with shortcuts and other icons, you can create folders to help organize the desktop. Right-click a blank area of the desktop, point to **New,** and click **Folder.**

Whoa!

Never delete program files, because doing so may incapacitate your program. If you want to remove a program use the Windows Add/Remove Program utility, which is explained in Chapter 10.

Inside Tip

To change the properties of the Recycle Bin, including the maximum amount of disk space it can use, right-click the **Recycle Bin** icon and click **Properties.** To empty the Recycle Bin, first make sure it contains only those files and folders you will never ever need. Then, right-click the **Recycle Bin** icon and click **Empty Recycle Bin.**

Dumping Files in the Recycle Bin

Windows comes complete with its own trash compactor. Whenever a file or icon has outlived its usefulness, either drag it over the trash can icon (the **Recycle Bin**) and release the mouse button, or click the file in My Computer or Windows Explorer to select it and then click the **Delete** button (the button with the X on it just below the menu bar) or press the **Del** key. Windows displays a dialog box asking you to confirm the deletion or cancel it; respond accordingly. If you confirm the deletion, Windows moves the file to the **Recycle Bin** without permanently deleting it, so you can recover it later if the need should arise.

Pulling things out of the **Recycle Bin** is as easy as dragging them into it. Double-click the **Recycle Bin** icon to display its contents. If the icon names are underlined, rest the mouse pointer on the icon you want to restore to highlight it. If the icon names are not underlined, click the item you want to restore to select it. **Ctrl+point** or **Ctrl+click** to select additional items. Open the **File** menu and click **Restore.**

Renaming Folders and Files

Managing your folders and files is an exercise in on-the-job training. As you create and use folders, you find yourself slapping any old name on them. Later, you find that the name doesn't really indicate the folder's contents, the name is too long, or you are just plain sick of seeing it snake across your screen. Fortunately, renaming a folder or file is easy:

◆ If you click files and folders to select them, click the icon for the file or folder you want to rename. The name appears highlighted, as shown in Figure 6.7. Click the name of the file or folder and type the new name. Click a blank area of the screen to make the name change official.

◆ If you point to files and folders to select them, right-click the file or folder you want to rename and click **Rename.** Type the new name and press **Enter** or click a blank area in the window.

◆ Whether you point to or click files or folders to select them, highlight the file or folder name by pointing at it or clicking it, press the **F2** key, and type the new name. Press **Enter.**

Whoa!

Windows uses the names of program folders to find the program files it needs to run the programs. If you rename a program folder or file, Windows usually throws a fit and won't run the program for you.

Type a new name

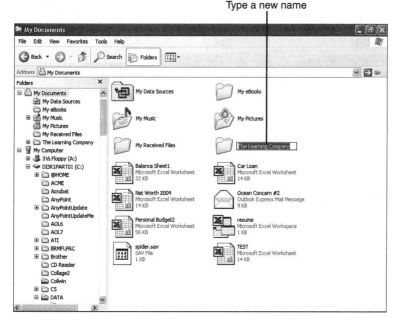

Figure 6.7

You can easily rename files and folders.

Moving and Copying Folders and Files

You can quickly move files and folders to reorganize them. To move an item, simply drag it over the folder or disk icon to which you want to move it. When moving or copying files and folders, keep the following in mind:

◆ To copy or move multiple files or folders, select the items as explained earlier in this chapter. When you copy or move one of the selected items, all the other items follow it.

◆ If you drag a folder or file to a different disk (or a folder on a different disk), Windows assumes that you want to *copy* the item to that disk. To move the item, hold down the **Shift** key while dragging.

◆ If you drag a folder or file to a different folder on the same disk, Windows assumes that you want to *move* the item into the destination folder. To copy the item, hold down the **Ctrl** key while dragging.

◆ To move a file or folder to the Windows desktop, drag it from My Computer or Windows Explorer onto a blank area on the desktop and release the mouse button.

◆ If you're not sure what you want to do, drag the folder or file with the right mouse button. When you release the button a context menu appears, presenting options for moving or copying the item.

Sometimes the easiest way to move a file or folder is to cut and paste it. Right-click the icon for the item you want to move and click **Cut.** Now change to the disk or folder in which you want the cut item placed. Right-click the disk or folder icon (or right-click a blank area in its contents window), and click **Paste.** You also can copy and move items in Windows Explorer by dragging items from the Contents list (right pane) over a disk or folder icon displayed in the left pane, as shown in Figure 6.8. You also can drag items from one My Computer window to another.

Drag selected file(s) or folder(s) over the destination icon.

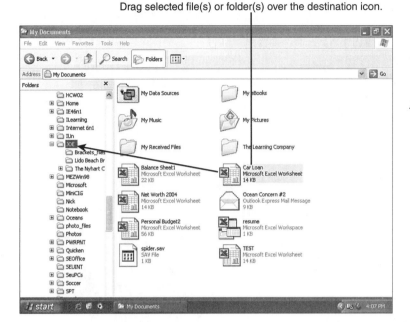

Figure 6.8

In Windows Explorer, you drag files or folders from the Contents list to a disk or folder icon.

The Least You Need to Know

♦ Your computer identifies your disk drives using letters: A and B for diskette drives; typically C for your hard drive; and D, E, F, and so on for additional drives, such as CD-ROM drives.

♦ Be gentle with diskettes, CDs, and DVDs.

♦ When inserting diskettes, CDs, and DVDs, never force the disk or disc into the drive. This can damage the disks and the drive's read/write head.

♦ When you create and save a document, it is stored as a named file on your computer's hard disk.

♦ Folders hold a group of related files on a disk.

♦ Use My Computer or Windows Explorer to see what's on your disks and to move, copy, rename, or delete files and folders.

Part 2

Personalizing Your Work Space

If you're like most people, you enjoy decorating your home or office to add your own personal touch. You might paint the walls a different color, hang a few photos of friends or family members, or populate your shelves with knickknacks or Beanie Babies.

In similar ways, you can decorate your computer desktop. Windows provides the tools you need to change the color of your desktop, pick a theme for icons and mouse pointers, turn on an animated screen saver, create your own icons and menus, and install additional games and other programs. This part shows you how to completely renovate your computerized desktop.

Chapter 7

Using a Cool Desktop Background and Sounds

In This Chapter

- ◆ Jazzing up the appearance of your desktop with themes
- ◆ Hanging some self-adhesive wallpaper
- ◆ Making your desktop look like a web page
- ◆ Turning on a screen saver included with Windows
- ◆ Making Windows play some different tunes

Are you tired of your Windows desktop? Do your shortcut icons look dumpy next to those of your friends and colleagues? Do you want to jazz up your work area? Put it in motion with some animated graphics? Play some cool sounds? Make your Windows desktop the envy of your department? Of course you do.

In this chapter, you make your personal computer more personal. Here you learn how to take control of the Windows desktop to make it look and act the way you want it to. You also learn how to customize the sounds that Windows plays whenever you select a particular command or perform a specific task.

Animating Your Desktop with Themes

Spreading your work out on the standard Windows desktop is about as exciting as spending an eight-hour day in a gray cubicle—the surroundings are anything but inspiring. Fortunately, Windows provides a selection of *desktop themes* to revitalize your working environment. Each desktop theme contains a graphical desktop background and specialized icons, mouse pointers, and sounds. For example, the Jungle theme places a jungle scene on the Windows background and plays animal sounds when certain events occur, such as Windows startup.

CAUTION

Whoa!

Windows XP comes with only a handful of desktop themes, none of which is very exciting. In order to obtain additional desktop themes, you must purchase Microsoft Plus! for Windows. (If you upgraded from an older version of Windows that had Desktop Themes installed on it, those themes will be available in Windows XP.)

Installing Desktop Themes

To use a desktop theme, first be sure that the desktop themes are installed on your computer. If your computer is running Windows XP, a couple desktop themes are installed automatically and are currently available. If you have an older version of Windows, check to make sure the desktop themes are installed. Open the **Start** menu, point to **Settings,** and click **Control Panel.** Click or double-click the **Add/Remove Programs** icon, and then click the **Windows Setup** tab. If the **Desktop Themes** check box is blank, click the box to place a check mark in it. Then insert the Windows CD into your computer's CD-ROM drive, click **OK,** and follow the onscreen instructions. When the installation is complete, you're ready to pick a theme that suits your tastes.

Picking Your Favorite Desktop Theme

Let the fun begin! To check out the available desktop themes and pick your favorite theme in Windows XP, right-click a blank area of the Windows desktop and click **Properties.** This calls up the Display Properties dialog box, as shown in Figure 7.1. Click the **Themes** tab. Open the **Theme** list and click the desired theme. (The **Browse** option enables you to poke around in the folders on your computer's hard disk to look in vain for more themes. The **More Themes Online** option opens an advertisement page for Microsoft Plus!)

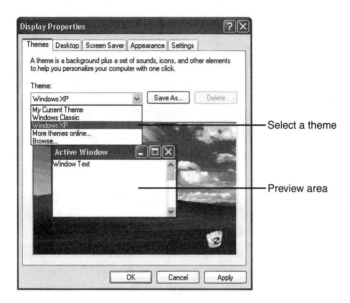

Figure 7.1

Windows XP features a couple desktop themes.

If you have Windows Me or Windows 98, and you installed the desktop themes, you have a wide selection of themes from which to choose. Take the following steps to check out the available desktop themes and pick your favorite theme:

1. Click the **Start** button, point to **Settings,** and click **Control Panel.**

2. In the Control Panel, double-click the **Desktop Themes** icon. If you're working in Windows Me, you have a simplified Control Panel that might not show all the Control Panel icons. Click **View all Control Panel options,** on the left side of the Control Panel window; then click the **Desktop Themes** icon. The Desktop Themes dialog box appears, as shown in Figure 7.2.

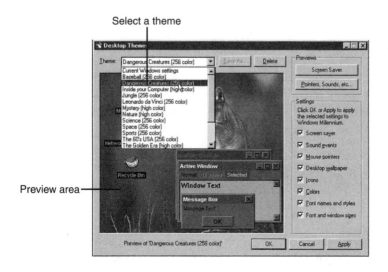

Figure 7.2

Select the desired desktop theme.

3. Open the **Theme** drop-down list and choose the desired desktop theme.

4. The selected theme appears in the preview area. To preview the screen saver, click the **Screen Saver** button. (You'll learn more about screen savers later in this chapter, in the section "Securing Some Privacy with a Screen Saver.")

5. Windows plays the screen saver. Move the mouse pointer or press the **Shift** key to turn it off.

6. To preview mouse pointers, sounds, and icons, click the **Pointers, Sounds, etc.** button.

CAUTION

Whoa!

If your computer seems a bit sluggish after you turn on a desktop theme, you might want to disable it. Desktop themes require disk space and memory that some computers just can't spare.

7. The Preview window appears. Click the tab for the type of object you want to preview: **Pointers, Sounds,** or **Visuals.** Double-click an item in the list to display it in the preview area or play a sound. When you're done, click the **Close** button.

8. You can disable individual components of the desktop theme by clicking the name of each component to remove the check mark from its box. Click **OK** to save your settings.

Messing with the Screen Colors

A desktop theme makes a nice novelty item, but the color combinations and fonts used in some of the themes can make it almost impossible to decipher the text and get any work done. If you're looking for a more subtle change in the desktop appearance, try tweaking the color scheme yourself.

To try out various color combinations, right-click a blank area of the desktop and click **Properties.** The Display Properties dialog box appears. Click the **Appearance** tab to access the color schemes, as shown in Figure 7.3. In Windows XP, you can use the options on the Appearance tab to choose a prefab design, color scheme, and font size that control all your windows. To make more specific adjustments, click the **Advanced** button.

In earlier versions of Windows, the Appearance tab provides controls for making specific adjustments to the display. (You can access these settings in Windows XP by clicking the **Advanced** button.) To change the overall appearance of your desktop, open the Scheme drop-down list and click the name of a theme that piques your interest. To change the properties of an object (the desktop, a window's title bar, a button, or some other item), click the object in the preview area in the top part of the dialog box, or open the **Item** drop-down list and click the object's name. Then, enter your preferences for the object's size, color, font, and other properties. Click **OK** when you're done.

Panic Attack

I've seen many a desktop with icons that overlap. If your desktop seems overly cluttered, try respacing the icons. In the **Item** list, choose **Icon Spacing (Horizontal)** or **Icon Spacing (Vertical)** and increase the **Size** setting.

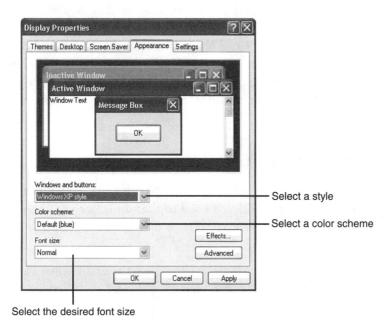

Figure 7.3

Pick a prefab color scheme and style.

Select a style

Select a color scheme

Select the desired font size

Hanging Wallpaper in the Background

Have you ever decorated your desk with wallpaper? Of course not! Maybe a new coat of varnish, some paint, or even contact paper, but never wallpaper. Well that's about to change. In Windows, you can use wallpaper to add a more graphic background to your desktop.

To hang wallpaper in Windows, first right-click a blank area of the desktop and click **Properties.** Click the **Desktop** or **Background** tab, if necessary, to bring it to the

Inside Tip _____

To use an image from the web as your desktop background, right-click the image and choose **Set as Background.**

front. In the list of backgrounds, near the bottom of the dialog box, click the name of the desired wallpaper. If the preview area shows a dinky icon in the middle of the screen, open the **Display** drop-down list and click **Tile** (to use the image as a pattern to fill the screen) or **Stretch** (to make the image as big as the desktop). Click **OK.**

Controlling the Desktop Icons and Visual Effects

A quick glance at the desktop icons might give you the impression that they're immutable. However, Windows does provide a set of options for controlling the appearance and behavior of these icons and other visual elements that make up the desktop. The steps for customizing the desktop icons vary considerably depending on whether your computer is running Windows XP or an earlier version of Windows. The following sections provide the instructions you need for whichever version of Windows your computer is running.

Customizing Desktop Icons in Windows XP

To take control of your desktop icons in Windows XP, right-click a blank area of the Windows desktop and click **Properties.** Click the **Desktop** tab and click the **Customize Desktop** button. This displays the Desktop Items dialog box, as shown in Figure 7.4.

Figure 7.4

The Desktop Items dialog box lets you change the appearance of icons and other desktop effects.

Using the Desktop Items dialog box, you can customize the desktop icons in any of the following ways:

♦ To display additional system icons on the desktop, including icons for My Computer, Internet Explorer, My Network Places, and My Documents, click the check box next to each icon you want placed on the desktop.

♦ To change the appearance of one of the desktop icons, click the icon, and then click the **Change Icon** button. Click the desired icon and click **OK.** You can return to the original icon by clicking it and clicking the **Restore Default** button.

♦ To have Windows automatically remove unused shortcut icons from the desktop after 60 days, click **Run Desktop Cleanup Wizard Every 60 Days** to place a check mark next to the option.

Click **OK** to save your settings and return to the Display Properties dialog box. To access additional preferences that control the overall appearance of the icons, click the **Appearance** tab and click the **Effects** button, and enter your preferences. When you're done, click **OK** to return to the Display Properties dialog box, and then click **OK** to save your settings and return to the Windows desktop.

Customizing Desktop Icons in Windows 2000, Me, and 98

To change the appearance of the icons in earlier versions of Windows, right-click a blank area of the Windows desktop and click **Properties.** In the Display Properties dialog box, click the **Effects** tab and take any of the following steps:

♦ To change the appearance of one of the desktop icons, click the icon, and then click the **Change Icon** button. Click the desired icon and click **OK.**

♦ To display only the icons' names when you choose to view the desktop as a web page, turn on **Hide icons when the desktop is viewed as a web page.** (This option is unavailable in Windows Me.)

♦ To display larger icons, turn on **Use large icons.**

♦ To make the icons look a little fancier, turn on **Show icons using all possible colors.** (This consumes slightly more memory.)

♦ To make windows, menus, and lists appear to spread out onto the desktop (instead of just popping up onscreen), turn on **Animate windows, menus, and lists** (in Windows 95 or 98) or **Use transition effects for menus and tooltips** (in Windows Me).

◆ To make the onscreen type appear less blocky, turn on **Smooth edges of screen fonts.**

◆ To display the contents of a window while you're dragging it across the screen, turn on **Show window contents while dragging.** (By default, Windows displays only an outline of the window you're dragging.)

When you're done entering your preferences, click **OK** to save your settings and return to the desktop.

What's This Web Tab For?

Microsoft was a little subtle about unveiling its plot for global domination. There were no great speeches, no press releases, not even the standard printed manifesto. Instead, Microsoft released a new version of Windows 95 that included a deceptively revamped Windows desktop, called the "Active Desktop," which it then included in Windows 98, Windows Me, Windows 2000, and Windows XP.

Although it's nearly identical in appearance to the old desktop, this new desktop includes several features designed to make it more customizable and to integrate it with the Internet (specifically, the web) and with any of your network connections. Here's a list of what the active desktop has to offer:

◆ **Web Style.** You met Web Style in Chapter 2. With Web Style on, Windows gives you one-click access to your files, folders, and programs.

◆ **Quick Launch toolbar.** You met the Quick Launch toolbar in Chapter 3. This toolbar and the whole taskbar-toolbar approach give you easy access to the programs you run most often.

◆ **Active desktop components.** Active desktop components are windows to the Internet. These objects can pull data from the Internet and display it on your desktop to provide you with up-to-the-minute news, stock prices, sports scores, weather reports, and much more. As you will see in this section, you can snatch active desktop components right off the web.

The **Web** tab is your key to mastering the active desktop and turning on active desktop components. If you don't have an Internet connection, or if you're not sure whether you do, work through Part 4 first. You can then add active components to your desktop by taking the following steps:

1. Right-click a blank area of the Windows desktop, and click **Properties.** The Display Properties dialog box appears.

2. Take one of the following steps to view the Web tab:

   ◆ **Windows XP:** Click the **Desktop** tab, click **Customize Desktop,** and click the **Web** tab.

   ◆ **Windows Me, 98, or 95:** Click the **Web** tab.

3. Click **New.** The New Active Desktop Item dialog box appears, asking if you want to go to the Gallery.

4. Click **Visit Gallery** (in Windows Me or XP) or **Yes** (in Windows 95 or 98). This runs Internet Explorer and connects you to the Internet if you are not already connected. Internet Explorer loads the Active Desktop Gallery web page.

5. Follow the trail of links to the desktop component you want. A page appears, as shown in Figure 7.5, describing the component and displaying a link or button for downloading it. (A *link* is an icon, graphic, or highlighted text that points to another web page or file.)

Click the link to add the active component to your desktop

Figure 7.5

Active desktop components are readily available on the web.

6. Click the link or button to download (copy) the component and place it on your desktop. Internet Explorer displays a dialog box, asking for your confirmation.

7. Click **Yes.**

8. A second dialog box appears, indicating that Windows will set up a subscription for this component. (A subscription simply tells Windows to download updated information automatically at a scheduled time.) Click **OK.** Internet Explorer downloads the component and places it on the desktop.

Locking Your Desktop Settings

As you saw in Chapter 4, Windows XP features user accounts, which enable each person to customize their Windows desktop without affecting other users' desktops. If your computer is running an earlier version of Windows, you can set up your computer for multiple users and lock the desktop settings for each user. To do so, take the following steps:

1. Click the **Start** button, point to **Settings,** and click **Control Panel.**

2. Double-click the **Passwords** icon. If you're working in Windows Me, the Control Panel might not display the **Passwords** icon. Click **View all Control Panel options,** on the left side of the Control Panel window; then click the **Passwords** icon.

3. Click the **User Profiles** tab.

4. Make sure the option **Users can customize their preferences and desktop settings** is selected.

5. Make sure both options under **User Profile Settings** are checked.

6. Click **OK.**

When you start Windows, a dialog box prompts you to enter your name and password. Instruct each person who uses your computer to enter a unique name and (optional) password when prompted to log on. Any preferences or desktop settings the user enters are then stored under that person's name. They do not affect settings that the other users enter.

When a user is done using the computer, he or she should log off. To log off, click the **Start** button and choose **Log Off** *yourname* (*yourname* varies, depending on who's logged on). When the confirmation dialog box appears, click **Yes.** (In earlier versions of Windows, you must choose **Start, Shut Down** to display the option for logging off.) Windows restarts without restarting your computer and displays a dialog box prompting the next user for his or her name and password.

Panic Attack

If you forget your password, you can still use Windows, but you'll lose your customized settings. Write down your password and keep it in a safe place. If you do lose your password, just press the **Esc** key when Windows prompts you to enter your name. Now, go to the Windows folder on drive C and find the file that has your user name. The file has a .pwl extension, but you might not see the extension. Delete this file and restart Windows. When Windows prompts you to type your name, type your name, type a new password, and click **OK**.

Securing Some Privacy with a Screen Saver

Have you ever seen a school of fish swimming across a computer screen? How 'bout a flock of flying toasters? A shower of meteors? A pack of creepy crawling cockroaches? If you've seen any of these animated patterns scurrying about a monitor, you have already witnessed screen savers in action.

In addition to functioning as an interesting conversation piece, screen savers serve a useful purpose: They deter passersby from snooping at your screen while you're away from your desk. For example, if you play Solitaire all day at work and you don't want your boss to know about it, you can activate a screen saver whenever you step away from your desk. You can even set up the screen saver with password protection so that nobody can turn it off without knowing the password.

Inside Tip

The best screen savers that are included with Windows are part of the desktop themes. If you selected a theme earlier in this chapter, you have already selected a screen saver. The following sections show you how to change the screen saver's properties.

Checking Out the Windows Screen Savers

Windows comes with several of its own screen savers. To check out the selection, right-click a blank area of the Windows desktop, click **Properties**, and click the **Screen Saver** tab. Open the **Screen Saver** drop-down list and click the name of a screen saver that appeals to you, as shown in Figure 7.6. To view the screen saver in action, click the **Preview** button. To deactivate the screen saver (and return to the Display Properties dialog box), roll the mouse or press the **Shift** key.

Figure 7.6

*Check out the screen savers
included with Windows.*

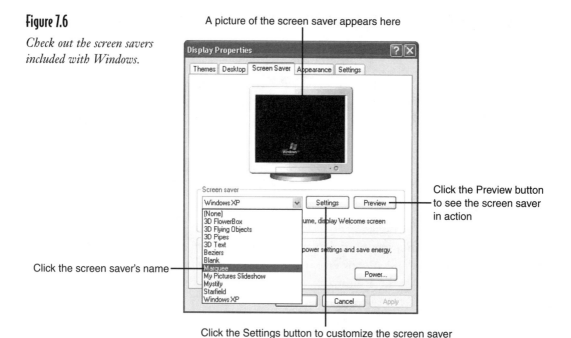

A picture of the screen saver appears here

Click the Preview button
to see the screen saver
in action

Click the screen saver's name

Click the Settings button to customize the screen saver

The Scrolling Marquee is great for keeping family members and co-workers informed when you're away from your desk. Open the **Screen Saver** list and click **Scrolling Marquee** (or **Marquee**). Click the **Settings** button. Drag over the text in the **Text** box, type the desired message, and click **OK.** Click **OK** to save your changes and close the Display Properties dialog box. When the Scrolling Marquee screen saver kicks in, it displays your message, scrolling across the screen.

Turning On and Off a Screen Saver

To turn on a screen saver, first select the desired screen saver, as explained in the preceding section. Click the arrows to the right of the **Wait ___ Minutes** spin box to specify how long your system must remain inactive (no typing and no mouse movement) before the screen saver kicks in. To specify how the screen saver operates (for example, the number of flying windows), click the **Settings** button, enter your preferences, and click **OK** to return to the Display Properties dialog box. To save your settings, click **OK.**

When your computer has been inactive for the specified period of time, the screen saver kicks in. To turn off the screen saver, simply move the mouse or press the **Shift** key.

Using a Password for Weak Security

If you're using a pre-Windows-XP version of Windows, don't let that **Password protected** option next to the screen saver lull you into a false sense of security. The screen saver password is designed only to prevent someone from taking a quick peak at your screen. As a deterrent against computer hackers, it's about as effective as locking your bike with a paper-clip chain. If someone wants to use your computer, all the person has to do is turn it off, turn it back on, and then disable the screen saver before it kicks in.

However, if you're looking for some free security, the screen saver password is better than nothing. To make the screen saver require a password, click the **Password protected** check box, and then click the **Change** button. Type the desired password in the **New password** and **Confirm new password** text boxes, and click **OK.** Whenever you return to your computer and move the mouse or press a key to turn off the screen saver, it will prompt you to enter your password.

In Windows XP, the screen saver has no password setting, because Windows handles the password through the user accounts. To add password protection to the screen saver, first set up your user account to require a password, as explained in Chapter 4. Then, right-click a blank area of the Windows desktop, click **Display Properties,** and make sure there is a check mark next to **On resume display Welcome screen.** Click **OK.** Whenever your screen saver kicks in and you return to your computer and press the **Shift** key or roll the mouse around, instead of returning to the Windows desktop, Windows displays the Welcome screen, prompting you to choose your user name and enter your password.

Making Your Computer Play Cool Sounds

In addition to the beeps and grunts your computer emits at startup, it's capable of producing more refined tones. When you start Windows, for instance, it ushers itself in with heavenly harp music or some other short audio clip. When you open a menu, close a window, or exit a program, Windows plays a unique audio clip for each of these actions or *events*. If you listen closely as you work in Windows, you'll be able to link each sound with its event.

If you keep listening closely (over several weeks), these sounds might start to annoy you and inspire an overwhelming desire to smash your speakers. Before you take such drastic action, read through the following sections. Here you'll learn how to pick a different sound scheme, assign different sounds to various Windows events, and even mute your system altogether.

Checking Your Audio Equipment

If you've ever prepared for a speech or presentation, you know how important it is to test your equipment before show time. After setting up and turning on the microphone, you hold it a few inches from your mouth and do the standard "Testing ... one ... two ... testing ..." thing. Well, before you start messing with audio clips in Windows, you should test your sound card and speakers to be sure they are operating properly. The procedure differs depending on which version of Windows your computer is running:

◆ **Windows XP.** Click the **Start** button, click **Control Panel,** and click **Sounds, Speech, and Audio Devices.** Click **Change the Sound Scheme,** and then under **Program Events** click an event that has a speaker next to it and click the **Play** button, as shown in Figure 7.7.

◆ **Windows Me, 98, or 95.** Open the **Start** menu, point to **Settings,** and click **Control Panel.** Double-click the **Sounds** icon. (If you're working in Windows Me, and you don't see the **Sounds** icon, click **View all Control Panel options,** on the left side of the Control Panel window.) Click the name of a Windows event that has a speaker icon next to it, and then click the **Play** button.

Figure 7.7

Use the Sounds and Multimedia Properties dialog box to test your computer's audio output.

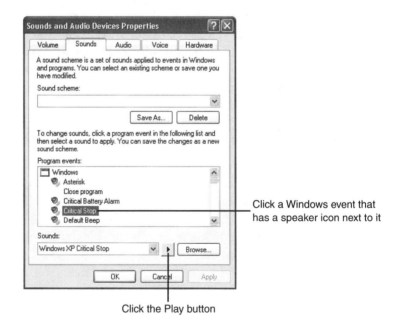

Click a Windows event that
has a speaker icon next to it

Click the Play button

At this point, Windows should play the audio clip that's assigned to the selected event. If you can't hear the clip, try adjusting the volume (as explained in the next section), or skip ahead to Chapter 29 to track down less-obvious causes.

Adjusting the Volume

The big problem with computer audio is that there are too many volume controls. You might find a volume control on the sound card (where the speakers plug in), on the speakers, and in Windows. In addition, if you're playing a computer game that has audio clips (most do), it might have its own volume control!

The trick to adjusting the volume is to start with the obvious controls first: the volume dials on the sound card and speakers. Set these controls to the desired level. If you're not sure which way to turn them, set them at the halfway point.

Next, check the volume control in Windows. Right-click the speaker icon in the lower-right corner of your screen and click **Open Volume Control** to display the Volume Control (or Play Control) window. (The Volume Control window's name varies, depending on your system's audio hardware, but the basic controls should be similar.) Open the **Options** menu and click **Properties.** In the **Show the following volume controls** list, be sure each check box (except **PC Speaker**) is marked, and then click **OK.** This gives you access to all the available volume controls, as shown in Figure 7.8.

Drag a balance slider to the left or right to adjust the balance

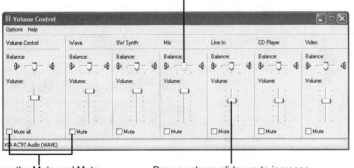

Figure 7.8

The Volume Control (or Play Control) window lets you set the volume and balance.

Be sure the Mute and Mute all options are not checked

Drag a volume slider up to increase volume or down to decrease it

Be sure the **Mute** option below each control is *not* checked (**Mute** disables a device). The **Mute all** option, below the leftmost control, can mute all the controls; make absolutely sure **Mute all** is *not* checked. Drag the slider for each volume control to the desired position. Repeat the steps from the preceding section to test the volume settings and readjust the settings as desired.

Choosing a Different Sound Scheme

When you're certain that your audio system is working properly, you can try out various sound schemes included with Windows. A sound scheme is a collection of audio clips assigned to various Windows events (such as opening or exiting a program).

To check out different sound schemes, double-click the **Sounds** icon in the Windows Control Panel (or **Sounds and Multimedia** in Windows Me or **Sounds, Speech, and Audio Devices** in Windows XP). Open the **Scheme** or **Sound Scheme** list and click the name of the sound scheme you want to try (refer to Figure 7.7). Click the **OK** button.

Panic Attack
If the **Scheme** list provides only the **Windows Default** and **No Sounds** options, the schemes are not installed. Run **Add/Remove Programs** from the Control Panel, click the **Windows Setup** tab, double-click **Multimedia,** and be sure **Multimedia Sound Schemes** is selected. Pop in the Windows CD, click **OK** to close the Multimedia dialog box, and click **OK** again to start the installation. To add sound schemes to Windows XP, you must purchase and install Microsoft Plus! for Windows.

Assigning Specific Sounds to Events

Picking a sound scheme is like choosing a vacation package. Each scheme provides all the settings you need for a consistent, thematic sound. If you want more control over which sounds Windows plays for the various events, you can assign a specific audio clip to each event.

Inside Tip

When you start poking around on the Internet, you might stumble upon some cool audio files. If the filename ends in .wav, you can assign the audio file to a Windows event. Save the file to the Windows/ Media folder on your hard drive, and it will appear in the **Sounds** list. See Part 4 of this book for more information.

To assign audio clips to events, display the Sounds and Multimedia Properties or Sounds and Audio Devices Properties dialog box as explained earlier in this chapter. In the **Sound Events** or **Program Events** list, click the event whose sound you want to change. Open the **Name** or **Sounds** list and click the name of the desired audio clip. To preview the sound, click the **Play** button. To save your settings, click **OK.**

The Least You Need to Know

◆ To install or remove Windows features, run **Add/Remove Programs** from the Control Panel and click the Windows **Setup** tab or click Add/Remove Windows Components.

◆ To preview and select from available desktop themes, right-click a blank area of the Windows desktop, click **Options,** and click the **Themes** tab.

◆ To give your desktop a graphic background, select the desired wallpaper on the **Background** or **Desktop** tab in the Display Properties dialog box.

◆ To turn on a screen saver, right-click the Windows desktop, click **Properties,** click the **Screen Saver** tab, open the **Screen Saver** drop-down list, and click the desired screen saver.

◆ To access the volume controls, double-click the speaker icon on the right end of the taskbar.

◆ To pick a different sound scheme, open the **Scheme** list in the Sounds and Multimedia Properties dialog box and click the desired sound scheme.

Chapter 8

Taking Control of Your Menus and Programs

In This Chapter

◆ Rearranging your **Start** menu with Windows Explorer

◆ Transforming the Windows desktop into a toolbar

◆ Transforming a folder into a toolbar

◆ Scheduling programs to run automatically

If you've ever spent a few hours cleaning and reorganizing your office, you know that, with a little effort, you can transform your office from a disorganized mess into a model of neatness and efficiency. The same is true of the Windows desktop.

By putting in a little time up front, you can redesign your desktop to conform to the way you work. You can place commands in more convenient locations on the **Start** menu, make your own desktop icons, transform folders into toolbars, and use Task Scheduler to automatically run programs for you. By the end of this chapter, you'll have the Windows desktop of your dreams!

Rearranging the Start Menu with Explorer

In Chapter 5, you learned how to drag program groups and individual programs to different locations on the **Start** menu. In the process, you probably noticed that dragging and dropping items on the **Start** menu is not the smoothest operation around. As you drag an object, menus open and close, making it difficult for you to drop the object in a precise location.

An easier way to rearrange items is to display the **Start** menu as a folder in Windows Explorer and then drag icons from one of the **Start** menu's folders to another. Try it yourself:

1. Right-click the **Start** button and click **Explore.** This starts Windows Explorer, which opens the **Start** folder.

2. Click the plus sign next to **Programs,** and then click the plus sign next to any subfolders that appear below the Programs folder.

3. To move a submenu, drag its icon to the desired location in the folder list. For example, to move the **Accessories** menu to the top of the **Start** menu, drag the Accessories folder over the Start folder. (To move it back to its original location, drag the Accessories folder over the Programs folder.)

4. To move a program, first change to the folder that currently contains the program (in the folder list, on the left).

5. In the folder list, be sure you can see the destination folder (the folder to which you want to move the program).

6. Drag the program's icon from the file list (on the right) over the destination folder and release the mouse button (see Figure 8.1).

Panic Attack

If you're wondering where all the program groups on the Windows XP All Programs menu are, you need to know that Windows keeps the programs in two folders: one for you and one for All Users. Click the plus sign next to **All Users,** click the plus sign next to **Start Menu,** and then click the **Programs** folder. This folder contains the program groups for all user accounts. Any changes you make here will affect the Start menu for every person who uses this computer.

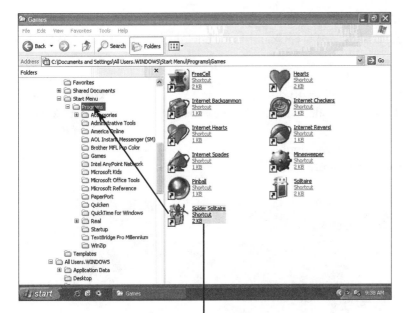

Figure 8.1

Windows Explorer is a great tool for restructuring your **Start** *menu.*

Drag the program icon over the desired destination folder

Making Your Own Toolbars

Chapter 5 showed you how to use the Windows Quick Launch toolbar to run programs with a single click. You even learned how to create your own Quick Launch buttons for your favorite programs.

However, the Quick Launch toolbar is much more powerful and versatile than Chapter 5 revealed. The following sections take you behind the scenes to show you how to turn on additional "Quick Launch" toolbars and create your own custom toolbars.

Turning on the Desktop Toolbar

If you think the Quick Launch toolbar is cool, you'll be happy to know that Windows has several more toolbars just like it:

◆ **Address** displays a text box into which you type a web page address to open a specific web page on the Internet. (You'll learn more about web pages and addresses in Part 4.)

◆ **Links** is another toolbar you can ignore for the time being. It contains buttons for connecting to popular websites.

◆ **Desktop** contains buttons for all the icons on the Windows desktop. Instead of double-clicking a desktop icon, you can simply click its button in the Desktop toolbar.

Let's check out the Desktop toolbar. Right-click a blank area on the taskbar, point to **Toolbars,** and click **Desktop**. Voilà! The Desktop toolbar appears. Because taskbar space is limited, you won't see many buttons. To see a complete collection of the Desktop toolbar's buttons, click the double-headed arrow (**>>**) at the right end of the Desktop toolbar, as shown in Figure 8.2.

Figure 8.2

*Your Windows desktop can
double as a toolbar.*

The Desktop toolbar   Click here to view
                          additional buttons

Transforming a Folder into a Toolbar

Gee, that was fun. But the Desktop, Address, and Links toolbars don't seem very useful, do they? I know I never use them. But wouldn't it be cool to have a Games toolbar with buttons for running Solitaire, FreeCell, Minesweeper, and Hearts? Let's make that toolbar right now:

1. Right-click a blank area of the taskbar, point to **Toolbars,** and click **New Toolbar.** The New Toolbar dialog box appears, prompting you to select the folder on which you want to base the toolbar.

2. Display the Games folder by taking one of the following steps, depending on which version of Windows you have:

   ◆ **Windows XP:** Click the plus signs next to **My Computer, C, Documents and Settings, All Users, Start Menu,** and **Programs.**

   ◆ **Windows Me:** Click the plus signs next to **C, Windows, Start Menu, and Programs.**

   ◆ **Windows 98:** Click the plus signs next to **C, Windows, Start Menu, Programs,** and **Accessories** to display the Games folder.

3. Click **Games.**

4. Click **OK.** Windows creates the Games toolbar and nests it inside the taskbar.

To turn off any of the toolbars, right-click a blank area of the taskbar, point to **Toolbars,** and click the name of the toolbar you want to turn off.

> **Computer Cheat**
>
> Instead of taking the standard steps for creating a toolbar, you can simply drag any folder from My Computer or Windows Explorer over a blank area of the taskbar and release the mouse button. Windows automatically converts the folder into a toolbar.

Automating Your Programs

I have one of those fancy coffee pots that brews a fresh pot of coffee every morning just before I roll out of bed—assuming I remember to feed it coffee and water before I hit the sack. Wouldn't it be great if Windows could run your favorite programs for you whenever you turn on your computer?

Well, you'll be happy to hear that Windows can do just that. With the Windows Task Scheduler, you simply tell Windows the days of the week and time of day you want it to run the program, and Windows runs the program at the scheduled time(s). Not only is Task Scheduler useful for running the programs you use most often, but it's great for running disk cleanup and maintenance utilities on a regular basis.

To schedule a program to run, take the following steps:

1. Open the **Start** menu, point to **Programs** (or **All Programs**), **Accessories, System Tools,** and then click or the **Scheduled Tasks** icon. The Scheduled Tasks window appears.

2. Click or double-click the **Add Scheduled Task** icon. This runs the Scheduled Task Wizard.

3. Read the Task Scheduler overview, and then click **Next.**

4. Click the program you want Task Scheduler to run, as shown in Figure 8.3, and click **Next.**

Click the program's name

Figure 8.3

Pick the program you want Task Scheduler to run for you.

Click Next

Computer Cheat

To have a program automatically run at startup, make a shortcut icon for the program and move it to the **Start, Programs, StartUp** folder (or **Start, All Programs, StartUp** folder).

5. Choose how often you want Task Scheduler to run the program, and then click **Next.** (For example, you can have Task Scheduler run the program daily, weekly, one time only, or whenever you start your computer.)

6. Specify the time of day and the days of the week on which you want Task Scheduler to run the program.

7. (Optional) Click **Open Advanced Properties** and enter additional preferences for running the program. (The available options vary from one program to another, so you'll have to improvise here.)

8. Click **Finish.**

When Task Scheduler is running, its icon appears in the system tray (at the right end of the taskbar). To disable Task Scheduler, double-click its icon, open the **Advanced** menu, and click **Stop Using Task Scheduler.**

The Least You Need to Know

- ◆ To display the contents of the **Start** menu in Windows Explorer, right-click the **Start** button and click **Explore.**

- ◆ To turn on the Desktop toolbar, right-click a blank area on the taskbar, point to **Toolbars,** and click **Desktop.**

- ◆ To transform any folder into a toolbar, drag the folder icon over a blank area of the taskbar and release the mouse button.

- ◆ Use the Task Scheduler to automatically run a favorite program on specified days and times.

- ◆ When Task Scheduler is running, an icon for it appears in the taskbar.

Chapter 9

Giving Yourself More Room to Work

In This Chapter

- ◆ Shrinking your desktop icons down to size
- ◆ Messing with your display's color settings
- ◆ Trashing icons you don't use
- ◆ Hiding the taskbar when you don't need it

Your Windows desktop can become every bit as cluttered and unmanageable as a real-life desktop. Fortunately, your Windows desktop is much easier to tidy up. You can shrink everything on your desktop to give yourself more room, rearrange the icons, dump icons that you don't use, and even hide the taskbar. This chapter shows you just what to do.

Clearing Desk Space by Making Everything Smaller

Wouldn't it be great if you could grab the edges of your monitor and stretch it? Maybe turn your 17-inch monitor into a big-screen, 21-inch version? Well, you can't, but you can do the next best thing—shrink everything on the desktop to give yourself a little more real estate. Here's what you do:

1. Right-click a blank area of the desktop and click **Properties.**

2. Click the **Settings** tab.

3. Drag the **Screen area** or **Screen Resolution** slider to the right one or more notches, as shown in Figure 9.1. As you drag, watch the preview area to see how the new setting affects the display.

The preview area shows the new desktop appearance

Figure 9.1

You can't make your display bigger, but you can make everything on it smaller.

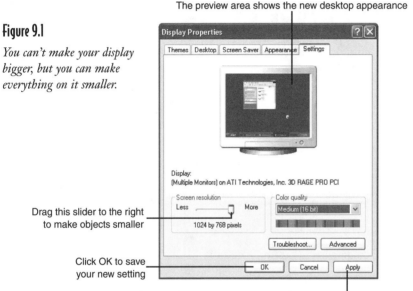

Drag this slider to the right to make objects smaller

Click OK to save your new setting

Click Apply to activate the new settings

4. When the preview area shows the desired desktop appearance (or the slider won't budge), click **Apply.**

5. Click **OK** to save your settings.

Panic Attack

If the icons have become too small to see, don't worry. You can make some adjustments. Open the Display Properties dialog box again. To make the icons and their labels bigger, click the **Settings** tab, click the **Advanced** button, open the drop-down list near the top of the General tab, and select the Large setting (**Large fonts** or **Large size**). If icons overlap, return to the Display Properties dialog box, click the **Appearance** tab, choose one of the **Icon spacing** options (**Vertical** or **Horizontal**) from the **Item** list, and increase the spacing.

What About the Color Settings?

As you were fiddling around with the screen area setting, you might have noticed the **Colors** drop-down list off to the left (refer to Figure 9.1). This list provides options for increasing or decreasing the number of colors used to display everything from icons to digitized photos. With more colors at its disposal, the monitor can display high-quality images more realistically.

So you want the highest setting possible, right? Well, not exactly. To display additional colors, your computer's display card and processor must work a little harder. Additional colors also consume more memory. The basic approach here is to choose the lowest setting that provides satisfactory quality. I set my display to Medium 16-bit, which does a good job of displaying photos and other detailed graphics. If you do any photo or video editing, you might want to bump up the setting. If you have an older computer, you might want to decrease the setting.

> **Inside Tip**
>
> A fancy desktop packed with animated shortcuts and designer wallpaper is cool, but all that spiffy stuff consumes precious resources. To keep your computer running at top speed, opt for a clean, simple desktop.

Rearranging Your Desktop Icons

Although the icons on the desktop provide convenient access to all of your programs and files, you can get a little carried away with them. In about 15 minutes, you can completely cover the surface of the desktop with shortcuts, making it nearly impossible to find anything. Fortunately, Windows has several tools to help you reorganize the icons on your desktop. Try the following techniques:

- To move an icon, drag it to the desired location.

- To have Windows XP rearrange the icons for you, right-click the desktop, point to **Arrange Icons By,** and click **Name, Size, Type,** or **Modified** (date on which the icon was created or changed). (In earlier versions of Windows, right-click the desktop, point to **Arrange Icons,** and click **By Name, By Size, By Type,** or **By Date**.)

> **Inside Tip**
>
> If you try to move an icon and it jumps to a different location, Auto Arrange is on. To turn it off, right-click the desktop, point to **Arrange Icons** or **Arrange Icons By,** and click **Auto Arrange** to remove the check mark and turn off the option.

◆ To have Windows XP line up the icons without rearranging them by name, size, type, or date, right-click the desktop, point to **Arrange Icons By,** and click **Align to Grid.** (In earlier versions of Windows, right-click the desktop and click **Line Up Icons.**)

◆ To have Windows automatically line up icons when you move them, right-click the desktop, point to **Arrange Icons** or **Arrange Icons By,** and click **Auto Arrange.**

Getting Rid of Icons You Don't Use

The best way to clear space on your desktop is to delete the icons you never use. First, select the icon you want to delete. If Web Style is on, point to the icon; if Web Style is off, click the icon. **Ctrl+point** or **Ctrl+click** to select additional icons. Then drag any one of the selected icons over the **Recycle Bin** icon and release the mouse button. Windows displays a dialog box asking for your confirmation. Click **Yes.**

Computer Cheat —————

To quickly delete icons, files, or folders, right-click any one of the selected items and click **Delete.** In Windows XP, right-click the desktop, point to **Arrange Icons By,** click **Run Desktop Cleanup Wizard,** and follow the onscreen instructions to move unused shortcut icons to the Unused Desktop Shortcuts folder.

Remember, if you delete an icon or other object by mistake, you can get it back. Double-click the **Recycle Bin** icon, click the icon that you accidentally deleted, and then open the **File** menu and click **Restore.**

Hiding the Taskbar

The taskbar is a great tool to have around, but when you're working on a document, playing a game, or viewing a web page, you need that extra half-inch of screen space where the taskbar resides. To reclaim the space, make the taskbar hide itself when you're doing other stuff:

1. Right-click a blank area of the taskbar and click **Properties.**

2. Click **Auto hide,** as shown in Figure 9.2.

3. Click **OK.**

Turn on Auto Hide

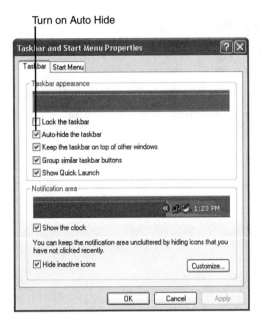

Figure 9.2

Give yourself some elbow-room.

As you work, the taskbar hides below the bottom of the screen (unless you moved the taskbar to a different edge of the screen). To bring the taskbar back into view, simply move the mouse pointer to the edge of the screen where the taskbar normally appears.

To make your taskbar larger, move the mouse pointer over the taskbar's top edge, so that the pointer appears as a two-headed arrow, and then drag up. With Auto hide on, you don't have to worry about the taskbar taking up too much screen space, because it hides itself when you're not using it.

Panic Attack

It's possible to make your taskbar so skinny that it becomes virtually invisible. If you can't find your taskbar, roll your mouse pointer around the edge of the screen to see if it pops up. If it does not appear, roll the mouse pointer around near the edge of the screen and see if the mouse pointer turns into a two-headed arrow, meaning that it is over the edge of the taskbar. Hold down the mouse button and drag the pointer toward the center of the screen to make the taskbar wider. This should bring it back into view.

The Least You Need to Know

- Use the Display Properties dialog box to shrink everything on the desktop and increase your work area.

- To have Windows automatically arrange the icons on the desktop, right-click the desktop, point to **Arrange Icons** or **Arrange Icons By,** and click **Auto Arrange.**

- If you don't use a particular shortcut icon, drag it to the Recycle Bin.

- To hide the taskbar, right-click it, choose **Properties,** and turn on **Auto hide.**

Chapter 10

Installing and Removing Programs

In This Chapter

- ◆ Picking programs your computer can run
- ◆ Finding out if your computer has room for a new program
- ◆ Installing a program in 10 minutes or less
- ◆ Running CD-ROM programs
- ◆ Getting rid of the programs you don't use

Although installing a program is typically less traumatic than installing a dishwasher or a central air conditioning system, the process can have similar, unforeseen problems. For instance, you might pick up the wrong version of the program—the Macintosh version rather than the Windows version. Or the program might have a quirky installation routine that doesn't install all of the components you need.

This chapter is designed to help you avoid the most common pitfalls, deal with unexpected problems, successfully install your new programs, and uninstall programs you never use.

Tech Term

Throughout this book, I use the terms **program, application,** and **software** interchangeably. These terms all refer to the instructions that tell a computer how to perform specific tasks.

Buying Software Your Hardware Can Run

Even the most experienced computer user occasionally slips up and buys a program that his or her computer can't run. The person might own a PC running Windows and pick up the Macintosh version of the program by mistake. Or maybe the program requires special audio or video equipment that the person doesn't have.

Before you purchase any program, read the minimum hardware requirements that are printed on the outside of the package to determine if your computer has what it takes to run the program:

♦ **Computer type.** Typically, you can't run a Macintosh program on an IBM-compatible computer (a *PC* or *personal computer* that runs *Windows*). If you have a PC, be sure the program is for an IBM PC or compatible computer. (Some programs include both the Macintosh and PC versions.)

♦ **Operating system.** Try to find programs that are designed specifically for the operating system you use. If your computer is running Windows Me, don't buy a program developed for Windows XP. (Although Windows XP can run most applications designed for Windows Me, Windows Me might have problems running some Windows XP programs.)

♦ **Free hard disk space.** When you install a program, the installation routine copies files from the installation diskettes or CDs to the hard disk. Be sure your hard disk has enough free disk space, as explained in the next section.

♦ **CPU requirements.** CPU stands for *central processing unit*. This is the brain of the computer. If the program requires at least a Pentium 4 processor, and you have a Pentium III, your computer won't be able to run the application effectively.

♦ **Type of monitor.** All newer monitors are SVGA (Super Video Graphics Array) or better, and most programs don't require anything better than SVGA. Some games and graphics programs require a specific type of display card, such as a 3D card or an advanced video card.

♦ **Mouse.** If you use Windows, you need a mouse (or some other pointing device). A standard two-button Microsoft mouse is sufficient. Some programs have special features you can use only with an IntelliMouse.

◆ **Joystick.** Although most computer games allow you to use your keyboard, games are usually more fun if you have a joystick.

◆ **CD-ROM or DVD-ROM drive.** If you have a CD-ROM or DVD-ROM drive, it usually pays to get the CD-ROM or DVD-ROM version of the application instead of using a diskette version. This simplifies the program installation, and the CD or DVD version might come with a few extras. Check for the required speed of the drive as well.

◆ **Sound card.** Most new applications require sound cards. If you plan on running any cool games, using a multimedia encyclopedia, or even exploring the Internet, you'll need a sound card. Some applications can use an old 8-bit sound card, but newer applications require a 16-bit or better sound card, which enables stereo output.

◆ **Amount of memory (RAM).** If your computer does not have the required memory (also known as *RAM*, short for *random access memory*), it might not be able to run the program, or the program might cause the computer to crash (freeze up).

Tech Term

Many people confuse memory (**RAM** or **random access memory**) with disk space. Your computer uses memory to store data and software instructions temporarily while your computer is actively processing the data and instructions. Memory provides the computer with fast access to data and instructions, but when you turn off your computer, whatever is stored in memory is erased. Disk storage, on the other hand, stores data and instructions permanently. When your computer needs data or instructions, it reads from the disk and stores the information in memory, where it can process it.

You can find out most of what you need to know about your computer from the System Properties dialog box. Hold down **Alt** and double-click **My Computer** to display the System Properties dialog box, as shown in Figure 10.1. The **General** tab displays the operating system type and version number, the type of processor, and the amount of RAM. Click the **Device Manager** tab and click the plus sign next to a device type to view its make and model number. For instance, click the plus sign next to **Display Adapters** to determine the type of video card that's installed.

Figure 10.1

The System Properties dialog box can tell you a lot about your computer.

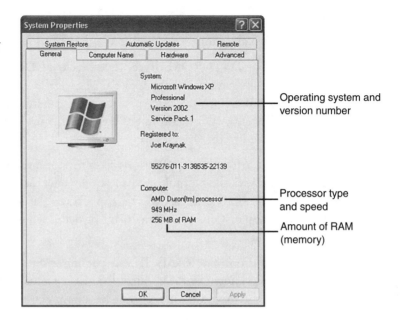

Operating system and version number

Processor type and speed

Amount of RAM (memory)

For more detailed system information, check out the Windows System Information tool. Open the **Start** menu, point to **Programs** or **All Programs, Accessories, System Tools,** and click **System Information.** (If you're running a version of Windows prior to Windows XP and **System Information** is not on the menu, you must install it from the Windows CD. Open the Windows Control Panel, click **Add/Remove Programs,** click the **Windows Setup** tab, and be sure **System Tools** is checked.)

Do You Have Enough Disk Space?

Most new computers sport a multi-gigabyte hard drive that has enough free space to last you well into the next decade. However, you should be sure that your new program will fit on the disk before you start the installation. If you try to stuff a program on a hard disk that's nearly full, you'll have some serious warning messages to deal with, and you can count on your system locking up sometime during the installation.

Checking the available disk space is easy. Right-click the icon for your hard disk drive in My Computer or Windows Explorer, and click **Properties.** The Properties dialog box displays the total disk space, the amount in use, and the amount that's free, as shown in Figure 10.2.

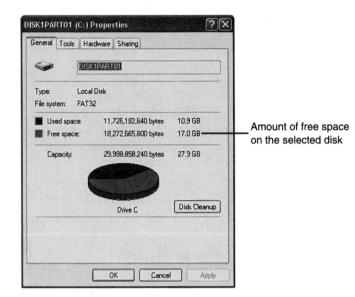

Figure 10.2

Windows displays the available space remaining on the disk.

Amount of free space on the selected disk

If your hard disk does not have sufficient free space for installing the program, you can free up some disk space by taking the following steps:

1. Display the disk's Properties dialog box. On the **General** tab, click the **Disk Cleanup** button (refer to Figure 10.2) and follow the onscreen instructions to clear unnecessary files from the disk.

2. Uninstall any programs you no longer use, as explained later in this chapter.

3. Be sure the Recycle Bin does not contain any files you might need by double-clicking the **Recycle Bin** icon. If the Recycle Bin contains no files you need, empty the Recycle Bin by opening the **File** menu and clicking **Empty Recycle Bin.**

4. Run Windows Setup and remove any Windows components you do not use. In Windows XP, open the Windows Control Panel, click **Add or Remove Programs,** click **Add/Remove Windows Components,** and use the resulting dialog box to remove unused components. (In earlier versions of Windows, open the Windows Control Panel, click **Add/Remove Programs,** click the **Windows Setup** tab, and remove the check mark next to any components you do not use.)

Inside Tip

Many programs create temporary files and then forget to delete them. Use the Windows **Start, Search** command or **Start, Find** command to search your computer's hard disk for temporary files (files whose names end in .tmp). When asked to specify the filename, type `*.tmp`. The asterisk is a wildcard character that stands in for any group of characters. Be sure **Include subfolders** is selected (in Windows Me, click **Search Options** and then click **Advanced Options**). Click **Find Now** or **Search Now**. After the search is complete, open the **Edit** menu, choose **Select All,** and then press the **Delete** key.

Installing Your New Program

Nearly every program on the market comes with an installation component (called Setup or Install) that does everything for you. If the program is on CD-ROM, you can usually pop the disc into your CD-ROM drive, click a few options to tell the program that it can install the program according to the default settings, and then kick back and watch the installation routine do its thing.

If the program comes on diskettes (floppy disks), or if the setup component on the CD doesn't start automatically when you insert the disc, take the following steps to kick start the setup routine:

1. If you haven't inserted the program CD or the first floppy disk into the drive, insert the CD or disk now.

2. Double-click **My Computer** on the Windows desktop or click the **Start** button and click **My Computer** (in Windows XP).

3. Double-click the icon for your CD-ROM or floppy drive. This displays a list of files and folders on the disk or CD.

4. Double-click the file named **Setup, Install,** or its equivalent (refer to the program's installation instructions if necessary). This starts the installation utility.

5. Follow the onscreen instructions to complete the installation.

Panic Attack

If you cannot find the Setup or Install file, Windows can help you locate the file that initiates the installation routine. Open the **Start** menu and click **Control Panel** (in Windows XP) or choose **Start, Settings, Control Panel** (in earlier Windows versions). Double-click the **Add/Remove Programs** or **Add or Remove Programs** icon. Click the **Install** button or **Add New Programs** link, and follow the onscreen instructions.

Selectively Installing Components

Many newer programs can consume several hundred megabytes of disk space. If your computer is running low on hard disk space, installing the entire program can be risky. These large programs typically offer the option to run the program from the CD or install only the most commonly used components.

If the setup routine gives you the option of running the program from the CD or hard disk, and your hard disk has plenty of free space, choose to run the program from the hard disk. You'll find that the program runs much faster, and you won't have to insert the CD every time you want to use the program. Choose to run the program from the CD only if your hard disk is running out of space.

Many setup routines provide an option for running the standard (typical), minimal, or custom installation, as shown in Figure 10.3. Again, unless your hard disk is running out of storage space, choose the standard installation. This installs the most common components. If you'd like to see what's available and order *a la carte*, perform a custom installation.

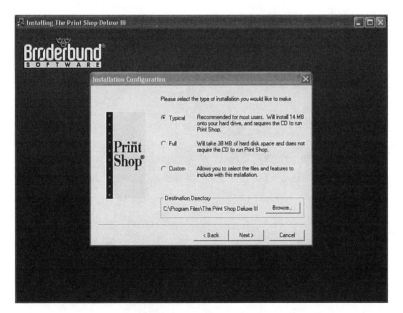

Figure 10.3

When in doubt, choose the standard or typical installation.

Removing a Program You Never Use

Your hard disk isn't an ever-expanding universe on which you can install an unlimited number of programs. As you install programs, create documents, send and receive e-mail messages, and view web pages, your disk can quickly become overpopulated.

One of the best ways to reclaim a hefty chunk of disk space is to remove (uninstall) programs that you don't use. Unfortunately, you cannot just nuke the program's main folder to purge it from your system. When you install a Windows program, it commonly installs files not only to the program's folder, but also to the \Windows, Windows\System, and other folders. It also edits a complicated system file called the Windows Registry. If you remove files without removing the lines in the Registry that refer to those files, you might encounter some serious problems. In short, you can't remove a program from your computer simply by deleting the program's files.

To remove the program safely and completely, you should use the Windows Add/Remove Programs utility. In Windows XP, click the **Start** button, click **Control Panel,** and click the **Add or Remove Programs** icon. This displays the Add or Remove Programs window, as shown in Figure 10.4. Click the name of the program you want to remove and then click the **Change/Remove** button. In most cases, a dialog box pops up on the screen asking if you want to completely remove the program from your computer. To confirm the removal, click **Yes.** In other cases, the program runs a custom setup routine, which provides instructions on removing the program entirely or removing only certain components. Follow the onscreen instructions.

Figure 10.4

Let Windows remove the program for you.

Click the program you want to remove

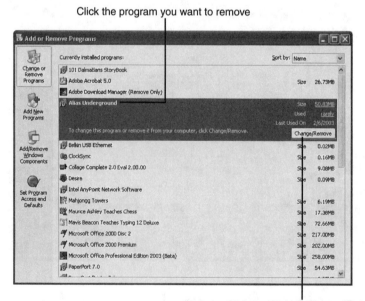

Click the Change/Remove button

If your computer is running a different version of Windows, take the following steps to remove a program:

1. Click the **Start** button, point to **Settings,** and click **Control Panel.**

2. Click the **Add/Remove Programs** icon. The Add/Remove Programs Properties dialog box appears.

3. Click the **Install/Uninstall** tab if it is not already selected. At the bottom of the window is a list of installed programs.

4. Click the name of the program you want to remove.

5. Click the **Add/Remove** button.

6. One or more dialog boxes leads you through the uninstall process, asking for your confirmation. Follow the onscreen instructions to complete the process.

7. If the program you removed has a shortcut icon on the desktop, you might have to delete this manually. Right-click the icon, and click **Delete.**

> **Inside Tip**
>
> If the name of the program you want to remove does not appear in the Add/Remove Programs list, use the program's own setup utility to remove the program. Search the program's submenu on the **Start, Programs** menu or in the program's folder for a Setup or Install option.

The Least You Need to Know

◆ Software provides the instructions your computer needs in order to perform a task.

◆ Not all programs run on all computers. Before buying a program, be sure your computer meets the requirements that are printed on the program's box.

◆ Hold down the **Alt** key while double-clicking **My Computer** to view important information about your computer.

◆ In most cases, you can simply pop a CD-ROM program into your computer's CD-ROM drive to start the installation routine.

◆ To install a program, use My Computer to change to the CD-ROM or floppy drive in which the program diskette or CD is loaded, and double-click the **Setup** or **Install** icon.

◆ To remove a program that you no longer use, open the Windows Control Panel and click **Add or Remove Programs** or double-click the **Add/Remove Programs** icon.

Part 3

Creating Letters, Greeting Cards, and Other Documents

Playing Solitaire and fiddling with the Windows desktop can keep you entertained for hours, but you didn't lay down a thousand bucks for a computer only to use it as a 99-cent deck of playing cards. You want to make something, print something, poke around on the Internet … you want to use the computer to get more out of life!

In this part, you become productive with your computer as you learn how to type and format letters, add images, create automated accounting worksheets, and print your documents. Along the way, you'll even learn how to perform some basic tasks, such as saving, naming, and opening the files you create.

Chapter 11

I Just Want to Type a Letter!

In This Chapter

- ◆ Typing on an electronic page
- ◆ Inserting the date and time from your computer
- ◆ Making your text big and pretty
- ◆ Shoving your paragraphs around on a page
- ◆ Saving the document you created

When my wife and I purchased a new computer for our home, I was dazzled by the hardware: the state-of-the-art processor, the all-in-one fax-copier-scanner-printer, the big-screen monitor, the surround sound audio system, and the super-speed cable modem. With this bad boy, we'd be cruising, rather than surfing, the Internet; building our own websites; scanning family photos; and editing videos!

As I ran down the list of all the cool things we could do with our new computer, my wife just stared at the screen. When I finished, she looked at me and said, "I just want to type a letter."

With the popularity of the Internet and other computer technologies, it's easy to forget that many people still use a computer primarily to type and print documents. In this chapter, you learn how to type, format (style), edit (cut and paste), and save a document using the most popular word processor on the planet—Microsoft Word.

Panic Attack

Although this chapter uses Microsoft Word to show you basic word processing features, don't worry if you're using a different word processor. The basic features and commands covered in this chapter differ only slightly between word processing programs. If you don't have Word or another high-end word processor installed on your computer, run WordPad, which is included with Windows. Open the **Start** menu, point to **Programs** or **All Programs,** point to **Accessories,** and then click **WordPad.**

Making the Transition to the Electronic Page

When you run Word (or whichever word processor is installed on your computer), it displays a blank "sheet of paper." The program also displays a vertical line called the *cursor* or *insertion point* to show you where the characters will appear when you start typing. Just below the insertion point is a horizontal line that marks the end of the document, as shown in Figure 11.1. As you type, this line moves down automatically to make room for your text. (You cannot move the cursor or insertion point past this line.)

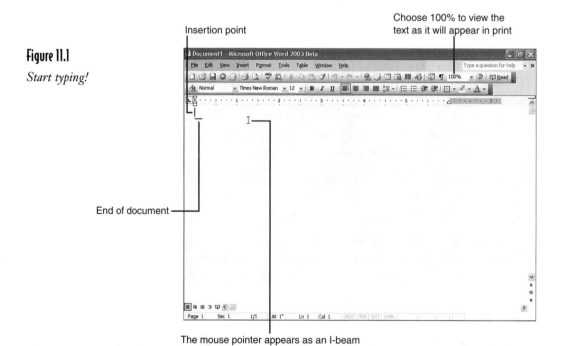

Figure 11.1

Start typing!

Insertion point

Choose 100% to view the text as it will appear in print

End of document

The mouse pointer appears as an I-beam to help you move the insertion point

The best way to learn how to type in a word processor is to start typing. As you type, keep the following information in mind:

♦ If the text is too small to read, open the **Zoom** list, as shown in Figure 11.1, and pick 100%. If the text is still too small, make it bigger, as explained in "Making the Text Bigger or Smaller" later in this chapter.

♦ Press the **Enter** key only to end a paragraph and start a new paragraph. Within a paragraph, the program automatically *wraps* the text from one line to the next as you type.

♦ Don't press the **Enter** key to insert a blank line between paragraphs. Later in this chapter, I'll show you a better way to add space between paragraphs.

♦ Use the mouse or the arrow keys to move the insertion point around in the document. If you're working on a long document, use the scroll bar to move more quickly.

♦ Delete to the right; Backspace to the left. To delete a character that's to the right of the insertion point, press the **Delete** key. To delete characters to the left of the insertion point, press the **Backspace** key.

In addition to allowing you to zoom in and out on a page, most word processing programs offer various views of a page. To change to a view, you typically open the **View** menu and click one of the following view options (in Word, you can quickly switch to a view by clicking a button for the desired view in the lower-left corner of the document window):

♦ **Normal** shows your document as one continuous document. In Normal view, the word processor hides complex page formatting, headers, footers, objects with wrapped text, floating graphics, and backgrounds. Scrolling is smooth because this view uses the least amount of memory.

♦ **Print or Page Layout** provides a more realistic view of how your pages will appear in print. Print Layout displays graphics, wrapping text, headers, footers, margins, and drawn objects. This uses a lot of memory, however, and might make scrolling a little jerky.

♦ **Web Layout** displays a document as it will appear when displayed in a web browser. In Web Layout view, a word processor displays web page backgrounds, wraps the text to fit inside a standard browser window, and positions the graphics as they will appear when viewed online.

Computer Cheat

If you really just want to type a letter, and you're using Microsoft Word, you can run Word's Letter Wizard to have Word format your letter for you. See "The Making of a Form Letter" in Chapter 14 for details.

◆ **Outline** allows you to quickly organize and reorganize your document by dragging headings from one location to another in the document.

What's with the Squiggly Red and Green Lines?!

As you type, you might get a strange feeling that your sixth-grade English teacher is inside your computer, underlining your spelling mistakes. Whenever you type a string of characters that Word can't find in its dictionary, Word draws a squiggly red line under the word to flag it for you so that you can immediately correct it. If the word is misspelled, right-click the word and choose the correct spelling from the context menu. (A squiggly green line marks a questionable grammatical construction.)

If the squiggly lines annoy you, you can turn off automatic spell checking. Open the **Tools** menu and click **Options.** Click the **Spelling & Grammar** tab, and turn off both **Check spelling as you type** and **Check grammar as you type.** Click **OK.**

Panic Attack

If the date or time is not current, your computer has the wrong information. Double-click the time display on the right end of the Windows taskbar and use the resulting dialog box to reset the date or time.

Inserting Today's Date

When you're typing a letter, you should include the date as part of the heading, just below your address. Of course, you could type the date, but that's too much like work. Have Word insert the date for you. Open the **Insert** menu and click **Date and Time.** Click the desired format and click **OK,** as shown in Figure 11.2.

Click the desired format

Figure 11.2

You can have your word processor insert the date or time for you.

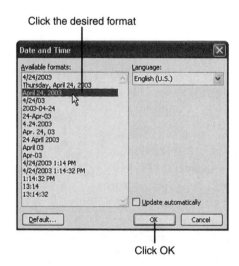

Click OK

Making the Text Bigger or Smaller

When you first start typing, you might notice that there's nothing fancy about the text. Word processors choose the dullest, dreariest-looking typestyle available. To give your text a facelift, try choosing a different typestyle (or *font*) and varying the size (measured in *points*) and attributes of the text.

To change the appearance of existing text, drag over the text to *highlight* it. Highlighting displays white text on a black background to indicate that the text is selected. Then choose the desired formatting options from the Formatting toolbar, as shown in Figure 11.3. (By the way, you also can change the properties of the text before you start typing.)

Tech Term _____

Technically, a **font** is a collection of characters that share the same typestyle and size. (Type size is measured in **points**; a point is approximately $\frac{1}{72}$ of an inch.) Most programs use the terms "font" and "typestyle" interchangeably.

Inside Tip _____

Where do you get fonts? Windows comes with dozens of fonts. Most word processors and desktop publishing programs come with additional font sets. You can purchase font collections on CD or download (copy) fonts from the Internet, but you probably already have more fonts than you will ever use.

Select the text size

Highlighted text

Make the text bold, italic, or underlined

Pick a different typestyle

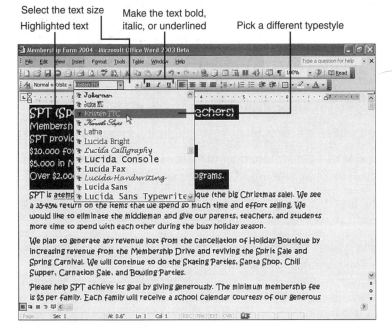

Figure 11.3

Use the Formatting toolbar to quickly change the text's appearance.

Shoving Text Left, Right, or Center

As you type a document, you might want to center a heading or push a date or address to the right side of the page to set it apart from surrounding text. To quickly change the text alignment, click anywhere inside the paragraph and then click one of the following buttons on the Formatting toolbar:

▤ **Align Left** pushes all lines of the paragraph against the left margin.

▤ **Center** positions each line of the paragraph at an equal distance from both the left and right margins.

▤ **Align Right** pushes all lines of the paragraph against the right margin. This is a useful option for placing a date in the upper-right corner of a page.

▤ **Justify** inserts spaces between the words as needed to make every line of the paragraph the same length, as in newspaper columns.

▤ ▤ The Formatting toolbar also contains buttons for creating numbered and bulleted lists. Simply highlight the paragraphs that you want to transform into a list and then click the desired button: **Numbering** or **Bullets.**

To indent the first line of a paragraph, you can press the **Tab** key at the beginning of the paragraph or enter a setting for the first line indent. Most word processors display a ruler, as shown in Figure 11.4, that lets you quickly indent paragraphs and set *tab stops*. (Tab stops determine where the insertion point stops when you press the **Tab** key.) To indent text and change margins and tab stop settings, here's what you do:

♦ To place a tab stop, click the button on the far-left end of the ruler to select the desired tab stop type (left, right, center, or decimal). Then click in the lower half of the ruler where you want the tab stop positioned.

♦ To move a tab stop, drag it left or right. To delete it, drag it off the ruler.

♦ To indent the right side of a paragraph, drag the right indent marker to the left.

♦ To indent the left side of a paragraph, drag the left indent marker to the right. (The left indent marker is the rectangle below the upward-pointing triangle.)

♦ To indent only the first line of a paragraph, drag the first line indent marker to the right. (This is the downward-pointing triangle on the left.)

♦ To create a hanging indent, drag the hanging indent marker to the right. (This is the upward-pointing triangle on the left.)

First line indent marker   Hanging indent marker   Right indent marker

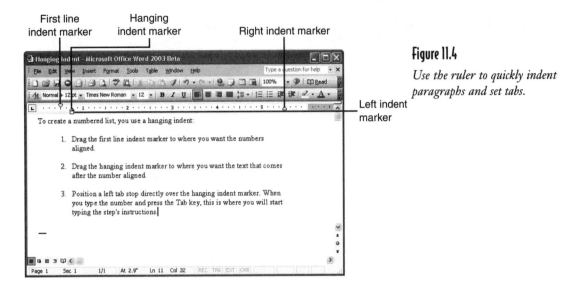

Left indent marker

Figure 11.4

Use the ruler to quickly indent paragraphs and set tabs.

Changing the Line Spacing

Here's a section just for kids. If you're working on a five-page paper for school, and you have only two-and-a-half pages of material, you can stretch this out by double-spacing:

1. Press **Ctrl+A** to select all the text.

2. Open the **Format** menu and click **Paragraph.** The Paragraph dialog box pops up on your screen.

3. Open the **Line spacing** list and click **Double.**

4. Click **OK.**

Computer Cheat

If your teacher wises up and issues formatting restrictions on your next assignment, bump up the text size by one point (this is barely noticeable), use the **File, Page Setup** command to increase the margins, and increase the line spacing by only a few points instead of double-spacing. An even more subtle technique is to use a larger font. Some fonts, such as Arial and Times New Roman, take up more space at the same point size than other fonts.

Inserting Space Between Paragraphs

Leaving space between paragraphs helps the reader easily see where one paragraph ends and another begins. Of course, you can insert blank lines between paragraphs by pressing the **Enter** key twice at the end of a paragraph, but that's a sloppy technique that limits your control over paragraph spacing later.

By specifying the exact amount of space you want inserted between paragraphs, you ensure that the amount of space between paragraphs is consistent throughout your document.

To change the space between paragraphs, drag over the paragraphs to highlight at least a portion of each paragraph. (You don't need to highlight all of the first and last paragraphs.) Open the **Format** menu and click **Paragraph.** Under **Spacing,** click the arrows to the right of **Before** or **After** to specify the amount of space (measured in points) you want to insert before or after each paragraph. In most cases, 6 points of extra spacing after each paragraph does the trick. Click **OK.**

Save It or Lose It

Unless you're the type of person who loves the thrill of risking everything for no potential gain, you should save your document soon after you type a paragraph or two. Why? Because right now, your computer is storing everything you type in RAM (Random Access Memory). A little dip in your local electric company's power grid can send your document off to never-never land. To prevent losing your work, save it to a permanent storage area—your computer's hard disk.

The first time you save a document, your program asks for two things: a name for the document, and the name of the drive and folder where you want the document stored. Here's the standard operating procedure for saving documents in most Windows programs:

1. Click the **Save** button on the toolbar, or open the **File** menu and click **Save.** The Save As dialog box appears, asking you to name the file.

2. Click in the **File name** text box and type a name for the file, as shown in Figure 11.5. The name can be up to 255 characters long, and you can use spaces, but you cannot use any of the following taboo characters: \ / : * ? " < > |

3. Open the **Save in** list and click the letter of the disk on which you want to save the document (typically drive C).

Select the folder here

Select a drive or folder here

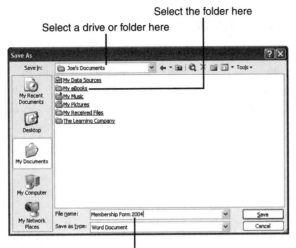

Figure 11.5

Use the Save As dialog box to save your document to your computer's hard disk.

Type a file name here

4. In the file/folder area, double-click the folder in which you want the document saved. (To save the document in a folder that's inside another folder, repeat this step.)

5. Click the **OK** or **Save** button. The file is saved to the disk.

Panic Attack

🖼 If you pass up the folder you wanted to select, you can back up. Click the **Up One Level** button.

From now on, saving this document is easy; you don't have to name it or tell the program where to store it ever again. The program saves your changes in the document you already created and named. You should save your document every 5 to 10 minutes to avoid losing any work. In most programs, you can quickly save a document by pressing **Ctrl+S** or by clicking the **Save** button on the program's toolbar.

Inside Tip

Most new word processors are set up to save files in the My Documents folder. If you create your own folders for storing documents, you might want to set up one of these folders as the one your word processor looks to first. In Word, open the **Tools** menu and click **Options**. Click the **File Locations** tab, click **Documents** (under **File types**), and click the **Modify** button. Use the Modify Location dialog box to pick the desired drive and folder, and then click **OK** to return to the Options dialog box. Click **OK** to save your changes. Now, whenever you choose to open or save a document, Word will display the contents of the folder you selected.

Editing Your Letters and Other Documents

Is your letter perfect? Are you sure? Take a 10-minute break, come back, and read it again with fresh eyes. Chances are your letter has at least a couple of minor flaws and possibly even some major organizational problems. To perform the required fixes and purge common errors from your letter, you need to master the tools of the trade. The following sections show you how to use your word processor's editing tools to copy, move, and delete text, and how to check for and correct spelling errors and typos.

Selecting Text

Before you can do anything with the text you just typed, you must select it. You can always just drag over text to select it (as explained earlier in this chapter), but Word offers several quicker ways to select text. The following table describes these techniques.

Quick Text Selection Techniques

To Select This	Do This
Single word	Double-click the word.
Sentence	**Ctrl+click** anywhere in the sentence.
Paragraph	Triple-click anywhere in the paragraph. Alternatively, position the pointer to the left of the paragraph until it changes to a right-pointing arrow, and then double-click.
Several paragraphs	Position the pointer to the left of the paragraphs until it changes to a right-pointing arrow. Then double-click and drag up or down.
One line of text	Position the pointer to the left of the line until it changes to a right-pointing arrow, and then click. (Click and drag to select additional lines.)
Large block of text	Click at the beginning of the text, scroll down to the end of the text, and **Shift+click.**
Entire document	Press **Ctrl+A.** Alternatively, position the pointer to the left of any text until it changes to a right-pointing arrow, and then triple-click.
Extend the selection	Hold down the **Shift** key while using the arrow keys, **Page Up, Page Down, Home,** or **End.**

Cutting and Pasting Without Scissors

Every word processor features the electronic equivalent of scissors and glue. With the cut, copy, and paste commands, you can cut or copy selected text and then insert it in a different location in your document. You can even copy or cut text from one document and paste it in another document!

 To cut or copy text, select it, and then click either the **Cut** or the **Copy** button on the toolbar. Move the insertion point to where you want the text inserted, and then click the **Paste** button. (Note that cutting a selection deletes it, whereas copying it leaves the selection in place and creates a duplicate.)

> **Inside Tip**
>
> To quickly move selected text, just drag it to the desired location in the document and release the mouse button. To copy the text, hold down the **Ctrl** key while you drag.

Whenever you cut or copy data in any Windows program, Windows places the data in a temporary storage area called the *Clipboard*. In the old days, the Clipboard could store only one chunk of data. If you cut one selection and then cut another selection, the second selection would bump the first selection off the Clipboard. Recent versions of Office, starting with Office 2000 and including Office XP and Office 2003 have upgraded the Clipboard to store twelve or more copied or cut items.

When you cut or copy two or more selections, the Clipboard toolbar or task pane appears, displaying an icon for each copied or cut selection. To paste the selection, click its icon. To paste all of the cut or copied selections, click the **Paste All** button. If the Clipboard toolbar does not appear in Word 2000, right-click any toolbar and click **Clipboard.** In Word 2002 and 2003, open the **Edit** menu and click **Office Clipboard.** This displays a Clipboard task pane on the right, providing a list of the 24 most recently cut or copied selections. Double-click the desired selection to paste it.

Oops! Undoing Changes

What if you highlight your entire document, intending to change the font size, and then press the **Delete** key by mistake? Is your entire document gone for good?

Nope.

As you cut, paste, delete, and perform similar acts of destruction, your Word processor keeps track of each command and lets you recover from the occasional blunder. To undo

> **Whoa!**
>
> Make sure you use the Undo feature before closing your document. After you save your document and close it, you cannot reopen it and undo actions you performed during a previous work session.

the most recent action, open the **Edit** menu and choose **Undo,** or click the **Undo** button (the button with the counterclockwise arrow on it) in the Standard toolbar. You can continue to click the **Undo** button to undo additional actions. Click the **Redo** button (the clockwise arrow) to undo Undo (or to again perform the action you just performed).

Checking Your Spelling and Grammar

Earlier in this chapter, you learned that Word automatically checks for typos and spelling errors as you type. If you turned off that option, you can initiate a spelling check by opening the **Tools** menu and selecting **Spelling and Grammar** or by clicking the **Spelling and Grammar** button on the Standard toolbar.

Word starts checking your document and stops on the first questionable word (a word not stored in the spelling checker's dictionary or a repeated word, such as *the the*). The Spelling and Grammar dialog box displays the word in red and usually displays a list of suggested corrections, as shown in Figure 11.6. (If the word appears in green, the grammar checker is questioning the word's usage, not its spelling.) You have several options:

◆ If the word is misspelled and the **Suggestions** list displays the correct spelling, click the correct spelling and then click **Change** to replace only this occurrence of the word.

◆ Double-click the word in the **Not in Dictionary** text box, type the correction, and click **Change.**

◆ To replace this misspelled word and all other occurrences of the word in this document, click the correct spelling in the **Suggestions** list and then click **Change All.**

◆ Click **Ignore** or **Ignore Once** if the word is spelled correctly and you want to skip it just this once. Word will stop on the next occurrence of the word.

◆ Click **Ignore All** if the word is spelled correctly but is not in the dictionary and you want Word to skip all other occurrences of this word in the document.

◆ Click **Add** or **Add to Dictionary** to add the word to the dictionary so that the spelling checker never questions it again in any of your Office documents (the dictionary is shared by all Office applications).

Don't place too much trust in your spell checker. It merely compares the words in its dictionary to the words in your document and highlights any string of text that's not in the dictionary. If you typed "its" when you should have typed "it's," the spelling checker won't flag the error. Likewise, if you type a scientific term correctly that is not in the spelling checker's dictionary, the spelling checker will flag the word, even if it is correct. Proofread your documents carefully before considering them final.

Inside Tip

To check the spelling of a single word or paragraph, double-click the word or triple-click the paragraph to select it before you start the spelling checker. When Word is done checking the selection, it displays a dialog box asking if you want to check the rest of the document.

Click the correct spelling if it's listed   Click Change or Change All

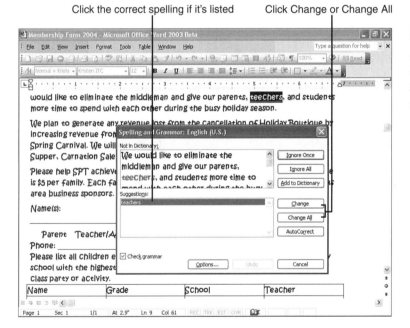

Figure 11.6

If Word finds a misspelling and displays the correct spelling, your options are easy.

When Word completes the spelling check, it displays a dialog box telling you so. Click **OK**.

The Least You Need to Know

◆ Use the **Zoom** list to zoom in if the text is too small.

◆ Use the arrow keys or the mouse to move the insertion point.

◆ Drag the mouse pointer over text to highlight it.

◆ Use the buttons in the Formatting toolbar to quickly style and align your text.

◆ To avoid losing your document, press **Ctrl+S** to save it to your computer's hard disk.

◆ To undo your most recent action, open the **Edit** menu and click **Undo** or click the **Undo** button.

Enhancing Your Documents with Clip Art and Other Objects

In This Chapter

♦ Add ready-made clip art to your documents

♦ Insert scanned images and digital photos

♦ Stretch, shrink, and drag graphics on a page

♦ Combine pictures and text (without losing anything)

♦ Make your text look more graphical

Nearly every program that enables you to type your own documents provides tools for sprucing up your documents with clip art, photos, lines, basic shapes, and other graphic objects. Using these tools, you can create your own illustrated newsletters, brochures, training manuals, reports, letterhead, and other publications for both business and personal use. However, combining graphics with text can often have unexpected, undesirable results. A clip art image may refuse to budge when you try to move it or may become distorted when you resize it. In addition, if you place several graphic objects on the same page, they frequently overlap in mysterious ways, causing layout nightmares.

This chapter provides basic instructions and techniques for inserting and manipulating graphic objects in your documents and helps you develop the skills you need to work around the inevitable problems you will encounter.

Inserting Ready-Made Clip Art Images

The easiest way to begin adorning your documents with graphic objects is to insert *clip art images*—small images rendered by professional graphics artists. With clip art, illustrating your publications is easy. Say you're creating a newsletter and you want to spruce it up with some pictures. Nothing fancy; maybe a picture of a fireworks display for a company newsletter or a picture of a baseball player to mark upcoming games for your softball league. You create the newsletter and then enter a command telling the program to insert a piece of clip art. You select the piece you want, click **OK,** and voilà, instant illustration, no talent required!

Get It Where You Can: Sources of Clip Art

Some programs (desktop publishing, word processing, business presentation, and spreadsheet programs) come with a collection of clip art on the installation disks or CDs. Microsoft Office, for example, includes a huge collection of clip art that you can use in all programs in the suite. Some of this "free" clip art is very good—but some isn't fit for open house at the local kindergarten.

You also can purchase separate clip art libraries on disk, just as you would purchase a program. These libraries typically include hundreds or even thousands of clip art images that are broken down into several categories: borders and backgrounds, computers, communications, people and places, animals, productivity and performance, time and money, travel and entertainment, words and symbols—you name it.

> **Inside Tip** _____
>
> You also can find gobs of graphics on the Internet; especially on the World Wide Web, as you'll see in Part 4. You can use a web search tool, as explained in Chapter 21, to find clip art libraries and samples. When you see an image you like, just right-click it and choose **Save Picture As.** (One warning, though: You shouldn't use a picture someone else created in your own publication without the artist's permission.) You can purchase clip art at Clipart.com; for a fixed fee, you can copy an unlimited number of clip art images from the site.

Pasting Clip Art on a Page

Now that you have a satchel full of clip art, how do you get it from the satchel into your documents? Well, that depends. Sometimes, you have to open the library, cut the picture you want, and paste it onto a page. Other times, you import or insert the image by specifying the name of the file in which the image is saved (it's sort of like opening a file). In Microsoft Word and other Office applications, you position the insertion point where you want the image inserted and then open the **Insert** menu, point to **Picture,** and click **Clip Art.** This opens the Clip Art task pane, shown in Figure 12.1. Click in the **Search for** text box, type a brief description of the desired image, and press **Enter.** The clip art task pane displays all the images in the collection that match your search term. Scroll down the list to check out the images, and then click an image to insert it.

Images that match your
search instructions

Figure 12.1

You can paste a piece of clip art onto a page.

Click an image to it

Hey, the Picture's Blocking My Text

When you lay a picture on top of text, the text typically moves to make room for the picture. In most programs you can set text wrap options to control the way that text behaves around the picture. To set the text wrap options, click the picture and then enter the command for formatting the picture (for example, enter **Format, Picture**).

The following list explains common text wrap options:

- **Square.** Places the picture on an imaginary rectangle and wraps the text around the rectangle. For example, if you have a circular picture, you can set text wrapping to square to make the text wrap in a more regular pattern around the image.

- **Tight.** Makes the text follow the contour of the picture.

- **None.** Places the picture right on top of the text. Choose this only if you have a see-through picture that you want to use as a watermark. Otherwise, it will hide your text.

- **Top and Bottom.** Places text above and below the picture, but does not wrap it around the sides.

- **Distance from Text.** Specifies how close the text can get to the image.

> **Panic Attack**
>
> Your choice in how to wrap text around an image seriously affects how the image moves when you drag it. Choosing no text wrapping gives you the most freedom—you can drag the image anywhere, even on top of a chunk of text. If the image refuses to budge when you drag it, the text wrap setting may be restricting its movement.

Resizing and Reshaping Images

When you plop a picture in a document, it rarely places itself in the perfect position. It's usually too big or too small, too far up or too far down, too far to the left or too far to the right. Fortunately, you have full control over the size and placement of the picture.

Changing the size of an image is a fairly standard operation. When you click the picture, squares or circles (called *handles*) surround it, as shown in Figure 12.2. To move the image, position the mouse pointer over the image itself (not over its handles) and drag the image to the desired location. To change the size and dimensions of the image, use the following techniques:

- Drag a top or bottom handle (not in the corner) to make the picture taller or shorter.

- Drag a side handle (not in the corner) to make the picture thinner or wider.

- Drag a corner handle to change both the height and width proportionally.

- If the image has a green circle handle floating above it, drag the green handle to spin the image around its center point.

◆ Hold down the **Ctrl** key while dragging to increase or decrease the size of the image from the center out. If you hold down the Ctrl key while dragging a handle on the right side out, for example, the picture gets wider on both the left and right sides. (If you hold down the Ctrl key while dragging the image itself, instead of one of its handles, you create a copy of the image instead of resizing it.)

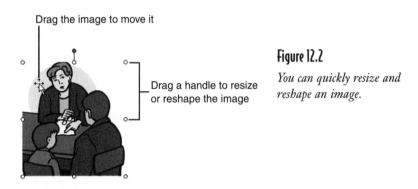

Drag the image to move it

Drag a handle to resize or reshape the image

Figure 12.2

You can quickly resize and reshape an image.

For more control over the size and dimensions of an image, right-click the image, click **Format Picture** (or **Format *Object,*** where *Object* is the name of the selected object), and click the **Size** tab. This page of options enables you to enter specific measurements for your picture. (The Size tab typically has an option called Lock Aspect Ratio, which is on by default. This ensures that when you change the height or width of a picture, the corresponding dimension is resized proportionally.)

Many programs also feature a cropping tool that lets you "trim" the edges off an image. Click the **Crop** button, and then drag a handle toward the center of the image to trim an edge off the image. (If you crop too much, drag the handle away from the image to uncrop it.) In Microsoft Office applications, you can find the **Crop** button on the Picture toolbar. (To turn on a toolbar, right-click any toolbar or the menu bar and click the name of the desired toolbar.)

Inserting Other Pictures

Clip art galleries are not the only source of graphic images. You can obtain digitized photos using a digital camera (as explained in Chapter 25), draw your own images, obtain images someone else has created and sent to you, or copy images from the web.

Digitized images are stored in a variety of *file formats*. The file format is computer code that a program uses to render a particular image onscreen and in print. Not all programs can translate all file formats, but most programs support numerous common

Inside Tip

You can tell a particular file's format by looking at its file name extension—the three characters tacked on to the end of a file name, after the period. Your computer may be set up to hide file name extensions, but if you right-click a file or a thumbnail view of the image and click **Properties** or **Preview/Properties,** you can see the complete file name, including its extension.

and uncommon graphic file formats, including WMF (Windows Meta File), TIFF (Tagged Image File Format), GIF (Graphics Interchange Format), PCX (PC Paintbrush), and BMP (Bitmapped), to name a few.

Though you can obtain images from numerous sources, the process for inserting an image in most programs is fairly standard:

1. Change to the document on which you want the picture inserted.

2. Open the **Insert** menu, point to **Picture,** and click **From File.** An Insert Picture dialog box appears, as shown in Figure 12.3.

Look in list

Figure 12.3

The Insert Picture dialog box.

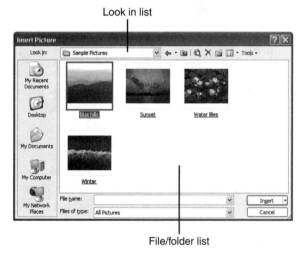

File/folder list

3. If the picture you want is stored on a different disk drive or in a folder other then My Pictures, open the **Look in** list and click the drive or folder where the picture is stored.

4. If necessary, in the folder/file list (the big area that shows the contents of the currently selected disk drive or folder), double-click the folder where the picture is stored.

5. If necessary, repeat step 4 until the file/folder list displays the contents of the disk or folder where the picture is stored.

6. If necessary, scroll down the file/folder list to bring the desired picture into view.

7. To insert the picture, double-click its name or click it and click the **Insert** button. The program inserts the selected picture into your document.

Scanning Photos, Drawings, and Illustrations

Another way that we, the artistically challenged, overcome our artistic handicap is to scan photos and other images into the computer using a gadget cleverly called a *scanner*. A scanner is sort of like a copy machine, but instead of creating a paper copy of the original, it creates a digital copy that can be saved as a file. You can then print the image, fax it, or even insert it in a document.

Most scanners on the market are *flatbed* scanners. You lay the picture face down on the scanner's glass, and then run the scan program by pressing a button on the scanner or selecting the program from the **Start, All Programs** menu. Another popular type of scanner is the *sheet fed*. With a sheet fed scanner, you load the original picture into a slot on the scanner, and the scanner pulls the original past its scanning mechanism to create the copy. The following steps run you through a typical scanning operation using a flatbed scanner:

1. Load the original image into the scanner as specified in the scanner's documentation.

2. Press the button (on the scanner) to initiate the scanning program or click the scan program's name on the Windows desktop or the **Start, All Programs** menu.

3. If necessary, select the command to start the scanning operation. This typically calls up a dialog box, like the one shown in the Figure 12.4, which prompts you to specify the type of document you're scanning and any preferences.

4. If the dialog box has a button for previewing the image, click the button so you can mark the area you want to scan. Don't be shocked if the preview looks bad; the preview area typically shows a low-resolution version of the image.

5. Enter your preferences and click the **Scan** button (or its equivalent) to start scanning.

If you have an application that features TWAIN support, you can scan an image directly into a document. For example, in Microsoft Word, position the insertion point where you want the image inserted and choose **Insert, Picture, From Scanner or Camera.** Word runs your scanning program. Scan the image as you normally would. Open the scan program's **File** menu and choose the option to exit and return to your document. Word displays the image you just scanned.

Figure 12.4

Enter your scanning preferences.

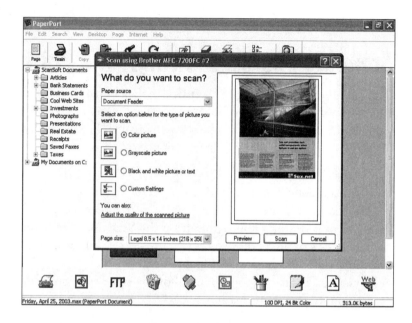

Drawing and Painting Your Own Illustrations

Clip art, photos, and scanned images are a great source of ready-made art, but when you need a custom illustration, draw it yourself. Most word-processing, desktop publishing, spreadsheet, and presentation programs include their own *drawing tools* that enable you to draw lines, arrows, basic shapes, and other objects in your documents. In addition, Windows includes its own *paint program* that transforms your monitor into a virtual canvas on which you can paint using an onscreen brush, pen, and "can" of spray paint. The following sections teach you the basic techniques for using paint and draw tools.

Drawing Lines, Squares, Circles, and Other Shapes

Drawing tools consist of onscreen pens, rulers, and templates that enable you to draw lines and basic shapes to create your own custom illustrations. By assembling a collection of these lines and shapes, you can create sophisticated illustrations to adorn your documents. But first, you need to know how to draw a line or shape onscreen. The following steps show you how to draw lines and shapes in most programs. If you're working in a Microsoft Office application, you can access the drawing tools by right-clicking the menu bar or any toolbar and clicking **Drawing.** To draw a line or shape, take the following steps:

1. Click the button or select the command for drawing the desired line, arrow, or shape on the Drawing Toolbar. When you move the mouse pointer over the page, it changes into a crosshair pointer.

2. Move the crosshair pointer to the position where you want one corner or one end of the object to appear.

3. Hold down the mouse button and drag the pointer away from the starting point in the desired direction until the object is the size and shape you want, as shown in Figure 12.5.

4. Release the mouse button.

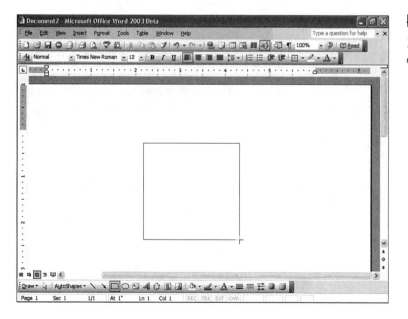

Figure 12.5

You can drag a line, arrow, or shape into existence.

To save some time and reduce the frustration when drawing objects, read through the following list of drawing tips:

- To draw several objects of the same shape, double-click the desired button and then use the mouse to create as many of those shapes as you like.

- To draw a uniform object (a perfect circle or square), hold down the **Shift** key while dragging.

- Hold down the **Ctrl** key while dragging to draw the object out from an imaginary center point. Without the Ctrl key, you drag the object out from its corner or starting point.

- Hold down **Ctrl+Shift** while dragging to draw the object out from its center point and create a uniform shape.

- To select an object, click it.

- To delete an object, select it and press **Del.**

- To move an object, select it and drag one of its lines.

- To resize or reshape an object, select it and drag one of its handles.

- To copy an object, hold down the **Ctrl** key while dragging it.

- To quickly change the appearance of an object, right-click it and select the desired option from the shortcut menu.

After you have an object on the page, you can use some of the other buttons in the Drawing toolbar to change qualities of the object, such as its fill color and the color and width of the line that defines it. First, select the shape whose qualities you want to change, and then click the button for the aspect of the object you want to change (line thickness, line color, or fill color) and choose the desired option.

Tech Term

Your computer screen is essentially a canvas made up of hundreds of thousands of tiny lights called **pixels**. Whenever you type a character in a word processing program, or draw a line with a paint or draw program, you activate a series of these pixels so that they form a recognizable shape onscreen.

Painting the Screen with Tiny Colored Dots

Have you ever seen a painting by Georges Seurat, the famous pointillist? His magnificent paintings consist of thousands of tiny dots. Paint programs use the same technique to generate an image. Each image you create in a paint program consists of thousands of tiny, onscreen colored dots called *pixels*.

Windows comes with a paint program, called Paint, which you can find on the **Start, All Programs, Accessories** menu. Run Paint to display the screen like the one shown in the Figure 12.6.

Drawing and painting tools

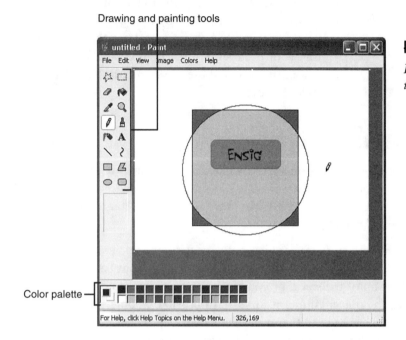

Figure 12.6

Paint is a paint program that comes with Windows.

Color palette

Once you have the Paint screen up, play around with some of the line, shape, and paint tools. The procedure is pretty basic: Click a line, shape, or paint tool (such as the Airbrush tool), choose a line thickness, and click a color. Then drag the mouse pointer over the "canvas." To create a filled shape, click the desired color for the inside of the shape, right-click the color for the outside of the shape and then drag your shape into existence. To fill a shape with color, click the paint can, click a color, and click anywhere inside the shape.

Text in a Box

As you saw earlier in this chapter, you can place text and images on the same page and have text wrap around the image. However, in some cases, you might need to add a label to an image or position a block of text in a precise location on a page. In such cases, you should add the text inside a text box. To place text in your publication, you must first draw a text box and then type something in that box. As you fine-tune your publication, you can drag and stretch the box as needed to position it on the page and accommodate your text.

Inside Tip

Moving a text box is kind of tricky. You can't just drag the center of the box, as you do when you move a picture. First, click the outline of the box so that handles appear around it. Then, drag the border that defines the box.

To create a text box, click the **Text Tool** or **Text Box** button. The mouse pointer turns into a cross-hair pointer. Position the pointer where you want the upper-left corner of the box to appear, and then drag down and to the right to create a box of the desired height and width. When you release the mouse button, your program inserts the text box. Type your text in the box, and use the Formatting toolbar to style the text.

Manipulating Overlapping Objects

Working with two or more objects on a page is like making your own collage. The trouble with objects is that when you place one object on top of another, the top object blocks the bottom one and prevents you from selecting it. You have to flip through the stack to find the object you want.

Most programs that allow you to stack objects on a page offer tools to help you re-arrange the objects in a stack. You can send an object that's up front back one layer or all the way to the bottom of the stack, or you can bring an object from the back to the front. First, click the object you want to move (if possible). Some objects are buried so deep that you can't get to them. In such a case, you have to move objects from the front to the back to get them out of the way until you find the one you want.

After selecting the object that you want to move, open the **Arrange** menu, point to **Order**, and select the desired movement: **Bring to Front, Send to Back, Bring Forward, Send Backward, Bring in Front of Text,** or **Send Behind Text.**

Inside Tip

If you have a half-dozen objects on a page and you want to nudge them all to the right, you don't have to move each object individually. **Shift+click** each object you want to move. Drag one of the objects, and all the rest will follow like little sheep. To group the objects and make them act as a single object, right-click one of the objects and click **Group**. (To ungroup the objects, right-click the grouped object and click **Ungroup**.)

The Least You Need to Know

♦ When you need some professionally drawn, ready-made art, check out the clip art collections included with your word processor and other programs and on the Internet.

♦ To move an image, drag any part of the image.

♦ To resize an image while retaining its relative dimensions, drag a corner handle.

♦ In any of the Office applications, you can insert images from the Internet or from a scanner, digital camera, or graphics program by using the **Insert, Picture, From File** command.

♦ To draw a line, shape, or text box onscreen, click the button for the object you want to draw, position the mouse pointer where you want one end or corner of the object to appear, and drag away from that point.

Chapter 13

Everything You Need to Know About Printing Documents

In This Chapter

- ◆ Installing a printer in Windows
- ◆ Previewing your document before you print
- ◆ Tweaking the page margins
- ◆ Printing your masterpiece
- ◆ Troubleshooting common printer problems

When printing goes as planned, it's a snap. You click the **Print** button and then kick back and play Solitaire while the printer spits out your document. However, rarely does a print job proceed without a hitch. You finish your game of Solitaire only to find a stack of papers covered with foreign symbols. Or you get an error message saying the printer's not ready. After hours of fiddling and fumbling, you find and correct the problem only to face a new problem: getting your printer back online. In this chapter, you will learn all you need to know to print glitch free and recover from the occasional print failure.

Setting Up Your Printer in Windows

You can't just plug your printer into the printer port on your system unit and expect it to work. No, that would be far too easy. You also need to install a printer driver—instructions that tell your programs how to use your printer. (If you have a printer that supports Plug-and-Play, Windows leads you through the installation at startup.)

In Windows, you install one printer driver that tells Windows how to communicate with the printer. All of your applications then communicate with the printer through Windows. When you set up a printer, Windows asks for the following information:

- **Printer make and model.** Windows comes with printer drivers for most common printers. In addition, your printer might have come with a disk containing an updated printer driver.

- **Printer port.** This is the connector at the back of the system unit into which you plug the printer. Most printers connect the LPT1 port, but many newer printers use the *USB* (*Universal Serial Bus*) port. (Some printers connect to the *serial port*.) If you're not sure, but you know that the printer is plugged into the *parallel* printer port, try LPT1. If the printer is plugged into the serial port, try COM1, COM2, or COM3.

Tech Term _____

All printers are commonly categorized as either **parallel, serial,** or **USB.** Parallel printers connect to one of the system unit's parallel printer ports: LPT1 or LPT2. A serial printer connects to the system unit's serial port: COM1, COM2, or COM3. USB printers plug into one of the computer's USB ports. Most people use parallel or USB printers because they're faster; parallel and USB cables can transfer several instructions at once, whereas a serial cable transfers them one at a time. Wireless printers are also available for wireless-enabled systems.

When you installed Windows, the installation program asked you to select your printer from a list. If you did that, Windows is already set up to use your printer. If you're not sure, open the **Start** menu and click **Printers and Faxes** (in Windows XP) or (in earlier versions of Windows) open the **Start** menu, point to **Settings,** and click **Printers.** If there's an icon for your printer, right-click it and make sure there's a check mark next to **Set As Default** or **Set As Default Printer.** If there is no icon for your printer, you must install a printer driver.

If your printer came with its own installation disk or CD, install the printer driver from that disk or CD. Insert the disk or CD, click the **Start** button, and click **Run.** When the Run dialog box appears, click the Browse button, change to the disk drive and folder that contains the **Setup** or **Install** file, double-click the Setup or Install file, and then click the **OK** button. Follow the onscreen instructions to complete the installation.

If you do not have a disk or CD for you printer, try installing one of the printer drivers included with Windows. Windows comes with printer drivers for hundreds of printers currently on the market (and many older printers, as well). To install one of the Windows printer drivers, take the following steps:

1. If the Printers window is not displayed, open the **Start** menu and click **Printers and Faxes** (in Windows XP) or (in earlier versions of Windows) open the **Start** menu, point to **Settings,** and click **Printers.**

2. Double-click the **Add a Printer** icon. The Add Printer Wizard appears.

3. Click the **Next** button. The next dialog box asks if you want to set up a network or local (desktop) printer.

4. Make sure **Local printer** is selected and click the **Next** button.

5. Select the port into which you plugged your printer. This usually is LPT1 or USB. Click the **Next** button. A list of printer manufacturers and printer makes and models appears.

6. Click the manufacturer of your printer in the **Manufacturers** list, click the specific printer model in the **Printers** list and then click the **Next** button, as shown in Figure 13.1. You now are asked to type a name for the printer.

Choose the make and model

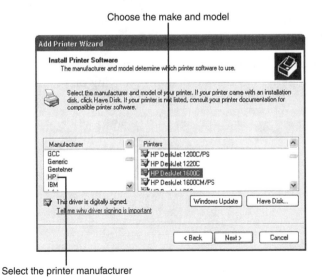

Figure 13.1

Windows includes printer drivers for most printers.

Select the printer manufacturer

7. This step is optional. Type a name for the printer. If you want to use this printer as the default printer, click **Yes;** then click the **Next** button. Windows asks if you want to print a test page.

8. Make sure your printer is on and has paper and then click Yes and click the Finish button. If you don't have a disk for the printer, a dialog box might appear telling you to insert the Windows CD. If prompted to insert the Windows CD, insert the CD into your computer's CD-ROM drive and click **OK.** Windows copies the specified printer driver and prints a test page to make sure the printer is working properly.

Preprint Checklist

Most programs display a print button in the toolbar that allows you to quickly send your document to the printer. It's tempting to click the button and see what happens. Resist the temptation. You can avoid nine out of ten printing problems by checking your document in Print Preview. Open the **File** menu and choose **Print Preview** (or its equivalent command), or click the **Print Preview** button in the toolbar. Figure 13.2 shows a sample document in Word's Print Preview window. Flip through the pages to see how they will appear in print and look for the following:

◆ **Chopped text.** Many printers have a nonprinting region near the margins. If you set your margins so that the text falls in these areas, the text will be chopped off (not printed).

◆ **Strange page breaks.** If you want a paragraph or picture to appear on one page and it appears on the next or previous page, you might need to insert a page break manually. Position the insertion point where you want the page break inserted and then press **Ctrl+Enter.**

◆ **Overall appearance.** Make sure your fonts look good next to one another, that text is aligned properly, and that no pictures are lying on top of text.

Make sure text and graphics don't overlap

Check the margins to see if text
falls in a nonprinting region

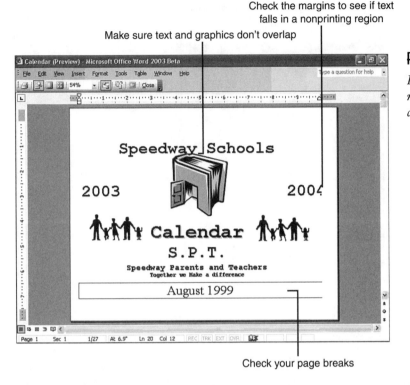

Figure 13.2

*Print Preview can reveal
many problems you should
correct before printing.*

Check your page breaks

Setting Your Margins and Page Layout

You can correct many undesirable page layout issues by checking and adjusting the
page margins and layout settings in your program. To display the page setup options,
open the **File** menu and select **Page Setup.** The Page Setup dialog box appears, presenting numerous options for changing the page layout and print settings. In the following sections, you learn how to use a typical page setup dialog box to set margins
and control how your program prints text on the pages. (If you checked your document in Print Preview and it looks fine, feel free to skip ahead to the section
"Sending Documents to the Printer," to start printing your document.)

Setting the Page Margins

A typical Page Setup dialog box displays the Margins tab up front, as shown in Figure
13.3. If it's hiding, click the **Margins** tab to bring it to the front. This tab lets you
change the top, bottom, left, and right margins. Click the up or down arrow to the
right of each margin setting to change the setting in increments of .1 inch, or click in
a margin setting text box and type the desired margin setting (usually measured in
inches).

Figure 13.3

Set the page margins for the entire document.

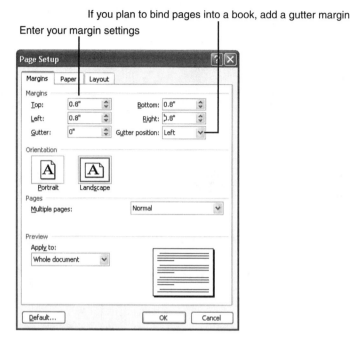

If you plan to bind pages into a book, add a gutter margin

Enter your margin settings

The **Margins** tab offers several additional options for special printing needs:

♦ **Gutter** lets you add margin space to the inside margin of the pages, in case you plan to insert the pages into a book or binder.

♦ **From edge** specifies the distance from the top of the page to the top of the *header* and from the bottom of the page to the bottom of the *footer*. (The **From edge** options are on the **Layout** tab in later versions of the Microsoft Office applications.)

Tech Term _____

A **header** is text that appears at the top of every page in a document. A **footer** is the same thing, but it appears at the bottom of every page. To add a header or footer, open the **View** menu and click **Header and Footer.** A word processor typically hides headers and footers in Normal view. To see how your header or footer will look on a page, change to Print Layout (or Page Layout) view, as explained in Chapter 11.

- **Mirror margins** is useful if you plan to print on both sides of a sheet of paper. When this option is on, your printer makes the inside margins of facing pages equal.

- **2 pages per sheet** or **Multiple pages** shrinks the pages of your document so that your printer can print two pages on a single sheet of paper.

- **Apply to** lets you apply the margin settings to the entire document, from this point forward in the document, or to only selected text. This is useful for long documents that might require different page layouts for some sections.

Picking a Paper Size and Print Direction

Usually, you print a document right side up on 8½ × 11-inch piece of paper. In some cases, however, you might need to print on legal-size paper or print a wide document, such as an announcement or sign, sideways on the page. If that's the case, check out the **Paper** or **Paper Size** tab. On this tab, you can pick from a list of standard paper sizes or specify a custom size. You can also select a print orientation: **Portrait** (to print normally, as in this book) or **Landscape** (to print with the longer edge of the paper at the bottom). **Landscape** is especially useful if you choose the **2 pages per sheet** option. (In later versions of the Office applications, you can find the **Portrait** and **Landscape** options on the **Margins** tab.)

Where's Your Paper Coming From?

If you always print on standard 8½ × 11-inch paper, you don't really need to worry about where the paper is coming from. Your printer is set up to use the default paper tray, which is typically loaded with 8½ × 11-inch paper, and all your programs know that. However, if you need to print envelopes, banners, or any other paper that's not 8½ × 11-inch, check the **Paper** or **Paper Source** tab before you start printing just to be sure that your program is set up to use the right tray.

Laying Out Your Pages

The last tab in the Page Setup dialog box is the **Layout** tab. You can safely ignore most of the options on the **Layout** tab. Just be sure you don't miss the following three options:

- **Vertical alignment.** The **Vertical alignment** list is very useful for making one-page documents (such as a short letter) look good on the page. Open the list and select **Center** to center the document on the page. This option is especially useful for printing cover pages and letters.

- ◆ **Line Numbers.** The **Line Numbers** button is useful for legal and literary pieces. These types of documents often contain line numbers so that people can refer to the line numbers when discussing the documents instead of quoting entire lines and sounding really boring.

- ◆ **Borders.** The **Borders** button opens the **Borders and Shading** dialog box, which allows you to add a border around your entire page or at the top, bottom, left, or right margin.

Sending Documents to the Printer

Once your printer is installed and online, printing is a snap. Although the procedure for printing might vary, the following steps work in most Windows programs. If you just want to print one copy of your document, using the default settings click the **Print** button on the toolbar. If you need to customize a bit, follow these steps:

1. Open the document you want to print.

2. Open the **File** menu and click **Print.** The Print dialog box appears, prompting you to enter instructions. Figure 13.4 shows a typical Print dialog box.

Figure 13.4

The Print dialog box lets you enter specific instructions.

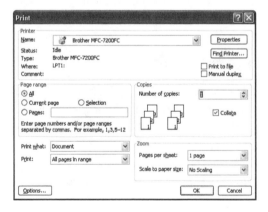

3. In the **Print range** section, select one of the following options:

   - ◆ **All** prints the entire document.

   - ◆ **Selection** is available only if you highlighted text before choosing the Print command. Selection prints only the highlighted portion of the document.

   - ◆ **Pages** prints only the specified pages. If you select this option, type entries in the **From** and **To** boxes to specify which pages you want to print. Some display a single text box into which you type the range of pages you want to print; for example, 3–10 or 3,5,7.

4. Click the arrow to the right of the **Print Quality** option (or click the **Options** or **Properties** button), and select the desired quality. (If you have a color printer, you might have the option of printing in grayscale or black and white.)

Inside Tip

To enter default settings for your printer (including the quality settings), click **Start, Printers and Faxes** (or **Start, Settings, Printers**) and then right-click the icon for your printer, and click **Properties**. Enter your preferences and click **OK**. The default settings control the operation of the printer for all programs.

5. To print more than one copy of the document, type the desired number of copies in the **Copies** text box.

6. Click **OK.** The program starts printing the document. This could take a while, depending on the print quality and on the document's length and complexity; documents that have lots of pictures take a long time.

Whoa!

Did your printer spit out an extra blank page at the end of your document? If it did, you might have told it to by pressing the **Enter** key three or four times at the end of your document. Doing this adds extra blank lines to your document, which can cause the program to insert a page break. If you see an extra page in Print Preview, delete everything after the last line of text in your document. Some programs also offer an option of spitting out a blank page to separate multiple documents. Check your printing options.

Managing Background Printing

If you ever need to stop, cancel, or resume printing, you must access the queue (a waiting line in which documents stand to be printed). Whenever you print a document in Windows, a picture of a printer appears next to the time in the taskbar. Double-click the printer icon to view the print queue, as shown in Figure 13.5. You then can perform the following steps to stop or resume printing:

◆ To pause all printing, open the **Printer** menu and select **Pause Printing.**

◆ To pause the printing of one or more documents, **Ctrl+click** each document in the queue, open the **Document** menu, and select **Pause Printing.**

- To resume printing, open the **Printer** or **Document** menu and click **Pause Printing.**

- To cancel all print jobs, open the **Printer** menu and select **Purge Print Jobs.**

- To cancel individual print jobs, **Ctrl+click** each print job you want to cancel, open the **Document** menu, and select **Cancel Printing.**

- To move a document in the print queue, drag it up or down.

If you choose to cancel printing, don't expect the printer to immediately cease and desist. Fancy printers have loads of memory and can store enough information to print several pages.

The Printer menu has options for controlling all printing

The Document menu controls printing for selected documents

Figure 13.5

You can supervise and control printing using Print Manager.

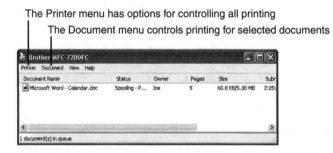

Panic Attack

If you chose to print only one copy of a document but your printer spit out several copies, this usually indicates that you printed the document more than once. When the printer doesn't start printing right away, many people lose patience and keep clicking the Print button. Each time you click the Print button, another copy of the document is sent to the queue, and your printer dutifully prints it.

Hey, It's Not Printing!

If your printer refuses to print your document, you'll have to do a little troubleshooting. The following questions can help you track down the cause:

- Is your printer plugged in and turned on?

- Does the display on the printer indicate that a problem, such as a paper jam, exists? Refer to your printer's manual for information on clearing paper jams and solving other common printer-related problems.

◆ Does your printer have paper? Is the paper tray inserted properly?

◆ Is the printer's On Line light on (not blinking)? If the On Line light is off or blinking, press the **On Line** button to turn on the light and make the printer print.

◆ Display the Print dialog box again and be sure **Print to file** is not selected. This option sends the document to a file on your disk instead of to the printer.

◆ Is your printer marked as the default printer? In My Computer, double-click the **Printers** icon. Right-click the icon for your printer, and be sure that **Set As Default** is checked. If there is no check mark, select **Set As Default.**

◆ Is the printer paused? Double-click the printer icon on the right end of the taskbar, open the **Printer** menu, and be sure that **Pause Printing** is not checked. If there is a check mark, click **Pause Printing.**

◆ Is the correct printer port selected? In My Computer, double-click the **Printers** icon and then right-click the icon for your printer and choose **Properties.** Click the **Details** tab and be sure that the correct printer port is selected—LPT1 in most cases.

The Least You Need to Know

◆ Before you print a document, click the **Print Preview** button to see how the document will appear when printed.

◆ To check the page layout settings, open the **File** menu and click **Page Setup.**

◆ To quickly print a document, no questions asked, click the **Print** button. For more control over printing, choose **File, Print.**

◆ To pause or cancel printing, double-click the printer icon on the right end of the taskbar to display the Print Manager, and then choose the desire option from the **File** menu.

◆ If your document doesn't start printing, double-click the printer icon on the right end of the taskbar to determine what's wrong.

Form Letters, Mailing Labels, and Envelopes

In This Chapter

- ◆ Making your very own form letter
- ◆ Automating mass mailings
- ◆ Printing mailing labels for your holiday cards
- ◆ Printing a stack of envelopes

Whether you run your own small business or just have lots of friends and relatives, mailing announcements, invitations, and greeting cards can become a major ordeal. Fortunately, Microsoft Word and most other popular word processors include a *mail merge* feature that can automate the task for you.

In this chapter, you learn how to create your own form letter and use Word's mail merge feature to merge that form letter with a list of names and addresses to generate a stack of personally addressed letters. You also learn how to use the mail merge feature to print a stack of matching envelopes. By the end of this chapter, all you'll have to do is stuff the envelopes and peel and stick the stamps.

The Incredible Power of the Mail Merge Feature

The mail merge feature is a powerful tool that merges a standard document, such as a form letter or mailing label, with a *data source*, such as an address list, to generate a series of unique documents. For example, the mail merge feature can merge a form letter with an address list to generate a stack of letters personally addressed to each person on the list.

Here's how it works: First, you create a database, such as an address book, that contains the data entries you want to insert in your form letter and mailing labels. Then, you create a form letter with *field codes* that tell your document which pieces of data to extract from the data source and where to insert them in your document. For instance, the field code <<LastName>> tells mail merge to grab data entries from the LastName column in the data source. When you execute the mail merge operation, mail merge generates a single document for each name in the data source. You can use mail merge to generate your form letters and print matching envelopes or mailing labels, as shown in Figure 14.1.

Tech Term

What's a **data source?**
A data source can be any document that contains a collection of records consisting of data entries. A data source may be a table, spreadsheet, database, or address book.

Figure 14.1

Mail merge generates a unique document for each record in a table.

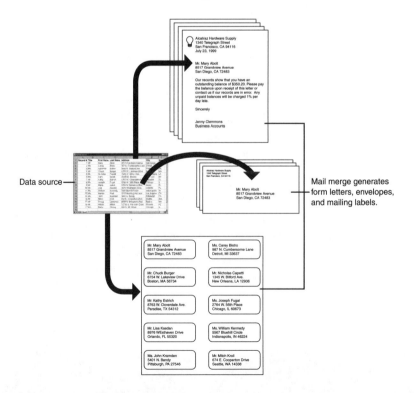

Data source

Mail merge generates form letters, envelopes, and mailing labels.

Making a Simple Address Book with a Word Table

As noted earlier in this chapter, the first step in performing a successful mail merge is to create a data source. The data source can be an address book you created in your e-mail program, a database created in a database application, a spreadsheet, or a table created in a word processing application. To make a simple address book data source in your word processor, create a table consisting of several columns and rows and then type in the names and addresses of your contacts, as shown in Figure 14.2.

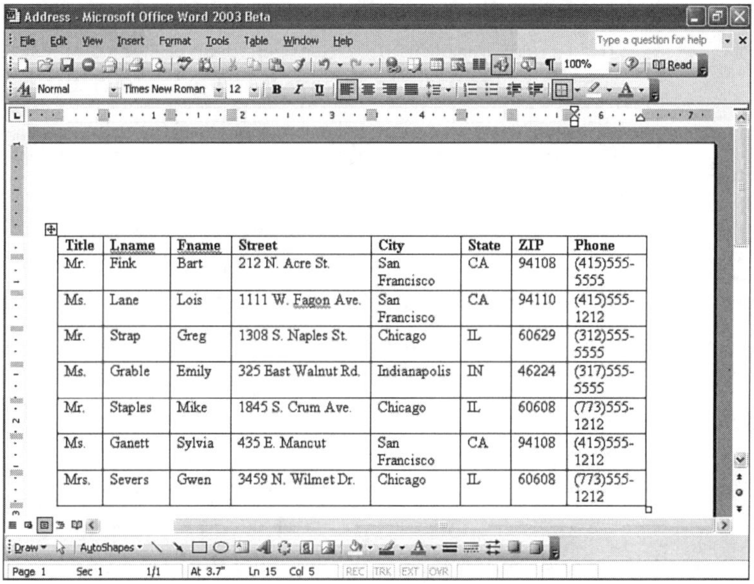

Figure 14.2

Word's table feature lets you create a basic address book.

To create a table in Word, click the **Insert Table** button. This opens a list showing a graphic representation of the columns and rows that make up a table. Drag down and to the right to highlight the desired number of rows and columns. If you need more columns or rows than first shown, drag beyond the bottom or right side of the grid to expand it. When you release the mouse button, Word inserts the table.

After the table is in place, start typing your entries. In the top row, type headings for each column; for instance, type LastName, FirstName, and Address. These headings allow Word to find and extract data from the table to create mailing labels and personally addressed letters, as explained later in this chapter.

Whoa!

When typing column headings, don't type any spaces. For example, use "LName" or "LastName" instead of "Last Name." Using spaces confuses the mail merge feature.

If an entry is too wide for the column, Word automatically resizes the columns or wraps text inside a cell to accommodate the entry. Press the **Tab** key to move from one cell (box) to the next, or click in the cell. When you reach the end of a row, press the **Tab** key to move to the next row. If you're in the last cell of the last row, pressing the **Tab** key creates a new row, so you can continue typing entries.

Computer Cheat

To have Word automatically adjust the row height and column width to accommodate your entries, select the row(s) or column(s) that you want to change, and then open the **Table** menu, point to **AutoFit**, and choose the desired option.

Adjusting the Row Height and Column Width

If your rows are too short or your columns are too narrow, resize them. The easiest way to adjust the row height and column width is to drag the lines that divide the columns and rows. When you move the mouse pointer over a line, the pointer changes into a double-headed arrow; that's when you can start dragging. If you hold down the **Alt** key and drag, the horizontal or vertical ruler shows the exact row height or column width measurement. (You can also drag the column or row markers inside the rulers to change the row height and column width.)

Sorting Your List

Tables commonly contain entries that you need to sort alphabetically or numerically. If you create a table of phone numbers for people and places that you frequently call, for example, you might want to sort the list alphabetically to make it easy to find people.

To sort entries in a table, first select the entire table (or the portion that contains the entries you want to sort). If you have a row at the top that contains descriptions of the contents in each column, be sure it is not selected; otherwise, it is sorted along with the other rows.

Open the **Table** menu and select **Sort**. Open the **Sort by** list and select the column that contains the entries to sort by. For example, if you want to sort by last name and the last names are in the second column, select **Column 2**. Open the **Type** drop-down list and select the type of items you want to sort (**Number, Text,** or **Date**). Select the desired sort order: **Ascending** (1, 2, 3 or A, B, C) or **Descending** (Z, Y, X or 10, 9, 8). Click **OK** to sort the entries.

The Making of a Form Letter

Now that your data source is complete, you can begin composing your form letter. How you compose your form letter is your business. You can type it from scratch, use a template, or seek help from the Letter Wizard (if you're using Microsoft Word). Omit any information that Word obtains from the data source during the merge, such as the person's name and address. After you complete the letter, you will insert field codes into the letter (one for the person's name, one for the address, and so on). These codes tell mail merge which entries to extract from the data source and where to insert those entries.

Computer Cheat

The easiest way to write and format a letter is to use the Letter Wizard. In Word 2002 or 2003, choose **Tools, Letters and Mailings, Letter Wizard.** In Word 2000, choose **Tools, Letter Wizard.** The Letter Wizard dialog box displays a fill-in-the-blank form that you can use to specify your preferences and enter information such as the inside address, the salutation, and the closing.

Inserting the Secret Codes

Assuming you created an address book in the preceding section, you should have everything you need to perform a mail merge: a form letter and a data source. You can now use the mail merge feature to insert field codes in your form letter.

The steps vary, depending on which version of Word you're using. In Word 2002 or 2003, follow these steps:

1. Create or open your form letter.

2. Crank down the **Tools** menu, point to **Letters and Mailings,** and select **Mail Merge.** The Mail Merge task pane appears, providing instructions on how to proceed.

3. Under **Select document type,** click **Letters** to tell Word to use your letter as the main document in the merge.

4. Click **Next: Starting document.** The Mail Merge Wizard prompts you to specify the document you want to use.

5. Be sure **Use the current document** is selected, and then click **Next: Select recipients.** The Mail Merge Wizard prompts you to specify your data source.

6. Select one of the following options and perform the necessary steps to select the source of data that you want to use for the merge:

- ◆ **Use an existing list** lets you use a data source you have already created. Select this option and then click **Browse** to display a dialog box that lets you pick the data source file. Follow the onscreen instructions to select the data you want to use.

- ◆ **Select from Outlook contacts** lets you use your Outlook contact list as the data source. Select this option and then click **Choose Contacts Folder** to select the contacts file you want to use as the data source.

- ◆ **Type a new list** leads you through the process of creating an address book containing the data that you want to merge with your form letter. Select this option and then click **Create** to display a fill-in-the-blank dialog box for adding names and addresses to your address book.

7. Click **Next: Write your letter.** The Mail Merge Wizard instructs you to compose your letter if you have not already done so and provides a list of options for inserting codes into your letter.

8. Position the insertion point where you want to insert a piece of data from the database. For example, you might move the insertion point just below the date to insert the person's name and address.

9. Click the link for inserting the desired information. For example, click **Address block** to insert the recipient's name and address, as shown in Figure 14.3. Click **Greeting line** to insert a greeting, such as "Dear Mr. Spock." To insert individual merge codes that correspond with fields in your database, click the **More items** link and pick the desired code.

10. Enter your preferences in the resulting dialog box and click **OK.** For example, if you chose to insert a greeting line, you can choose to insert the person's first name, title, and last name, or just the last name, in the greeting. The Mail Merge Wizard inserts a merge code into the document, such as `{{{{AddressBlock}}}}`, which will extract the corresponding data from the data source.

Panic Attack

The Mail Merge Wizard in Word 2002/2003 tries its best to match its fields to the fields in your data source, but it's not perfect. Click the **Match Fields** button in the lower-left corner of the Insert Address Block or Insert Greeting Line dialog box to adjust the matchups.

---

11. Repeat steps 8 through 10 to insert additional merge field codes.

12. Click **Next: Preview your letters.** The Mail Merge Wizard merges your form letter with your data source, creates a collection of personalized letters, and displays the first letter.

13. Click the **>>** button to preview the next letter or the **<<** button to preview the previous letter. (You can edit individual letters if desired.)

Click the Address block link to
the recipient's name and address

Select the information you want to include

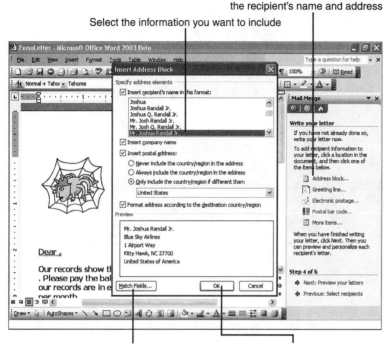

Figure 14.3

Insert field codes to pull entries from the data source into your letter.

Click Match Fields to make sure Word is looking for
the information in the correct data source fields

Click OK

In Word 2000 or 2003, the process is a little more straightforward, because you insert a code for each individual data entry. The Mail Merge Helper can lead you through the process. Here's what you do:

1. With your form letter displayed onscreen, crank down the **Tools** menu and select **Mail Merge.** The Mail Merge Helper dialog box appears. It leads you step by step through the merge operation.

2. Click **Create** (under **Main Document**), select **Form Letters,** and click **Active Window.** This tells Word to use your letter as the main document in the merge.

3. Under **Data Source,** click **Get Data** and click **Open Data Source.**

4. Select the document that contains the desired records, and click **Open.** (This might be a spreadsheet, a database file, or a Word document containing a table.)

5. The Microsoft Word dialog box appears, telling you that your form letter has no merge fields (as if you didn't know). Click **Edit Main Document.** Word returns you to your form letter and displays the Mail Merge toolbar.

6. Position the insertion point where you want to insert a piece of data from the database. For example, you might move the insertion point a couple lines down from the date to insert the person's name and address.

7. Open the **Insert Merge Field** drop-down list and click the desired field, as shown in Figure 14.4. This inserts a code (such as <<FirstName>>) that will pull specified data (a person's first name, in this case) from the data source and insert it into your letter.

Figure 14.4

Insert field codes by selecting them from the **Insert Merge Field** *list.*

Click the desired field

Click Merge Field

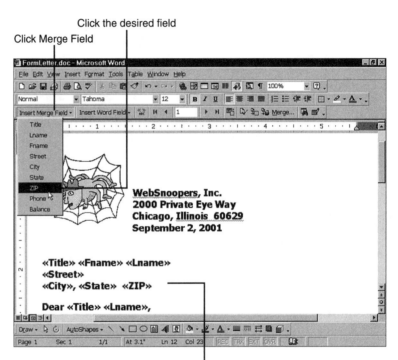

Word plugs in the field codes at the insertion point

Whoa!

Don't type your field codes. Typing field codes into your form letter doesn't work. No matter how easy it is, Word just doesn't recognize these codes. You must select the code from the **Insert Field Code** list.

8. Repeat step 7 to insert additional merge field codes. Add punctuation and spaces between the codes as necessary. For example, if you are assembling codes to insert the recipient's address, you need to add spaces and commas in the following way:

```
<<Title>> <<FirstName>> <<LastName>>
<<Address>>
<<City>>, <<State>> <<ZIP>>
```

9. If your database contains information that you want to insert in the salutation or body of the letter, insert a field merge code wherever you want that information to appear. You might, for example, use the following salutation:

```
Dear <<Title>> <<LastName>>,
```

Initiating the Merge Operation

Now comes the fun part. After you have inserted the desired field codes, you're ready to initiate the merge operation and generate your personalized letters. Again, the steps vary slightly, depending on whether you're using Word 2002 or 2003 or an early version.

In Word 2002 or 2003, click **Next: Complete the merge.** You can then click the **Print** link to print the letters or click **Edit Individual Letters** to create a new document consisting of a personally addressed letter for everyone in the data source. (I always choose to edit individual letters so that I can check for errors before printing.) When you're ready to print, just click the **Print** button.

If you're using an earlier version of Word, follow these steps:

1. Click the **Merge** button (on the Merge toolbar). The Merge dialog box appears, offering the following options for controlling how Word merges the form letter and data source:

   ◆ **Merge to** lets you merge to the printer, to a new document, or to your e-mail program. It's a good idea to merge to a new document so that you can check for errors before printing. You can also flip through the merged document and personalize the form letters that Word generates.

   ◆ **Records to be merged** lets you select a range of records so that you can create letters for only selected records in the data source.

   ◆ **When merging records** tells Word whether to insert blank lines when a particular field in a record is blank.

   ◆ **Query options** displays a dialog box that lets you sort the merged letters or create letters for a specific collection of records.

2. Enter your merge preferences, and then click the **Merge** button. If you choose to merge to the printer, Word starts printing the letters. If you choose to merge to a new file, Word opens a new document window and places the merged letters in this window. You can then print them as you would print any document.

Printing Addresses on Mailing Labels

Now that you have a stack of letters, you need to address them. You can do this by using a mailing label as your main document and merging it with the data source.

In Word 2002 or 2003, follow the same steps that you followed earlier in this chapter in the section "Inserting the Secret Codes," but when you get to step 3, select **Labels.** There's nothing tricky here; follow the Mail Merge Wizard's instructions in the task pane, and you'll be ready to start stuffing envelopes in no time.

In earlier versions of Word, open the **Tools** menu, select **Mail Merge,** and follow the Mail Merge Helper's instructions to set up a new main document for printing mailing labels. Complete the merge by specifying the location of your data source and inserting the required field codes. After you have entered the field codes, you're ready to execute the merge operation and print your mailing labels. Follow the same steps you performed earlier in this chapter in the section "Initiating the Merge Operation."

Inside Tip

Print your mailing labels on inexpensive printer paper and hold the printed addresses over a sheet of labels to check the alignment. You can move the addresses down by adding blank lines before the first line of field codes or by using the **Format, Paragraph** command to add space before the first line. To move the addresses to the right, add spaces to the left of each line.

Printing a Stack of Envelopes for Mass Mailing

At the beginning of this chapter, I promised that after you learned how to use mail merge, all you would need to do is stuff envelopes and peel and stick mailing labels. I lied. You can reduce your workload even more by printing the addresses directly on your envelopes.

To use the mail merge feature to print envelopes, follow the same steps you followed to create mailing labels, but when prompted to choose the document type, choose **Envelopes.** After you enter the field codes and give your okay, Mail Merge Helper returns you to the main document, where your field codes are laid out on an "envelope." Type your name and return address in the upper-left corner to have it printed on the envelope. You can then click the option for executing the merge and printing your envelopes.

To print a single envelope, without using the mail merge feature, first highlight the address of the recipient as it appears on your letter. Then, open the **Tools** menu, point to **Letters and Mailings,** and click **Envelopes and Labels.** The Envelopes and Labels dialog box appears, with the Envelopes tab up front, and the address you highlighted is in the Delivery Address text box. If your address is not in the Return Address text box, click inside the box and type your name and address. Load an envelope into your printer, and then click the **Print** button.

Inside Tip

If you're mailing tri-fold newsletters or brochures, you don't need an envelope. Simply create a new main document and position the field codes where you want the addresses printed (typically the center of the page). You can then print the addresses directly on the back of the brochures or newsletters.

The Least You Need to Know

◆ To use the mail merge feature, you need a main document and a data source.

◆ To use the mail merge feature in Word 2002, open the **Tools** menu, point to **Letters and Mailings,** and click **Mail Merge Wizard.** In earlier versions of Word, open the **Tools** menu and click **Mail Merge.**

◆ To prepare for a successful mail merge, you select the type of document you want to create, specify the location of your data source, and insert field codes in your main document where you want specific data entries inserted.

◆ To initiate the merge, click **Next: Complete the merge** (in Word 2002) or click the **Merge** button on the Merge toolbar (in earlier versions of Word).

Making a Spreadsheet Do Your Math Homework

In This Chapter

- See the similarities between your checkbook and a spreadsheet
- Type text, numbers, and dates in a spreadsheet cell
- Add formulas to a spreadsheet to perform calculations on the values you entered
- Graph the values in a spreadsheet even if you don't know how to graph

There's no mystery to spreadsheets. A checkbook is a spreadsheet. A calendar is a spreadsheet. Your 1040 tax form is a spreadsheet. Any sheet that has boxes you can fill in is a type of spreadsheet.

So what's so special about computerized spreadsheets? For one thing, they do the math for you. For example, a computerized grade book spreadsheet can add each student's grades, determine the average for each student, and even assign the correct letter grade for each average. And that's not all. The spreadsheet can also display the averages as a graph, showing how each student is doing in relation to the other students or showing a student's progress or decline in performance. In this chapter, you learn what it takes to create your own spreadsheets, and some of the things you can do with spreadsheets.

A Computerized Ledger Sheet

A spreadsheet is a grid consisting of a series of columns and rows that intersect to form thousands of small boxes called *cells*, as shown in Figure 15.1. Most spreadsheet applications display a collection of spreadsheets (also called *worksheets*) in a workbook. You can flip the pages in the workbook by clicking the spreadsheet *tabs*.

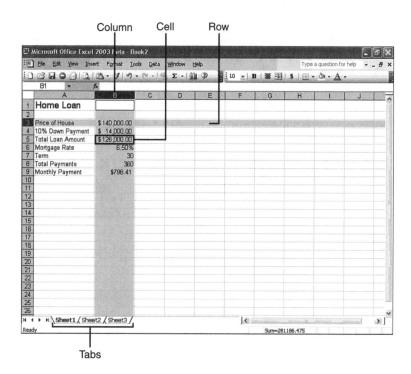

Figure 15.1

A popular spreadsheet application with a sample file open.

Why Did the Column Cross the Row?

Look across the top of any computer spreadsheet, and you'll see the alphabet (A, B, C, and so on). Each letter stands at the top of a *column*. Along the left side of the spreadsheet, you'll see numbers representing *rows*. The place where a column and row intersect forms a box, called a *cell*. This is the basic unit of any spreadsheet. You will type text, values, and formulas in the cells to make your spreadsheet.

Knowing Where a Cell Lives

To keep track of where each cell is located and what each cell contains, the spreadsheet uses *cell addresses*. Each cell has an address made up of a column letter and row number. For example, the cell that's formed by the intersection of column B and row 3 has the address B3.

Inside Tip

Some spreadsheet applications let you name individual cells or groups of cells (*ranges*). You can then use the names, instead of the cell addresses, to refer to the cells.

Cell Hopping

To select a block of cells, drag over the cells to highlight them. To select a row, click the row number that's to the left of the desired row or drag over two or more row numbers to select multiple rows. To select a column, click the letter that's above the desired column or drag over two or more column letters to select multiple columns.

When you move to a cell, its address is usually displayed at the top or bottom of the spreadsheet

Input line

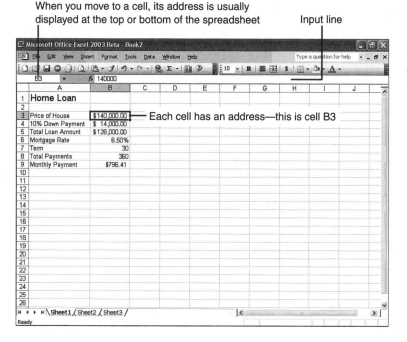

Each cell has an address—this is cell B3

Figure 15.2

A cell's contents appear in the input line.

Building a Spreadsheet from the Ground Up

I bet you're just dying to know how you go about making a spreadsheet. The easiest way is to get a friend to set it up for you—to insert all the formulas and other complicated stuff. Then, all you have to do is type in your data and watch the spreadsheet do its thing. If you're a do-it-yourselfer, however, you'll need to take the following steps (don't worry, I'll go into more detail later in this chapter):

Step 1: Design the spreadsheet.

Step 2: Label the columns and rows.

Step 3: Enter your data: labels (text), values (numbers), and dates.

Step 4: Enter the formulas and functions that the spreadsheet will use to perform calculations.

Step 5: Format the cells (to display dollar signs, for instance).

There's no law that says you have to perform the steps in this order. Some users like to enter their formulas before entering their data, so the formulas calculate results as they work. Regardless of how you proceed, you will probably have to go back to previous steps to fine-tune your spreadsheet.

Computer Cheat

If you need a spreadsheet for a common task, such as determining a loan payment, check to see if your spreadsheet program features a template for the task you want to perform. Open the **File** menu, select **New,** and choose the option for creating a spreadsheet from a template. Excel comes with dozens of templates, and later versions of Excel enable you to copy additional templates from Microsoft's "Office on the Web" site. With a template, everything is laid out for you; you simply plug in the specific data you want to use.

Step 1: Designing the Spreadsheet

If you have a form that you want the spreadsheet to look like, lay the form down by your keyboard and use it as a model. For example, if you're going to use the spreadsheet to balance your checkbook, use your most recent bank statement or your checkbook register to model the columns and rows.

If you don't have a form, draw your spreadsheet on a piece of paper or a napkin to determine the columns and rows you need. (It doesn't have to be perfect, just something to get you started.)

Step 2: Labeling Your Columns and Rows

When you have some idea of the basic structure of your spreadsheet, you're ready to enter *labels*. Labels are commonsense names for the columns and rows.

To enter a label, click in the cell where you want it to appear, type the label, and press **Enter**. If your label starts with a number (for example, 2004 Sales), you may have to type something in front of it to tell the spreadsheet to treat it as text rather than as a value. In most applications you type an apostrophe (') or a quotation mark ("). Usually, whatever you type appears only in the input line until you press **Enter.** Then the label is inserted into the current cell. (If you type an apostrophe, it remains invisible in the cell, though you can see it when the entry is displayed on the input line.)

If an entry is too wide for a cell, it will overlap cells to the right of it … unless the cell to the right has its own entry. In such a case, the entry on the left will appear chopped off (hidden). If you click the cell, you can view the entire entry on the input line. If you want to see the entire entry in the cell, you can widen the column, usually by dragging the right side of the column header, as shown in Figure 15.3.

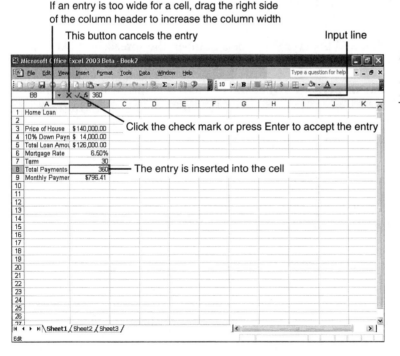

If an entry is too wide for a cell, drag the right side of the column header to increase the column width

This button cancels the entry

Input line

Click the check mark or press Enter to accept the entry

The entry is inserted into the cell

Figure 15.3

Select a cell, and then type your entry.

Step 2½: Editing Your Entries

When you make mistakes or change your mind about what you entered, the best way to make corrections usually is to replace the entry. **Tab** to the cell that contains the entry, type the replacement, and press **Enter.** That's all there is to it.

To edit an entry, click in the cell you want to change, and then click inside the entry in the input line or press the key for editing the entry (the **F2** key in Excel). This puts you in *Edit mode*, and allows you to edit the entry on the input line. You can then use the arrow keys to move the cursor or insertion point and type your change. Press **Enter** when you're done. Newer versions of most spreadsheet applications offer something called *in-cell editing*. Instead of editing the entry on the input line, you edit it directly inside the cell. To edit an entry, you simply double-click it, and then enter your changes.

Step 3: Entering Values and Dates

Once you have labeled your rows and columns, you're ready to enter your raw data: the values and/or dates that make up your spreadsheet. As you type your entries, keep the following in mind:

- **Values are numbers.** Whenever you type a number, the spreadsheet "knows" it is a value. You don't have to do anything special.

- **Don't enter dollar or percent signs.** You can have the spreadsheet add these symbols for you when you format the cells. Type only the number. (In some spreadsheets, you must pick a number format before you start typing. For instance, you might type a date and have it appear as a number rather than as a date. See "Step 5: Making the Cells Look Pretty," later in this chapter for more information on how to do this.)

- **Type dates in the proper format for your spreadsheet.** In most spreadsheets, you must type the date in the format mm/dd/yy (02/25/04) or dd-mmm-yy (02-FEB-04).

- **Dates are handled as numbers.** Although the spreadsheet displays dates in a format that people understand, it treats a date as a numerical value (typically the number of days since January 1, 1900). You can then have the spreadsheet use the date in a formula to calculate when a payment or delivery is due.

- **######## Long entries.** If a value you type is too wide for a cell, the spreadsheet may display a series of number signs (#) or asterisks (*) instead of the value. Don't worry—your entry is still there. You can click on the cell to see the entry in the input line, and if you widen the column, the spreadsheet will display the entire value.

To enter values or labels quickly, many spreadsheets let you copy entries into one or more cells or *fill* selected cells with a series of entries. For example, in an Excel spreadsheet, you can type January in one cell, and then use the Fill command to have Excel insert the remaining 11 months in 11 cells to the right. Fill also allows you to duplicate entries. For example, you can type 250 in one cell, and then use the Fill command (or drag the Fill handle down, as shown in Figure 15.4) to enter 250 into the next 10 cells down.

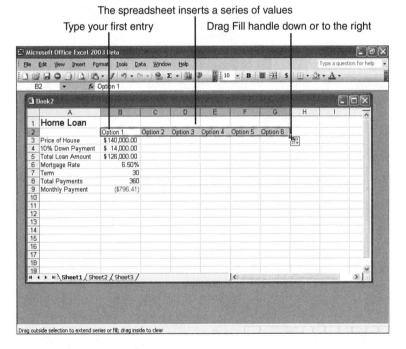

Figure 15.4

Excel's Fill feature in action.

Step 4: Calculating with Formulas and Functions

At this point, you should have rows and columns of values. You need some way to total the values, determine an average, or perform other mathematical operations. That's where formulas and functions come in. They do all the busy work for you … once you set them up.

What Are Formulas?

Spreadsheets use formulas to perform calculations on the data you enter. With formulas, you can perform addition, subtraction, multiplication, or division using the values contained in various cells.

Formulas typically consist of one or more cell addresses and/or values and a mathematical operator, such as + (addition), – (subtraction), * (multiplication), or / (division). For example, if you wanted to determine the average of the three values contained in cells A1, B1, and C1, you would use the following formula:

(A1+B1+C1)/3

Entering Formulas in Your Spreadsheet

To enter a formula, move to the cell in which you want the formula to appear, type the formula, and press **Enter.** Some spreadsheets assume that you want to type a formula if you start your entry with a column letter. Other spreadsheets require you to start the formula with a mathematical operator, such as an equal sign (=) or plus sign (+). Figure 15.5 shows some basic formulas in action.

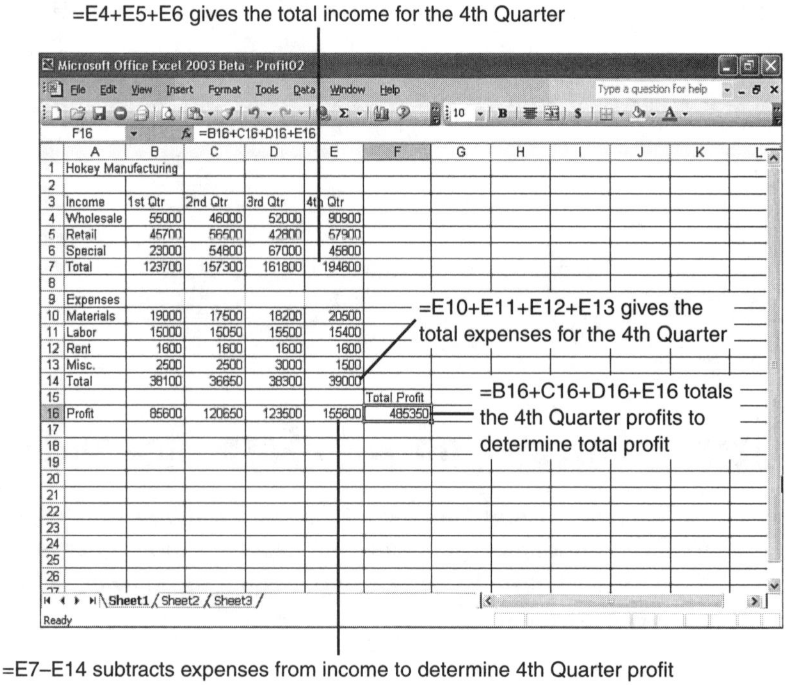

Figure 15.5

Some formulas at work.

=E4+E5+E6 gives the total income for the 4th Quarter

=E10+E11+E12+E13 gives the total expenses for the 4th Quarter

=B16+C16+D16+E16 totals the 4th Quarter profits to determine total profit

=E7–E14 subtracts expenses from income to determine 4th Quarter profit

Most spreadsheets let you enter formulas in either of two ways. You can type the formula directly in the cell in which you want the result inserted, or you can use the mouse to point and click on the cells whose values you want inserted in the formula. To use the second method, called *pointing*, you would use the keyboard and mouse together. For example, to determine the total of the values in B4, B5, and B6, you would perform the following steps:

1. Click the cell in which you want to enter the formula. The formula's result will appear in this cell.

2. Type = to mark this as a formula.

3. Click cell **B4** to add the cell's address to your formula.

4. Type + to add another cell address to the formula.

5. Click cell **B5.**

6. Type + to add the final cell address to the formula.

7. Click cell **B6.**

8. Press **Enter** to accept the formula. If any of the cells in the formula (B4, B5, or B6) contains a value, the formula's result appears in the cell in which you entered the formula.

Inside Tip _____

If your spreadsheet application has a toolbar, it probably has a Sum button that looks like Â. To quickly determine a total, the cell in which you want the total inserted, click the **Sum** button (Â), and then drag over the cells that contain the values you want to add. When you release the mouse button and press **Enter**, the spreadsheet performs the required calculations and inserts the result.

Using Ready-Made Functions for Fancy Calculations

Creating simple formulas (such as one for adding a column of numbers) is a piece of cake, but creating the formulas required for a mortgage refinance spreadsheet can pose quite a challenge. To help you in such cases, many spreadsheet applications offer predefined formulas called *functions*.

Functions are complex ready-made formulas that perform a series of operations on a specified *range* of values. For example, to determine the sum of a series of numbers in cells A1 through H1, you can enter the function =SUM(A1..H1), instead of entering =A1+B1+C1+ and so on. Every function consists of three elements:

◆ The **@** or **=** sign indicates that what follows is a function.

◆ The **function name** (for example, SUM) indicates the operation to be performed.

◆ The **argument** (for example A1:H1) gives the cell addresses of the values the function will act on. For example, =SUM(A1:H1) determines the total of the values in cells A1 through H1.

Inside Tip

Use this mnemonic device to remember the order in which a spreadsheet performs mathematical operations: My (Multiplication) Dear (Division) Aunt (Addition) Sally (Subtraction). To change the order of operations, use parentheses. Any operation inside parentheses is performed first.

Although functions are fairly complicated and intimidating, many spreadsheets have tools to help. For example, Microsoft Excel offers a tool called the Function Wizard (or Insert Function tool), which leads you through the process of inserting functions. It displays a series of dialog boxes asking you to select the function you want to use, and pick the values for the argument. Figure 15.6 shows the Insert Function tool in action.

Select a type of function

Figure 15.6

Tools such as Insert Function tool makes it easier to work with functions.

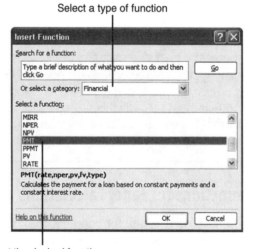

Select the desired function

Step 5: Making the Cells Look Pretty

Once you have the basic layout of your spreadsheet under control, you can *format* the cells, to give the spreadsheet the desired "look." The first thing you might want to do is change the column width and row height to give your entries some breathing room. You may also want to format the values—tell the application to display values as dollar amounts or to use commas to mark the thousand's place.

In addition, you can change the type style and type size for your column or row headings, change the text color, and align the text in the cells. For example, you may want to center the headings or align the values in a column so that the decimal points line up. To improve the look of the cells themselves, and to distinguish one set of data from another, you can add borders around the cells and add shading and color to the cells.

To format cells, select the cells you want to format and then use the controls on the Formatting toolbar or the options on the Format menu to apply the desired formatting.

Many newer spreadsheet applications have an AutoFormat feature that allows you to select the look you want your spreadsheet to have. The application then applies the lines, shading, and fonts to give your spreadsheet a makeover, as shown in Figure 15.7.

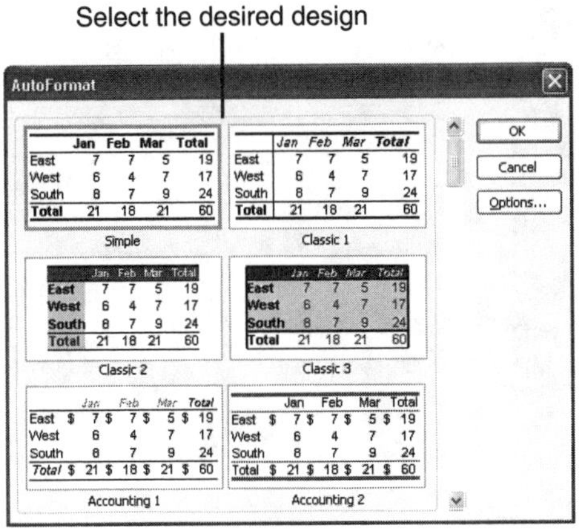

Tech Term

Formatting cells means to improve the look of the cells or cell entries without changing their content. Formatting usually includes changing the type style and size of type, adding borders and shading to the cells, and telling the application how to display values (for example, as currency or in scientific notation).

Select the desired design

Figure 15.7

Some applications can format your spreadsheet for you.

Once you've formatted your spreadsheet, you can print it. With some spreadsheet applications, such as the latest version of Excel, you can publish your spreadsheet and graphs electronically on the World Wide Web.

Instant Graphs (Just Add Data)

People, especially management types, like to look at graphs. They don't want to have to compare a bunch of numbers; they want the bottom line. They want to see immediately how the numbers stack up. Most spreadsheet applications offer a graphing feature to transform the values you entered into any type of graph (a.k.a. *chart*) you want: bar, line, pie, area, or high-low (to analyze stock trends). The steps for creating a graph are simple:

1. Drag with the mouse over the labels and values that you want to include in the graph. (Labels are used for the *axes*.)

2. Enter the **Graph** or **Chart** command. (This command varies from application to application.)

3. Select the type of graph you want to create.

4. Select the **OK** option. The application transforms your data into a graph and inserts it into the spreadsheet, as shown in Figure 15.8.

Figure 15.8

Most spreadsheet applications can quickly throw together any type of graph you need.

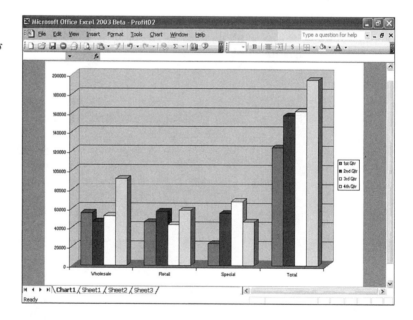

Special Spreadsheet Printing Considerations

When you print a letter or other document created in a word processing application, you typically don't need to worry that your paragraphs will be too wide for the pages. The word processor automatically wraps the text to make it fit. Spreadsheets, however, can be much wider than a typical 8½ × 11-inch sheet of paper. To accommodate extra wide spreadsheets, your spreadsheet application features special print options. The following sections explain some of these options in greater detail.

Previewing Your Worksheets Before Printing

Before you start tweaking the worksheet layout and adjusting print settings to make a worksheet fit on 8½ × 11-inch pages, check your page setup to determine how your spreadsheet application is prepared to print your worksheet(s). Frequently, the application inserts awkward page breaks, omits titles and column headings from some of the pages, and uses additional settings that result in an unacceptable printout.

To check your worksheet before printing, click the **Print Preview** button (or select **File, Print Preview**). This displays your worksheet in Print Preview mode, as shown in Figure 15.9.

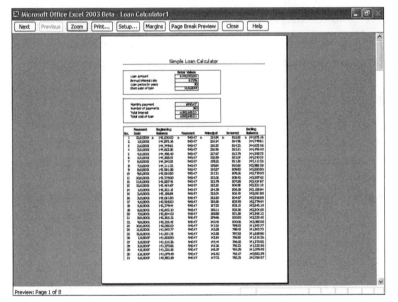

Figure 15.9

Excel's Print Preview lets you see how a worksheet will print before you print it.

Along the top of the preview area are several buttons that enable you to flip pages, zoom in and zoom out on the page, and change some common print settings. If your spreadsheet application displays a **Margins** button, click it to display margin and column markers; you can drag the markers to adjust column widths and page margins right onscreen. If your application displays a **Page Break Preview** button, click the button to see how the application plans on dividing your spreadsheet into pages; you can drag the page break bars to adjust the page breaks before printing.

Changing the Page Setup

If your worksheet is close to fitting on a single page, you usually can adjust the left and right margins to pull another column or two (or a couple rows) onto the page. If the worksheet still doesn't fit, you may need to adjust the page setup, via the Page Setup dialog box. To display the Page Setup dialog box, open the **File** menu and click **Page Setup,** or click the **Setup** button on the Print Preview screen. In Excel, the Page Setup dialog box features the following four tabs:

- ◆ **Page.** This tab contains options for specifying the page orientation (portrait or landscape), the paper size, print quality, and at the number at which Excel starts numbering the pages. This tab also offers an interesting feature that can shrink your worksheet to fit on one or more pages.

- ◆ **Margins.** This tab contains spin boxes for setting the top, bottom, left, and right margins and for specifying the distance between the top edge of the page and the header and the distance between the bottom edge of the page and the footer. You may prefer to set margins in Print Preview.

- ◆ **Header/Footer.** This tab provides options for printing a footer (on the bottom of each page) or a header (at the top of each page) that automatically numbers the worksheet pages for you and prints the file's name, the worksheet title, the date and time, and any other information you want to include.

- ◆ **Sheet.** The Sheet tab enables you to specify the order in which you want your pages printed and to designate one or more rows you want to print at the top of every page and one or more columns you want printed along the left side of every page. This tab includes several additional options, including an option for specifying a print area, so you can print only a select portion of the spreadsheet.

Hiding Columns and Rows

If you're having trouble fitting your worksheet on the desired number of pages, or you want to prevent someone viewing the printout from seeing some confidential data, you can hide selected columns or rows. To hide columns or rows and prevent Excel from printing them, take the following steps:

1. Drag over the column or row headers for the columns or rows you want to hide.

2. Open the **Format** menu and select **Column, Hide** or **Row, Hide.** (Alternatively, right-click one of the selected columns or rows and select **Hide** from the context menu.) The selected columns or rows disappear, and a dark line appears on the worksheet to indicate that rows or columns are hidden.

3. Click the **Print Preview** button. Excel displays the worksheet, omitting the hidden columns or rows.

Bringing hidden rows or columns back into view isn't the most intuitive operation. First, drag over the column or row headings before and after the hidden columns and rows. If columns C, D, and E are hidden, for example, drag over column headings B and F to select them. Open the **Format** menu and select **Columns, Unhide** or **Rows, Unhide.**

Printing Your Worksheets

When you're satisfied with the way your worksheet looks in Print Preview, you're ready to send it to your printer. The quickest way to print is to click the tab for the worksheet you want to print and then click the **Print** button. This sends the worksheet off to the printer, no questions asked. To print more than one worksheet or set additional printing preferences, open the **File** menu, click **Print,** and enter your preferences.

Five Cool Things You Can Do with a Spreadsheet

I already mentioned a couple practical uses for spreadsheets: averaging grades and balancing your checkbook (although a personal finance application, such as Quicken, works much better). I sat around awhile and thought up some other practical things you can use spreadsheets for:

♦ **Schedules.** Use a spreadsheet to keep track of your various projects. You can use a separate row for each project and a separate column for each stage in the project.

♦ **Invoices.** Create an invoice that lists the parts delivered, the number of parts, and the price per part. The invoice can calculate the total due for each part, the subtotal of all parts, the amount of sales tax due, and the grand total (total plus tax).

♦ **Loan amortization.** If you are purchasing a house or car or taking out a loan to start your business, you can use a spreadsheet to determine how much interest and principal you will be paying on various loans.

♦ **Home or business inventory.** Use a spreadsheet to keep track of each item you own and how much it is worth. Such a record is invaluable in the event of a fire or theft. (Assuming the record doesn't get burned or stolen.)

◆ **Play tic-tac-toe.** Those little boxes are just begging for some Xs and Os. You can crank up your font size and have a ball playing tic-tac-toe onscreen.

The Least You Need to Know

◆ A cell can contain any of the following entries: a row or column heading, a formula, a function with an argument, or a value.

◆ Formulas perform calculations on the values in the cells. Each formula consists of one or more cell addresses and a math operator.

◆ A function is a ready-made complex formula that performs calculations on a range of values.

◆ You can format the cells in a spreadsheet to control the text size and style, row height, column width, borders, and shading.

◆ Spreadsheet programs include several special page setup options to cram wide spreadsheets on narrow sheets of paper.

Part 4

Getting Wired to the Internet

Faster than Federal Express. More powerful than the Home Shopping Network. Able to leap wide continents in a single click. Look, up on your desktop. It's a phone! It's a network! No, it's the Internet!

With your computer, a modem, and a standard phone line, you have access to the single most powerful communications and information network in the world—the Internet. The chapters in this part show you how to get wired to the Internet and use its features to exchange electronic mail, chat with friends and strangers, shop for deals, manage your investments, plan your next vacation, research interesting topics, and even publish your own creations via the web!

Chapter 16

Connecting to the Outside World with a Modem

In This Chapter

- ◆ Ten good reasons to buy a modem
- ◆ Grasping the basic principles of modem talk
- ◆ Understanding ISDN, DSL, and other modem acronyms
- ◆ Getting your modem up and running
- ◆ Connecting to the Internet with your modem

How would you like to access the latest news, weather, and sports without stepping away from your computer? Track investments without having to call a broker or wait for tomorrow's newspaper? Connect to an online encyclopedia, complete with sounds and pictures? Order items from a computerized catalog? Send a postage-free letter and have it arrive at its destination in a matter of seconds? Mingle with friends and strangers in online chat rooms? Transfer files from your computer to a colleague's computer anywhere in the world?

With your computer, a modem, and a subscription to an online service or Internet service provider, you can do all this and more. This chapter introduces you to the wonderful world of modems and shows you how to connect your computer to the outside world.

What Can I Do with My Modem?

A modem is the single most liberating tool for your computer. With a modem and a computer, you can connect to other computers located down the block, across town, or anywhere in the world—assuming that the remote computer lets you in. Here's a sample of some of the cool stuff you can do with your modem:

♦ Get the latest news, up-to-the-minute stock prices, sports scores, weather reports, and travel information.

♦ Shop anywhere in the world, track down hard-to-find products, and even place an order on the web.

♦ Research any topic imaginable without leaving your home or office.

♦ Take classes on everything from using your computer to speaking Spanish.

♦ Exchange e-mail (electronic mail) with anyone in the world who has an e-mail account.

♦ Chat with friends, relatives, and complete strangers by typing and transmitting messages back and forth.

♦ Save on long-distance service by placing long-distance calls over the Internet. (By connecting a video camera to your computer, you can even talk face to face.)

♦ Play games in two-player mode. If you have a game that lets you play games in two-player mode by using a modem, the program probably contains all the tools you need to play the game over the phone lines. Refer to the user manual that came with the game.

♦ Transfer files between your computer at work and your computer at home.

♦ Publish your own documents electronically on the web. You can publish a personal page, family page, or business page, including photos, original drawings, and even audio and video clips.

♦ Create your own interactive journal, called a *blog*, where you can speak your mind and provide your friends and relatives with a convenient meeting place. (In Chapter 22, you learn how to create and publish your own web pages and blogs.)

How This Modem Thing Works

A *modem* (short for MODulator DEModulator) is essentially a phone for computers. A phone converts incoming signals from a phone line into audio output that you can hear. In a similar manner, a standard modem converts the analog signals that travel over phone lines into digital signals that the computer can process. To send a signal, a standard modem converts the digital signal from your computer into an analog signal that can be transmitted over phone lines. A cable modem converts cable signals into digital signals and acts as a tuner, network interface, and modem all rolled into one.

Modems transfer data at different speeds, commonly measured in *bits per second (bps)*. The higher the number, the faster the modem can transfer data. Common rates for standard modems include 28,800bps, 33,600bps, and 56,800bps. Because these modem speed numbers are becoming so long, manufacturers have started to abbreviate them by quoting speeds in *Kbps* and *Mbps*. You'll commonly see speeds listed as 33.6Kbps or 58.8Kbps. When they start dropping the "bps" and list something like 56K, you know it's fast, and when they start quoting speeds in mbps (or megabits per second), they're referring to a super-speedy connection.

Tech Term

Kbps stands for kilobits per second, which is equivalent to 1,000 bits per second. Faster speeds, such as those achieved over cable and network connections, are commonly expressed in **Mbps,** or megabits per second, which is roughly equivalent to 1,000,000 bits.

Modem Types: Standard, ISDN, DSL, and Cable

If your computer is not equipped with a modem, you need to do a little shopping. However, before you visit your local computer store, do a little homework and check out your modem options. The following sections explain the major differences between modems and introduce special features you might want to consider.

Chugging Along with Standard Modems

Because standard modems are the least expensive of the lot and because they can send and receive signals over standard phone lines, they remain the most popular type of modems. However, not all standard modems are created equal. As you shop for a modem, you should consider the following features:

◆ **Speed.** Don't settle for anything slower than 56Kbps.

◆ **Internal versus external.** Most computers come with an internal modem that's built into the computer. All you see of the modem are jacks for connecting the modem to a phone line and (optionally) plugging in a phone so you can use the line for phone calls when you're not connected to the Internet. An external modem sits outside the computer and connects to the computer's serial (COM, or communications) port or a USB (Universal Serial Bus) port using a cable. External modems typically have indicator lights that can help you troubleshoot connection problems. Before you purchase an internal modem, be sure your computer has an open *expansion slot* on the *motherboard* for plugging in an *expansion card*. Before purchasing an external modem, be sure you have an open serial or USB port.

Tech Term

Your computer has a big circuit board inside it that everything else plugs into. This board is called the **motherboard.** The motherboard typically has five or more **expansion slots** that are about a half-inch wide and 4 to 6 inches long, depending on the slot type. On most computers, the expansion slots are located in the back. You can plug smaller circuit boards, called **expansion cards,** into these slots to upgrade your computer and add capabilities. For example, you can add a network card for connecting your computer to a network or add a modem card to dial into an online service.

◆ **Serial port or USB connection.** If you decide to purchase an external modem, and your computer is equipped with one or more USB ports, opt for the USB modem. USB allows you to connect up to 127 devices to a single port, giving your computer virtually unlimited expandability. This leaves your sole serial port open for other devices.

◆ **ITU or V.90 support.** ITU or V.90 is the international standard for 56K modems. You might find modems that advertise the x2 standard. In the past, these modems did not conform to the V.90 standard, but newer x2 modems support V.90.

◆ **Fax support.** Like fully equipped fax machines, a fax/modem allows you to exchange faxes with a conventional fax machine or another computer that has a fax/modem.

◆ **Voice support.** If you plan on having your computer answer the phone and take messages, be sure the modem offers voice support. Without voice support, your modem can answer the phone, but it can only emit annoying screeching noises—which is useful for making telemarketers back off.

♦ **Videoconferencing support.** Some modems are also designed to handle video calls, sort of like on *The Jetsons*. Of course, you'll need a video camera to take advantage of this feature.

Whoa!

56K pushes the limits of phone line communications. The phone company limits connection speeds to 53K, although there is some talk of raising the speed limit. You will rarely see data transfers at 56Kps. Expect a maximum speed of about 40 to 45Kbps, and that's only when your modem is receiving data. A 56K modem still sends data at 28.8 to 33.6Kbps due to other limitations, such as line noise (static caused by loose connections, moisture, faulty wiring, or interference from nearby electrical or radio-frequency appliances).

Standard modems offer three benefits: the modem itself is inexpensive and easy to install, the modem plugs into a standard phone jack, and online services offer modem connections at bargain rates. However, for speedy Internet connections, consider the options described in the following sections.

Speeding Up Your Connections with ISDN

Unlike standard modems that must perform analog-to-digital conversions, ISDN (Integrated Services Digital Network) deals only with digital signals, supporting much higher data transfer rates: 128Kbps, which is more than twice as fast as 56K modems. ISDN modems use two separate 64Kbps channels, called *B channels*, that, when used simultaneously, achieve the 128Kbps transfer rates. This two-channel approach also lets you talk on the phone while surfing the web; one channel carries your voice while the other carries computer signals at 64Kbps (half speed). When you hang up, the modem can use both channels for computer communications. A third, slower, channel (channel D) is used by the phone company to identify callers and do basic line checking, so you don't really need to think about it.

Shop for the ISDN service before you shop for an IDSN modem or adapter, and ask your phone company for recommendations. The performance of your ISDN connection relies on how well your ISDN adapter works with your phone company's connection.

Whoa!

Although ISDN might sound like the ideal solution for home and small-business use, ISDN setup and service can be expensive. Call your phone company and add up the costs before you decide.

The New Kid on the Block: DSL Modems

Short for *digital subscriber line*, DSL has put a big dent in the ISDN market and has stiffened the competition between the phone and cable companies. Using standard phone lines, DSL can achieve data transfer rates of up to 1.5Mbps, or even 9Mbps if you're within 2 miles of a DSL connection center. At 1.5Mbps, a DSL modem is about 25 times faster than a standard 56Kbps modem and compares in speed to a cable modem. DSL achieves these rates over standard analog phone lines by using frequencies not used by voice signals. The only drawback is that because DSL is a relatively new product (although the technology has been around a while), it might not be available in your area or supported by your online service.

Several types of DSL are available, including ADSL and SDSL. In North America, ADSL (Asynchronous DSL) is most common. "Asynchronous" indicates that the system uses different data transfer rates for upstream and downstream communications—typically 1 to 2Mbps for downstream traffic and 32Kbps to 1Mbps for upstream traffic. In Europe, SDSL (Symmetric DSL) is most common. SDSL lines use the same data transfer rates for both upstream and downstream traffic (typically about 3Mbps).

Because there is no single DSL standard, don't purchase a modem without first checking with your phone company. Most DSL providers market their service as a package deal and include a DSL modem that works with the service.

Whoa!

Before you jump on the DSL bandwagon, do some research and ask your phone company to provide details on the cost, reliability, and performance boost you can expect from your DSL service.

Inside Tip

Although a satellite service, such as DirecPC, offers speedy connections, it's tough to set up, the satellite connection is iffy at times, and the service is relatively expensive. However, if you live in the boonies where cable and DSL service are unavailable, satellite service may be the only way you can obtain a broadband (fast) connection.

The Pros and Cons of Cable Modems

Like cable television connections, a cable Internet connection supports high-speed data transfers to your PC, allowing you to cruise the Internet at the same speed you can flip TV channels. In addition to speed, cable modems are relatively inexpensive (starting at about $100) and are easy to install. You can expect to pay about $40 to $60 per month for cable Internet access, which makes it competitive with ISDN service. However, cable modems do have a few drawbacks:

◆ **Availability.** Your cable company might not offer Internet cable service.

◆ **Variable connection speeds.** Cable service is set up to serve a pool of users. The more users connected to one service station, the slower the connection. Although cable companies commonly advertise 8Mbps data transfer rates, the rate you'll experience will likely be around 1 to 2Mbps.

◆ **Security issues.** A cable connection is considered an "always on" connection, which keeps your computer connected to the Internet all the time. This places your computer more at risk to be accessed by unauthorized individuals. To prevent unauthorized access, you can use a firewall, as explained in Chapter 23, but a firewall is not foolproof.

Connecting Your Modem to an Outside Line

Most computers are equipped with a standard internal modem (the 56Kbps variety). If your computer does not have a modem, you have several options:

◆ Get an external serial modem and (with the computer turned off) plug the modem into your computer's serial port (commonly labeled COM1 or COM2). When you restart your computer, Windows leads you through the process of installing the modem's software.

◆ Get an external USB modem, plug it into your computer's USB port, and follow the onscreen instructions to install the software. (One of the benefits of USB is that it allows you to safely connect devices to your computer when the power is on.)

◆ Hire a service technician or get help from a knowledgeable friend to install and set up an internal modem. Although installing and setting up an internal modem is usually easy, you need to follow a long list of safety precautions to ensure that you don't damage any equipment. In addition, internal modems occasionally cause conflicts with other devices, and troubleshooting these conflicts can be a very complicated process.

Plugging In a Standard, ISDN, or DSL Modem

After the modem is installed, connect it to the phone line. If you're setting up a standard or DSL modem, use a phone cord (with RJ-11 connectors) to connect the line-in or telco jack on the modem to the phone jack on the wall. If you're setting up an ISDN adapter, use an ISDN cable (with RJ-45 jacks) to connect the ISDN-U port or NT-1 port with the ISDN wall jack.

To share the phone line with a phone or fax machine, use another phone cord to connect the phone jack on the modem to the phone or fax machine, as shown in Figure 16.1.

Side view of modem

Figure 16.1

Connect a phone to your modem so that you can place calls when you're not using your modem.

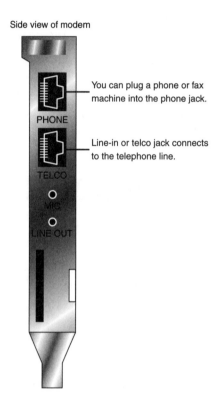

You can plug a phone or fax machine into the phone jack.

Line-in or telco jack connects to the telephone line.

Connecting a Cable Modem

Unless you're the resident handyman in your neighborhood, I strongly recommend that you shell out the 50 bucks to your cable company to hire a professional to install your cable modem, or try to talk them into giving you a free installation, because they'll make a ton of money off you in the long run. The installation can be fairly complex:

◆ If your computer does not have a network card, you must install a new network card, typically called an *Ethernet adapter*. This card has an outlet on the back that allows you to plug your cable modem into the computer. (If your computer has a USB port, you can purchase a USB/Ethernet adapter that allows you to connect the cable modem to the USB port.)

♦ If there is no cable connection to your computer, you must add a splitter to an existing cable and run a cable to your modem. Because most cable modems are external, you'll need to plug the cable modem into a power source.

♦ After your cable modem is connected to the cable, to the network card, and to a power source, you must install network protocols that let your computer communicate with the cable company's network. Installing the correct protocols and entering the required settings can be a real headache.

I recommend that you hire a professional installer, because a professional has the equipment needed to test for and repair any cable problems, install the required networking protocols, enter the correct settings, and get your cable connection up and running in a hurry. And if you have trouble connecting, you have someone to call for help.

Testing ... One ... Two ... Three ...

If your computer has a standard modem, you can run the Windows modem diagnostics to make sure the modem is installed properly. In Windows XP or 2000, take the following steps:

1. Click the **Start** button and click **Control Panel.** The Windows Control Panel appears.

2. Click **Printers and Other Hardware.** The Printers and Other Hardware window appears.

3. Click **Phone and Modem Options.** The Phone and Modem Options dialog box appears.

4. Click the **Modems** tab.

5. Click the name of your modem and click the **Properties** button. The Properties dialog box for the selected modem appears.

6. Click the **Diagnostics** tab and click the **Query Modem** button. Windows sends some test commands to your modem and logs the responses. Watch the message area for any indication that your modem failed to respond to a command.

> **Panic Attack**
>
> If your computer is experiencing technical difficulties when using the modem, refer to Chapter 29 for troubleshooting tips.

Of course, you can't dial out with your cable modem, so is there any way to test it? Most cable modems are external and have several indicator lights on the front. Typically, one or more lights must be lit, not flashing, to indicate a stable connection. Check the modem manual to determine what these status lights indicate. In general, if the lights are all out, be sure your modem is plugged in and turned on. If two or more lights are flashing, the modem is either trying to establish a connection or telling you there's a problem.

In addition, if you plugged the cable modem into a network card, the network card should have a light that indicates a stable network connection. In most cases, the light should be solid.

The Least You Need to Know

♦ You can use a modem to connect to the Internet or a commercial online service, play multiplayer games over the phone lines or a cable connection, connect to a desktop computer from a remote location, or place free long-distance phone calls over the Internet.

♦ Although you can squeak by with a 28.8Kbps modem, a 56Kbps modem makes cruising the web much more enjoyable. A DSL, cable modem, or satellite service is even better.

♦ ISDN modems are preferable to standard modems because ISDN deals with digital-to-digital signals, which support significantly higher data transfer rates than standard analog-to-digital modems.

♦ DSL modems offer faster connections rates than even ISDN and have the included advantage of being used through regular phone lines.

♦ To use a phone along with a standard modem, plug the phone into the modem's phone jack and connect the line jack on the modem to the incoming phone line jack on the wall.

Finding an Information FREEway

In This Chapter

- Connecting to America Online and other commercial services
- Getting free training through free trial offers
- Canceling your subscription before you have to pay
- Connecting cheaply through Internet service providers
- Solving your own Internet connection problems

You have the required hardware for connecting to the digital world—a computer and a modem—but something's missing. Who will your modem call? How can you use it to send e-mail, check the weather forecast, and track your mutual funds?

Inside Tip

For one-stop shopping, try a commercial online service, such as America Online or SBC Prodigy. A commercial service provides you with a connection to the Internet in addition to members-only services. An ISP typically provides a less expensive connection to the Internet (no member-only services), and you must use your own software (provided with Windows) to access the Internet.

Whoa!

Before signing up for a "free" trial offer, read the contract. Some services require you to pay for the first month and give you the second month free. Other services might attach conditions to your cancellation or charge you a fee if you cancel before the trial period ends.

To connect to the digital world, you need one more essential element—a commercial online service (such as America Online) or an Internet service provider (ISP). Both online services and ISPs provide you with a local phone number for dialing in to a special network that connects you with other users and services. Think of it as your doorway to the digital world.

Getting a Free Trial Offer to an Online Service

The best way to learn how to use an online service, exchange e-mail, chat, and surf the web is to do it. Most online services provide free trial offers. Sign up for a service, use it to practice the basics, and then, if you decide to try a different service or an ISP, cancel your subscription before the free trial period expires. I know it sounds unethical, but just think of it as being a savvy shopper.

The following is a rundown of the four major commercial online services. (Keep in mind that the prices quoted here were current at the time this book was written but are subject to change. In addition, many services offer annual plans and rebate programs that could affect the rates. Check with the service for price specifics.)

- **America Online.** AOL offers several payment plans: $23.90 per month for unlimited use ($239.40 for the year or $19.95 per month if you pay for one year in advance), $14.95 per month for unlimited access if you already have an Internet connection, $9.95 for 5 hours per month (plus $2.95 for each additional hour), or $4.95 per month for 3 hours (plus $2.50 for each additional hour). America Online is the most popular online service on the planet. It offers simple navigational tools, great services, and a friendly, hip social scene. Call 1-800-827-6364 for more information. If you have web access through a friend, your local library, or work, you can sign up for AOL at www.aol.com.

- **CompuServe.** CompuServe charges $9.95 for 20 hours per month, plus $2.95 for each additional hour, or $19.95 per month for unlimited use, or $199 per year for unlimited use (about 17 bucks a month), or $9.95 per month for unlimited access if you already have an Internet connection. CompuServe has traditionally been more technical and business-oriented. Call 1-800-848-8990 or visit www.compuserve.com for more information.

◆ **Microsoft Network.** MSN Internet Access is essentially an Internet service provider that offers some specialized content. The Unlimited plan costs $21.95 per month, or you can opt for the hourly plan at $9.95 per month for 20 hours ($1.50 for each additional hour), or opt for the Disney plan at $21.95 per month for a more family-oriented service. Call 1-800-FREE-MSN (1-800-373-3676) or visit www.msn.com for more information and a free month trial.

◆ **SBC Yahoo!** SBC Yahoo! provides unlimited access for $15.95 per month. Call 1-866-SBC-YAHOO (1-866-722-9246) or visit sbc.com/sbcyahoo/for more information.

> **Whoa!**
> The rates listed here do not include phone charges. If the service does not have a local phone number for where you live, you might end up paying long-distance rates to connect. Some services offer 800 numbers but typically charge a per-minute rate to use that number.

The next section shows you how to sign up for a subscription to these services. When you sign up as a new member, the service provides information about its free trial period.

Signing Up for Your Membership

When you register for a subscription to one of these services, you can download (copy) the required software online or the service will send you a version on CD. Install the software as explained in Chapter 10 and then follow the onscreen instructions to choose a user name (member name) and password.

The installation program uses the modem to dial a toll-free number that lists local numbers. After you select a local number (and usually an alternative number in case the first number is busy), the installation program disconnects from the toll-free connection and then reconnects you locally. Most services then ask you to supply the following information:

◆ Your modem's COM port. To determine the COM port, double-click the **Modems** icon in the Control Panel, click your modem's name, and click **Properties.** (If your computer has a cable modem, an always-on connection, you do not need to enter modem settings.)

◆ Your modem's maximum speed. (Most services support up to 56K connections. Many services also offer ISDN and DSL support.)

◆ Any special dialing instructions, such as a number you must dial to connect to an outside line.

> **Whoa!**
>
> If you have call waiting, it will disconnect you if anyone calls when you're online. Before typing the phone number, type the code required to disable call waiting (in most cases, *70) followed by a couple of commas. The commas insert delay times so that the code can take effect before the program dials the phone number. (Check with your phone company to determine the code you must enter to disable call waiting, and ask if a service charge is added each time you disable call waiting.) In some cases, you can disable call waiting by selecting the option in the software you use to connect to the service.

◆ Your name, address, and telephone number.

◆ A credit card number and expiration date. (Even if the service offers a free trial membership, you typically must enter a credit card number.)

◆ The name (screen name) and password you want to use to log on to the service. (Write down your screen name and password in case you forget it. Without this information, you will not be able to connect.)

◆ An acceptance of the terms of service (TOS) or rules you must follow to continue using the service. If you break the rules, the service might terminate your account. Read the TOS so that you know what you're getting into.

Getting Help Online

Because online services differ, I can't give you specific instructions on how to navigate each service, send e-mail messages, post notes on message boards, or chat online. The steps vary from one service to another.

However, all online services display a toolbar or other navigational tool with buttons or links that point to popular features. For example, in America Online, you click the **You've Got Mail** button to access your electronic mailbox. Click the **Internet** button to open a menu for accessing various Internet features, such as the web, newsgroups (Internet message boards), or the Internet Yellow Pages.

In addition, all commercial services have their own help systems, which typically consist of both online and offline help. Offline help is installed on your hard drive as part of the program and provides general instructions on how to use the service. Online help typically provides assistance for more-specific issues, such as problems you encounter when trying to read e-mail messages. Simply open the **Help** menu and choose the desired type of help. Figure 17.1 shows a typical online help screen in America Online.

Choose a subject   Double-click a specific article

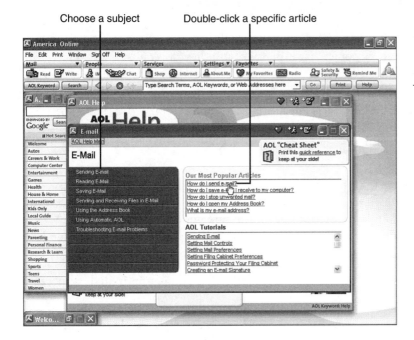

Figure 17.1

Online help is a great tool for troubleshooting problems.

Canceling Your Membership

If you're not satisfied with your online service, don't just stop using the service. Unless you cancel your membership, your online service will dutifully charge the monthly fee to your credit card whether you use the service or not. If you choose to no longer use the service, be sure you cancel your membership before the next month's billing period begins.

Of course, most services don't let you cancel your membership online. You need to call a customer service representative so that the person can grill you on why you want to dump the service. Here's a list of the customer service numbers for the major online services:

America Online: 1-888-265-8008

CompuServe: 1-800-848-8990

Panic Attack
If the phone number printed here doesn't work, check the online help system or the service's billing area for a customer service phone number.

SBC Yahoo!: 1-866-722-3425

Microsoft Network: 1-800-386-5550

Finding Alternative Internet Connections

Online services are great if you like the member-only services or desire a sense of community, but they can be somewhat expensive, and they don't always provide fastest, most reliable Internet service. In addition, online services often have quirky e-mail systems that can make it difficult to exchange e-mails and attached files with nonmembers. If you're looking for a cheap way to establish a pure Internet connection, and you're not interested in any members-only perks, consider connecting through an ISP.

Locating a Local Internet Service Provider

To find an ISP, flip through the Yellow Pages and look under Internet Service Providers or Internet Online Service Providers. To find a good ISP, ask your friends, relatives, and colleagues for recommendations. Ask the following questions:

- ◆ How much does the service charge per month? Do you get unlimited connect time for one price?

- ◆ Was it easy to set up the connection?

- ◆ If you had trouble setting up the connection, did the company offer quality assistance?

- ◆ Do you ever have trouble connecting to the service? (Some ISPs oversell their service, making it difficult to connect during high-traffic hours.)

- ◆ Does the ISP provide a fast, reliable connection? (Again, ISPs who oversell their service might provide slow Internet connections or be quick to disconnect users during busy hours.)

- ◆ Has the ISP ever messed up your bill? I once had an ISP double-charge me for three months running and then threaten to cancel my account. Be sure the company has its act together. This is good advice even if you're going with a big-name national service.

If you don't have the Yellow Pages or any friends, relatives, or colleagues, skip ahead to the section called "Setting Up Your Internet Connection" later in this chapter. The Windows Internet Connection Wizard can help you track down an ISP.

If you don't mind putting up with a steady stream of onscreen advertisements, try a free Internet service, such as NetZero (at www.netzero.com or call 1-877-638-9376), Juno (at www.juno.com or call 1-800-879-5866), or Address.com (at www.address. com). Many of these "free" Internet services started to feel the financial pinch late in the year 2000 and either went out of business or began to limit the number of hours of free connect time. Don't be surprised if one of the companies mentioned here is no longer in business. If the company still is in business and is offering free service, be sure to read the fine print.

> **Inside Tip** _____
>
> A fast, reliable Internet connection is most important, but tracking down a bottleneck can be difficult. At times, the entire Internet can slow down due to high traffic or multiple system failures. A bad phone connection or outdated telephone company equipment can restrict the data flow to your computer. Even your own computer, if it's bogged down trying to run too many programs, can make a fast connection seem slow.

Gathering the Information You Need to Connect

To set up your account, you need information and settings that tell your computer how to connect to the ISP's computer. Obtain the following information:

◆ **Phone number or network settings.** If you're using a standard, ISDN, or DSL modem to connect, you must have the phone number of the connection site nearest to you. If you have a high-speed cable or satellite connection, your computer connects to the cable company's network, so you must obtain the required network settings, including the computer name and address.

◆ **User name.** This is the name that identifies you to the ISP's computer. It is typically an abbreviation of your first and last names. For example, Jill Eikenhorn might use jeikenhorn as her user name. If you have a unique last name and you're concerned that someone might use your name to stalk you, use a cryptic nickname. You can choose any name you like, as long as it is not already being used by another user.

◆ **Password.** The ISP might let you select your own password or might assign you a password. Be sure to write down the password in case you forget it.

◆ **Connection type.** Most ISPs offer PPP (Point-to-Point Protocol), but ask to be sure. PPP is simply a "language" that two computers agree to speak in order to communicate over the Internet. An older protocol called SLIP (Serial Line Internet Protocol) is a little slower and less reliable, but some ISPs still support it.

◆ **Domain name server.** The domain name server (DNS) is a computer that's set up to locate computers on the Internet. Each computer on the Internet has a unique number that identifies it, such as 197.72.34.74. Each computer also has a domain name, such as www.hollywood.com, which makes it easier for people to remember the computer's address. When you enter a domain name, the domain name server looks up the computer's number and locates it.

◆ **Domain name.** This is the domain name of your service provider's computer, such as internet.com. You use the domain name in conjunction with your user name as your e-mail address—for example, jeikenhorn@internet.com.

◆ **News server.** The news server lets you connect to any of thousands of newsgroups on the Internet to read and post messages. Newsgroups are electronic bulletin boards for special-interest groups. The news server name typically starts with news and is followed by the service provider's domain name—for example, news.internet.com.

◆ **Mail server.** The mail server is in charge of electronic mail. You need to specify two mail servers: POP (Post Office Protocol) for incoming mail, and SMTP (Simplified Mail Transfer Protocol) for mail you send. The POP server's name typically starts with pop and is followed by the service provider's domain name, such as pop.internet.com. The SMTP server's name typically starts with smtp or mail and is followed by the service provider's domain name, such as smtp. internet.com. (See Chapter 18 for details.)

◆ **E-mail address.** If you plan to receive e-mail messages, you need an e-mail address. Your address typically begins with your user name, followed by an "at" sign (@) and the domain name of your service provider—for example, jeikenhorn@internet.com.

Setting Up Your Internet Connection

After you have all the information you need, you can run the Internet Connection Wizard and enter the connection settings (as discussed in a moment). The wizard displays a series of screens prompting you to enter each piece of information. If you're using a standard, ISDN, or DSL modem to connect, the wizard creates a Dial-Up Networking icon that you can click to establish your connection. If you're connecting via cable modem or over a network, the wizard enters settings instructing your web browser and e-mail program to establish a connection via the Local Area Network (LAN).

Whoa!

Before you connect to the Internet, a Windows component called Dial-Up Networking must be installed. If your computer is running Windows XP or 2000, the dial-up feature is already installed. If your computer is running an older version of Windows, open **My Computer** to see if the **Dial-Up Networking** icon is there. If it's missing, open the Windows Control Panel, double-click **Add/Remove Programs,** click the **Windows Setup** tab, double-click **Communications,** and place a check mark next to **Dial-Up Networking.** Click **OK,** click **OK** again, and follow the onscreen instructions to install Dial-Up Networking.

Although I would really like to give you step-by-step instructions for using the Internet Connection Wizard, the steps vary depending on which Internet Connection Wizard you're using and whether you're dialing to connect or are connecting over a LAN; Microsoft keeps changing it. However, I can tell you how to start the wizard and tell you what to watch out for:

◆ To start the Internet Connection Wizard, click the **The Internet, Internet Explorer,** or **Connect to the Internet** icon on your Windows desktop.

◆ If your desktop does not contain one of the icons mentioned in the previous item, the Connection Wizard might be hiding on the Start menu. In Windows XP or 2000, choose **Start, All Programs, Accessories, Communications, New Connection Wizard.** In Windows Me, check the **Start, Programs, Accessories, Communications** menu for the **Internet Connection Wizard** option. In older versions of Windows, check the **Start, Programs, Accessories, Internet Tools** menu for an option named **Get on the Internet,** or check the **Start, Programs, Internet Explorer** menu for an option called **Connection Wizard.**

◆ After the wizard starts, follow the onscreen instructions to set up your Internet account. The first or second screen displays several options for setting up your account. If you already have an ISP, choose the option for using your existing ISP. If you are connecting via cable modem or satellite, or if your computer is on a network, choose the option for connecting via LAN. If you have a modem and you don't have an ISP, choose the option for locating a new ISP and setting up an account. The wizard will dial a toll-free number to obtain a list of available ISPs and local numbers.

◆ If you need to find an ISP, the wizard asks for your area code and the first three digits of your phone number. It then downloads a list of ISPs available in your area, as shown in Figure 17.2. You need to register with the service and provide a credit card number. The wizard downloads the required connection settings for you, so you don't have to enter them manually.

Select an Internet service provider

Figure 17.2

The Internet Connection Wizard can help you locate an ISP in your area.

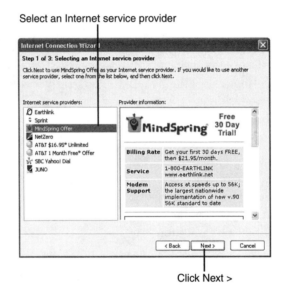

Click Next >

◆ If you already set up an account with a service provider in your area, you must manually enter the connection settings. This is no biggie; the wizard steps you through the process. When asked whether you want to view the Advanced settings, however, click **Yes** so that you can enter the required settings yourself.

◆ If asked to specify a logon procedure, leave **I don't need to type anything when logging on** selected, even though your ISP requires you to enter a name and password. This option is for services that require you to manually log on using a terminal window or logon script. Most ISPs do not require this.

◆ Most ISPs automatically assign you an IP (Internet Protocol) address when you log on, so don't choose to use a specific IP address unless your ISP gave you one.

♦ If your ISP requires you to use a specific DNS server address, choose **Always use the following** and enter the DNS address in the **DNS Server** text box. If your ISP offers a secondary DNS, enter it so that you can still navigate if the first DNS is busy. Many ISPs now use dynamic DNS addressing, which automatically routes you to the best DNS server for your location.

♦ The wizard also asks you to enter settings for connecting to the ISP's news and mail server. You can do this later or enter the settings now.

If you ran the Internet Connection Wizard to set up a standard, ISDN, or DSL modem connection, take one of the following steps to place a shortcut icon for your connection on the desktop (if you're connecting via cable or network, you don't need an icon on the desktop, because your computer remains connected to the Internet at all times):

♦ In Windows XP or 2000, click the **Start** button, point to **Connect To,** right-click the icon for your Internet connection, point to **Send To,** and click **Desktop (create shortcut).**

♦ In earlier versions of Windows, run My Computer and double-click the **Dial-Up Networking** icon. The Dial-Up Networking folder contains icons for any ISPs that you have set up. Right-drag the icon for your ISP to a blank area of the Windows desktop, release the mouse button, and click **Create Shortcut(s) Here.**

Testing Your Dial-Up Connection

After you have an icon, you can double-click it to connect to the Internet. When you double-click the icon, a dialog box appears, as shown in Figure 17.3, prompting you to type your user name and password (supplied by your ISP).

Type your user name and password. If desired, check the **Save password** check box. This saves your user name and password, so you won't have to type them the next time you log on. If you share your computer with someone else, and you do not want that person using your Internet connection, leave the check box blank. Click the **Connect** button.

Enter your user name

Figure 17.3

When you double-click the icon you just created, this dialog box appears.

Type your password

Click the Connect or Dial button

Panic Attack

If your computer is running Windows Me or an earlier version and you don't have the **Save password** option, Client for Microsoft Networks is not installed. In the Control Panel, double-click the **Network** icon, click the **Add** button, and double-click **Client**. Click **Microsoft** and then double-click **Client for Microsoft Networks**. Be sure that **Client for Microsoft Networks** is selected as the **Primary Network Logon,** and then click **OK**.

After you click the **Connect** button, Dial-Up Networking dials into your service provider's computer and displays messages indicating the progress, such as Dialing..., Checking user name and password..., and Connecting... Assuming that Dial-Up Networking could establish a connection, a dialog box appears, indicating that the computer is now connected. You can now run Internet programs (as explained in later chapters) to navigate the World Wide Web, send and receive e-mail, and so on.

Inside Tip

To disconnect, right-click the Dial-Up Networking icon on the right end of the taskbar, and then click **Disconnect**. (The icon looks like two tiny overlapping computers.)

If your connection proceeds smoothly the first time, lucky you. Most first attempts fail for some reason or another. You might have forgotten to type your password, or your Dial-Up Networking connection might have a wrong setting. If the connection fails, check the following:

◆ Did you type your user name and password correctly? (If you mistyped this information, or if your ISP entered it incorrectly on the system, Dial-Up Networking typically displays a message indicating that the system did not accept your password.) Retype your user name and password, and try connecting again. (Passwords are typically case sensitive, so type the password *exactly* as your service provider specifies.)

◆ Was the line busy? Again, Dial-Up Networking typically displays a message indicating that the line was busy. If several people are connected to the service, you might have to wait until someone signs off. Keep trying.

◆ Check your Dial-Up Adapter settings. In Windows XP or 2000, click the **Start** button, point to **Connect To,** right-click the icon you use to connect to the Internet, click **Properties,** and make sure **Internet Protocol (TCP/IP)** is checked, as shown in Figure 17.4. In earlier versions of Windows, display the Windows Control Panel and double-click the **Network** icon. Click **Dial-Up Adapter,** and click the **Properties** button. Click the **Bindings** tab, and be sure there is a check mark next to **TCP/IP->Dial-Up Adapter.** (If NetBEUI or IPX/SPX are listed, be sure they are *not* checked.)

◆ Be sure you have selected the correct server type. In Windows XP or 2000, click the **Start** button, point to **Connect To,** right-click the icon you use to connect to the Internet, click **Properties,** click the Networking tab, and make sure the correct server type is specified (usually **PPP**). In earlier versions of Windows, display the Control Panel, double-click the **Dial-Up Networking** icon. Right-click the icon for connecting to your ISP, and choose **Properties.** Click the **Server Type** tab. Open the **Type of Dial-Up Server** drop-down list and choose the correct server type (specified by your service provider)—usually **PPP.**

◆ Did your modem even dial? Go to the Windows Control Panel and check your modem setup. Be sure that you've selected the correct modem and COM port.

◆ Do you have reliable phone lines? Unplug your modem from the phone jack and plug a phone into the jack. Do you get a dial tone? Does the line sound fuzzy? If you don't hear a dial tone, the jack is not working. If the line is fuzzy when you make a voice call, it has line noise, which might be enough to disconnect you.

Tech Term _____

TCP/IP stands for **Transmission Control Protocol/ Internet Protocol.** More simply, TCP/IP is the language that two computers use to communicate over the Internet. NetBEUI and IPX/SPX are two protocols commonly used for networks.

Figure 17.4

Be sure TCP/IP is linked to your dial-up adapter.

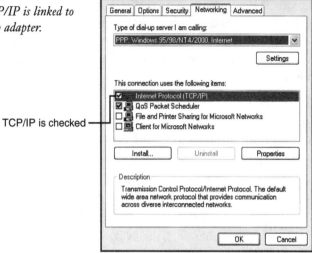

TCP/IP is checked ──

Testing a Broadband Cable Connection

If your computer connects to the Internet by way of a cable connection, the easiest way to test your connection in all versions of Windows is to run Internet Explorer or whichever web browser you plan on using and see if it opens a web page. In Windows XP and 2000, you also can test the connection by doing the following: Open the Control Panel, click **Network and Internet Connections,** and click **Network Connections.** Right-click the icon for your network connection and click **Status.** The resulting dialog box shows the amount of time your computer has been connected and the connection speed.

Inside Tip

To test the speed of your connection, go to bandwidthplace. com/speedtest/. Follow the onscreen instructions to test the actual speed of your connection.

The Least You Need to Know

◆ To get some free practice, sign up for a trial offer with America Online, Microsoft Network, or SBC Yahoo!, and check out everything it has to offer.

◆ If you sign up for a free trial offer and you decide not to use the service after the trial period, don't forget to call and cancel your membership.

♦ To sign up for most online services or establish an account with an ISP, you must enter a valid credit card number and information about the type of connection you're using.

♦ To enter settings for your Internet connection, run the Internet Connection Wizard and follow its instructions.

♦ If you have trouble connecting to your online service or ISP, check your settings to make sure you entered your user name and password correctly.

♦ If you have trouble establishing a DSL or cable modem connection, check the network settings to make sure you entered them correctly.

Sending E-Mail: Postage-Free Same-Day Delivery

In This Chapter

- ◆ Giving your e-mail program directions to the post office
- ◆ Addressing and sending e-mail messages
- ◆ Checking your electronic mailbox
- ◆ Jazzing up your messages with photos and fancy fonts
- ◆ Attaching files to outgoing messages
- ◆ Following proper e-mail etiquette

How would you like to send a message to your friend and have it arrive in a matter of seconds instead of days? Send dozens of messages every day without paying a single cent in postage? Never again stare out your window waiting for the mail carrier?!

Well, your dreams are about to come true. When you have a connection to the Internet and an e-mail program, all of these benefits are yours. In this chapter, you learn how to start taking advantage of them.

Running Your E-Mail Program for the First Time

The hardest part about e-mail is getting your e-mail program to connect to your Internet service provider's *mail server*, an electronic post office that routes your incoming and outgoing messages to their proper destinations. If you are using one of the major commercial online services, such as America Online or SBC Prodigy, you can relax; the installation program took care of all the details for you. You simply click the e-mail or mailbox button and start using it.

However, if you connect through an ISP, you must use a separate e-mail program (such as Outlook Express or Netscape Messenger) and enter settings that tell it how to connect to the *mail server*. Before you start your e-mail program, be sure you have the following information from your ISP:

♦ **E-mail address.** Your e-mail address is usually all lowercase and starts with your first initial and last name (for example, jsmith@iway.com). However, if your name is John Smith (or Jill Smith), you might have to use something more unique, such as JohnHubertSmith@iway.com. (All e-mail addresses must contain the @ sign to separate the recipient's name from the mail server's address.)

♦ **Outgoing mail (SMTP).** The SMTP (Simple Mail Transfer Protocol) server is the mailbox into which you drop your outgoing messages. It's actually your Internet service provider's computer. The address usually starts with mail or smtp, such as mail.iway.com or smtp.iway.com.

♦ **Incoming mail (POP3).** The POP (Post Office Protocol) server is like your neighborhood post office. It receives incoming messages and places them in your personal mailbox. The address usually starts with pop, such as pop. iway.com.

♦ **Account.** This one is tricky. It could be your user name, the name you use to log on to your service provider (for example, jsmith), or something entirely different assigned to your account by your ISP.

♦ **Password.** Typically, you use the same password for logging on and for checking e-mail. I can't help you here; you picked the password or had one assigned to you.

After you have the preceding information, you must enter it into your e-mail program. The following sections show you how to enter e-mail connection settings in Outlook Express and Netscape Messenger.

Entering E-Mail Settings in Outlook Express

Before you can enter connection settings, you must run Outlook Express. Click the **Outlook Express** icon on the Windows desktop or on the Quick Launch toolbar, or run the program from the **Start, All Programs** or **Start, Programs, Internet Explorer** menu.

When you first run Outlook Express, the Internet Connection Wizard starts and steps you through the process of entering the required information, as shown in Figure 18.1. Just follow the onscreen instructions. If the Internet Connection Wizard does not start, or you need to enter information for a different e-mail account, open the **Tools** menu and choose **Accounts.** Click the **Add** button, choose **Mail,** and follow the onscreen instructions to enter the settings.

Figure 18.1

Before you can use Outlook Express, you must enter connection settings.

Entering E-Mail Settings in Netscape Messenger

To enter connection settings in Netscape Messenger, first run the program. Click **Start, All Programs, Netscape, Mail & Newsgroups.** After it's running, take the following steps to enter settings for your mail server:

1. Open the **Edit** menu and choose **Mail & Newsgroup Account Settings.** The Mail & Newsgroup Account Settings dialog box appears.

2. Click the **Add Account** button. The Account Wizard appears, prompting you to specify the account type.

3. Click **E-mail Account** and click the **Next** button. The Account Wizard prompts you to enter your name and e-mail address.

4. Enter your full name and your e-mail address in the appropriate text boxes and click the **Next** button. The Account Wizard prompts you to enter the e-mail server information, as shown in Figure 18.2

Enter the addresses for the
incoming and outgoing mail servers

Figure 18.2

Specify the addresses of the incoming and outgoing mail servers.

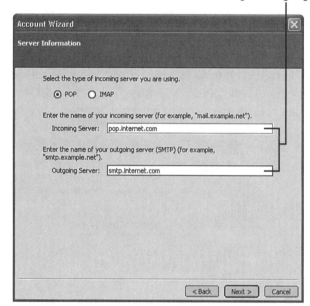

5. Enter the information you received from your ISP concerning their incoming and outgoing mail servers and click the **Next** button. The Account Wizard prompts you to type your user name.

6. Type your user name and click the **Next** button. The Account Wizard prompts you to type a descriptive name for the account.

7. Type a name for this account and click the **Next** button. The Account Wizard displays a summary of the information you entered for this account.

8. Click the **Finish** button. You are returned to the Accounts window, where you will find the new account added to the account list.

9. To make your new account the default account for sending and receiving e-mail, click the account's name and then click the **Set As Default** button.

Addressing an Outgoing Message

The procedure for sending messages over the Internet varies, depending on which e-mail program or online service you're using. In most cases, you first click the button for composing a new message. For example, in Outlook Express, you click the **New Mail** or **Create Mail** button. A window appears, prompting you to compose your message.

Click in the **To** box and type the person's e-mail address (see Figure 18.3). Then click in the **Subject** box and type a brief description of the message. Click in the large box near the bottom of the window and type your message. When you're ready to "mail" your message, click the **Send** button.

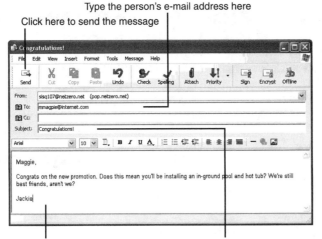

Type the person's e-mail address here

Click here to send the message

Type your message here

Type a brief description of the message here

Figure 18.3

Sending mail with a typical Internet e-mail program (Outlook Express).

Some e-mail programs send the message immediately. Other programs place the messages you send in a temporary outbox; then, when you're ready to send the messages, you click the button to initiate the send operation. For example, in Outlook Express, you click the **Send and Receive** or **Send/Recv** button. Outlook Express then sends all messages from the Outbox and checks for incoming messages.

> **Inside Tip** _____
>
> Most e-mail programs, including Outlook Express and Netscape Messenger, include e-mail address books. Instead of typing the person's e-mail address, you simply select it from a list. To quickly display the address book, press **Ctrl+Shift+B** in Outlook Express or **Ctrl+Shift+2** in Messenger. To add someone to your address book, click the button for creating a new contact, and then enter the person's name, e-mail address, and other contact information.

Checking Your E-Mail Box

When someone sends you an e-mail message, it doesn't just pop up on your screen. The message sits on your service provider's mail server until you connect and retrieve your messages. There's no trick to connecting to the mail server—assuming that you entered the correct connection settings. Most programs check for messages automatically on startup or display a button you can click to fetch your mail. The program retrieves your mail and then displays a list of message descriptions. To display a message, click or double-click its description, as shown in Figure 18.4.

Figure 18.4

You can quickly display the contents of messages you receive.

Click the message description

Double-click the message to display it in its own window

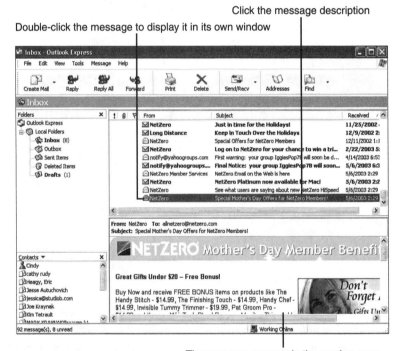

The message appears in the preview pane

Inside Tip

Most e-mail programs use several folders to help you keep your messages organized. For example, Outlook Express stores the messages you receive in the Inbox folder, messages that are waiting to be sent in the Outbox folder, messages you sent in the Sent Items folder, messages you deleted in the Deleted Items folder, and messages you composed but chose not to send in the Drafts folder. To switch from one folder to another, click the desired folder. To display a message you received, for instance, click the Inbox folder and then click the description of the message.

Sending Replies

To reply to a message in most e-mail programs, you select the message and then click the **Reply** or **Respond To** button. This opens a window that automatically inserts the e-mail address of the person who sent the message, along with the sender's description of the message, usually preceded by "Re:". Many e-mail programs also include the contents of the previous message so that the recipient can easily follow the conversation. To differentiate between the sender's original message and your reply, some e-mail programs add a right angle bracket (>) at the beginning of each line of the original message. To respond, type your message in the message area, and then click the **Send** button.

> **Inside Tip**
>
> When replying to a long message, delete most of the original material from the message you received, leaving only one or two lines to establish the context. This makes the message travel faster and takes up less disk space on the recipient's computer.

If you received a message that you would like to pass along to other recipients, you can *forward* the message. First, click the message you want to forward, and then click the **Forward** button. In the **To** text box, enter the e-mail addresses of the people to whom you want to forward the message. Your e-mail program automatically inserts the original message in the message area. If you would like to add an introduction to or comment about the original message, type this text in the message area. When you're ready to forward the message, click the **Send** button.

Adding Photos and Other Cool Stuff

How would you like to add a photo to your message or jazz it up with some fancy fonts? Most e-mail programs let you use special type styles and sizes, add backgrounds, insert pictures, and embellish your messages with other formatting options.

Both Netscape Messenger and Outlook Express offer a toolbar that contains buttons for the most common enhancements. In Outlook Express, you can use the toolbar to make text bold or italic, add bulleted and numbered lists,

> **Whoa!**
>
> When you send a message that has pictures, lines, and fancy fonts, the e-mail program sends it as a web page. The recipient's e-mail program must support web page formatting (most do); otherwise, the message will appear to be packed with cryptic codes.

and insert pictures, horizontal lines, links, and other objects. (If the toolbar does not appear, check the **Format** menu for an **HTML** option. HTML stands for Hypertext Markup Language, the coding system used to format web pages.)

The buttons for inserting pictures and formatting text work the same way as in your word processing and desktop publishing programs. The only new thing here is the button for inserting links. (A *link* is highlighted text that points to another web page.) To insert a link, first you drag over the text you want to appear as the link. You then click the button for inserting the link, type the address of the web page you want it to point to, and click **OK.** You can also drag links from a web page into the message area and plop them right down in the message area. (You'll learn more about links in Chapter 20.)

Inside Tip

Most e-mail programs automatically convert any web page addresses or e-mail addresses you type in the message area into links. Just type the address and press the **spacebar** or **Enter** key.

Attaching Documents to Your Messages

You can fit most e-mail messages on a Post-it note. A person typically rifles off a message or reply in less than a minute. However, there are times when you might want to send something more substantial—perhaps an outline for a book, a photo of yourself, a copy of an article you found on the web, or a document with its formatting intact.

Whatever the case, you can send files along with your messages by creating *attachments*. An attachment is a file in its original condition and format that you tack on to the message. For instance, if you have a resumé you created in Word, you can e-mail it as an attachment to a prospective employer. That person could then open the resumé in Word and view or print it. Without attachments, you would need to copy the text of the resumé and paste it into your e-mail message, losing any formatting you applied to the text and any graphics you inserted.

The process for attaching a file is fairly simple, but the steps vary, depending on which e-mail program you use. In most e-mail programs, you follow the same steps as you do for composing and addressing the message. To attach a file to the message, you click a button (for example, **Attach** or **Insert File**). This displays a dialog box that lets you select the file you want to send. The dialog box looks just like the dialog box you use to open files. Change to the folder that contains the file you want to send, and then double-click the file's name. When you are ready to send the message, along with the attachment, simply click the **Send** button.

Many word processing and spreadsheet programs have built-in support for e-mail, allowing you to send a document right from the program. In Word, for instance, you open the document you want to send, and then you open the **File** menu, point to **Send To,** and click **Mail Recipient.** This displays the e-mail program's toolbar with text boxes for typing the recipient's e-mail address and a description of the message.

If you receive a message that contains an attached file, your e-mail program usually displays some indication that a file is attached. For example, Outlook Express displays a paper clip icon. If you double-click the message (to display it in its own window), an icon appears at the bottom of the window or in an attachments text box. You can double-click the icon to open the file, or right-click and choose **Save** to save the file to a separate folder on your hard drive.

Panic Attack

When you receive an attachment, you should use an antivirus program to scan the file before opening it (if it's a document) or running it (if it's a program). Programs are especially notorious for carrying viruses, but documents can contain macro viruses, which can cause as much havoc. (Most antivirus programs have an option to run in the background, and they automatically scan attachments when you choose to open them or save them to disk.)

In many cases, when someone forwards a message to you, the person's e-mail program sends the forwarded message as an attachment. If the message has been forwarded several times, you might need to meander through a long line of attachments to view the original message.

What About Hotmail and Other Free E-Mail Services?

You probably have heard of "free e-mail" services, such as Hotmail, Yahoo!, and Juno, and wondered why anyone would need free e-mail. Isn't all e-mail free? Does your ISP charge extra for it? Of course, your e-mail account is included with the service that your ISP provides; your ISP does not charge extra for it. But there are several good reasons to explore these free e-mail services:

- Free e-mail is typically web based, allowing you to send messages and check your mail on the web. If you travel, you can manage your e-mail from anywhere in the world using any computer that's connected to the Internet. You don't need a computer that has your e-mail account settings on it.

- Free e-mail lets everyone in your home or business have his or her own e-mail account. When Junior starts corresponding with his chat room buddies, he'll want his privacy, and he can have it with his own e-mail program.

◆ Free e-mail gives you another e-mail address for registering "anonymously" for free stuff. Whenever you register for contests, shareware, and other freebies on the Internet, you must enter your e-mail address. Use your free e-mail account to register so that companies will send any junk mail to that address, and keep your real e-mail address private.

◆ Free e-mail provides you with a stable e-mail address. In the event that you change ISPs, you don't need to notify all your friends, relatives, and colleagues that you changed your e-mail address.

To get a free e-mail account, connect to any of the following sites, click the link for free e-mail, register, and follow the instructions at the site to start using your free e-mail account:

MSN Hotmail	www.hotmail.com
ICQ Mail	www.icqmail.com
Yahoo!	mail.yahoo.com
address.com	www.address.com
Excite	mail.excite.com

To find more free e-mail services, use your favorite web search page to search for the phrase "free e-mail."

E-Mail Shorthand and Emoticons

If you want to look like an e-mail veteran, pepper your messages with any of the following *emoticons* (pronounced *ee-mow-tick-ons*); these are icons that look like facial expressions or act as abbreviations for specific emotions. (You might need to turn your head sideways in order for them to look like tiny faces.) You can use these symbols to show your pleasure or displeasure with a particular comment, to take the edge off a comment you think might be misinterpreted, and to express your moods:

:) or :-)	I'm happy, or it's good to see you, or I'm smiling as I'm saying this. You can often use this to show you're joking.
:D or :-D	I'm really happy or laughing.
;) or ;-)	Winking.
:(or :-(	Unhappy. You hurt me, you big brute.

;(or ;-(	Crying.
:| or :-|	I don't really care.
:/ or :-/	Skeptical.
:# or :-#	My lips are sealed. I can keep a secret.
:> or :->	Devilish grin.
;^)	Smirking.
%-)	I've been at this too long.
:p or :-p	Sticking my tongue out.
<g>	Grinning. Usually takes the edge off whatever you just said.
<vbg>	Very big grin.
<l>	Laughing.
<lol>	Laughing out loud.
<i>	Ironic.
<s>	Sighing.
<jk>	Just kidding (these are also my initials).
<>	No comment.

In addition to the language of emoticons, Internet chat and e-mail messages are commonly seasoned with a fair share of abbreviations. The following is a sample of some of the abbreviations you'll encounter and be expected to know:

AFAIK	As far as I know
BRB	Be right back
BTW	By the way
CUL8R	See you later
F2F	Face to face (usually in reference to meeting somebody in person)
FAQ	Frequently asked questions. (Many sites post a list of questions that many users ask, along with the answers. They call this list a FAQ—pronounced like *fact* without the "t.")
FOTCL	Falling off the chair laughing

FTF	Another version of face to face
FYA	For your amusement
FYI	For your information
HHOK	Ha ha; only kidding
IMHO	In my humble opinion
IMO	In my opinion
IOW	In other words
KISS	Keep it simple, stupid
LOL	Laughing out loud
MOTOS	Member of the opposite sex
OIC	Oh, I see
PONA	Person of no account
ROTFL	Rolling on the floor laughing
SO	Significant other
TIC	Tongue in cheek
TTFN	Ta ta for now

E-Mail No-No's

To avoid getting yourself into trouble by unintentionally sending an insulting e-mail message, you might want to consider the proper protocol for composing e-mail messages. The most important rule is to NEVER EVER TYPE IN ALL UPPERCASE CHARACTERS. This is the equivalent of shouting, and people become edgy when they see this text on their screen. Likewise, take it easy on the exclamation points!!!

Secondly, avoid sending bitter, sarcastic messages (*flames*) via e-mail. When you disagree with somebody, a personal visit or a phone call is usually more tactful than a long e-mail message that painfully describes how stupid and inconsiderate the other person is. Besides, you never know who might see your message; the recipient could decide to forward your message to a few choice recipients as retribution.

If you are in marketing or sales, avoid sending unsolicited ads and other missives. Few people appreciate such advertising. In fact, few people appreciate receiving anything that's unsolicited, cute, "funny," or otherwise inapplicable to their business or personal life. In short, don't forward every little cute or funny e-mail message, "true" story, chain letter, joke, phony virus warning, or free offer you receive.

Finally, avoid forwarding warnings about the latest viruses and other threats to human happiness. Most of these warnings are hoaxes, and when you forward a hoax, you're just playing into the hands of the hoaxers. If you think that the warning is serious, check the source to verify the information before you forward the warning to everyone in your address book.

Tech Term

When you strongly disagree with someone on the Internet, via e-mail or (more commonly) in newsgroups, it's tempting to **flame** the person with a stinging, sarcastic message. It's even more tempting to respond to a flaming message with your own barb. The resulting flame war is usually a waste of time and makes both people look bad. Also, don't bombard your enemy's e-mail account with a billion messages in an attempt to make the person's e-mail server crash. Even if it works, it's not very nice.

The Least You Need to Know

♦ To set up a new e-mail account in Outlook Express, open the **Tools** menu, choose **Accounts,** click the **Add** button, choose **Mail,** and follow the onscreen instructions.

♦ To access the e-mail settings in Netscape Messenger, open the **Edit** menu, click **Preferences,** and click **Mail & Newsgroups.**

♦ To create a new e-mail message, click the **Compose** or **New Message** button or its equivalent in your e-mail program.

♦ Incoming e-mail messages are often stored in the Inbox. Simply click the **Inbox** folder and then click the desired message to display its contents.

♦ To reply to a message, select the message and then click the **Reply** button.

♦ To attach a document to an outgoing message, click the button for attaching a file and then select the desired document file.

Chatting with Friends, Relatives, and Complete Strangers

In This Chapter

- ◆ Experiencing the lively banter in chat rooms
- ◆ Sneaking a peek at a chatter's identity
- ◆ Chatting in private rooms
- ◆ Contacting friends and relatives with instant messages
- ◆ Adding other dimensions with audio and video

Every couple months, I come across a news story about a couple who met in an online chat room and decided to get married. The woman usually sounds as dumb as a brick, and the guy typically looks like some shady character who probably has three other wives and a dozen kids waiting for their child support checks. I could be wrong, but the negative speculation is a lot more interesting than the gushy story they put in the news.

Be that as it may, online chat does provide a fun and inexpensive way to meet people and "talk" with friends, relatives, colleagues, and complete strangers. In the right chat room, you can even make new business contacts and find a new job! When you're in a chat room, you simply type and send a message, and it immediately pops up on the screen of every person in the chat room. When anyone else in the chat room sends a message, it pops up on your screen. This makes for a frenetic conversation that can be fun to watch.

This chapter shows you how to use various chat tools in commercial online programs and on the Internet. You learn how to converse in chat rooms, check out a person's profile (identity), use instant-message programs to chat privately with friends and relatives, and use the audio and video features of your computer to place video "phone calls" on the Internet.

Hanging Out in Chat Rooms

Commercial online services, such as America Online, have their own exclusive chat rooms, where members gather during all hours of the day and night to share interests, argue politics, discuss movies, flirt with one another, and explore various topics. If you subscribe to one of these online services, you can enter any of the standard chat rooms and start conversing, or just sit back and watch the messages scroll by.

To enter a chat room on America Online, first sign on to view the Welcome window. Click **People & Chat** to display the People & Chat window, and then click **Chat Room Listings.** Double-click the desired chat category in the list on the left, and then double-click the desired chat room on the right. (The number next to each chat room indicates the number of people currently in the room.) America Online displays a chat window, as shown in Figure 19.1.

> **Panic Attack**
>
> America Online chat rooms are limited to 36 members. If a room is full, America Online automatically bumps you into a room like the one you selected. For instance, if you chose The Flirts Nook, and it's full, America Online might bump you into The Flirts Nook 103.

Before you start chatting, read the messages to get a feel for the content and tone of the room. When you're ready to jump in, type your message and press **Enter** or click the **Send** button. To leave the chat room, simply close its window. You can then select a different room from the Find a Chat window. In the following sections, you learn how to use more cool chat tools in America Online.

Messages from all chatters appear here   List of chatters

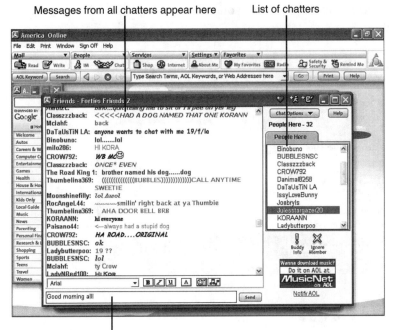

Type your message here and press Enter

Figure 19.1

The chat window contains the controls you need to start chatting.

Checking Out the People Who Are Checking You Out

Every member of America Online has the opportunity to create a *profile* that lists the person's age, marital status, geographical location, hobbies, and other pertinent information. In most cases, the profile information is either overly cryptic or an outright lie, so you can't rely on it. However, the lies people tell usually reveal something about them, and they provide a key to understanding the individual.

To check out a person's profile, double-click the person's name in the list of chatters displayed on the right side of the window. This displays the profile information that the person entered, as shown in Figure 19.2.

To check and edit your own profile, press **Ctrl+K,** type profile, press **Enter,** and then, when the Member Directory dialog box appears, click the **My Profile** button near the right side of the dialog box. Read the warning box that tells you that whatever information you enter is publicly accessible, and click **OK.**

Whoa!

Although most America Online members are fairly nice folks, there are plenty of creeps online. Don't give out personal information such as your last name, phone number, address, or passwords. People have been known to pose as customer service reps and request this information. Don't believe them.

Enter your personal information (or whatever you want people to think about you) and click the **Save** button.

Figure 19.2

As my profile reveals, I'm as exciting as I think I am.

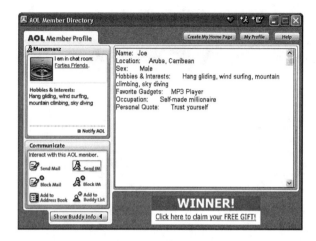

Sending Private Messages

If you strike up a conversation with someone who has completely captured your interest, you might want to grab a table for two in the corner and have your own private conversation. How do you do this?

Well, you have two options. The easiest way is to send the person an IM, or instant message. An IM appears only on your screen and the recipient's screen. To send an IM, right-click the person's name in the list of chatters on the right, and then click **Send IM.** Type your message and click the **Send** button. The Send Instant Message window remains on your screen, displaying a running dialog between you and your friend, but you both remain in the public chat room.

If you would like to leave the public chat room, or if you want to chat in private with two or more other people, create your own private room. Above the list of chatters, click **Chat Options** and click **Private Chat.** Type a name for your chat room, and click **GO CHAT.** You must then send an IM to your friend to tell the person the name of your private chat room. (To quickly display the Send Instant Message window, press **Ctrl+I.**) Private rooms are great if you and your pals are trying to have a serious discussion and some moron keeps interrupting and hassling you; simply create your own private room and invite only your select group of friends.

> **Inside Tip**
>
> If someone invites you to a private chat room, the person must tell you the name of the room. To go to the room, click the **Chat Options** and select **Private Chat**, type the name of the room, and click **Go Chat.**

Making Your Own Public Chat Room

Are you the consummate host or hostess? Do you love throwing parties and mingling with your guests? Do you live for the thrill of greeting people and making them feel welcome? If you answered "Yes" to these questions, or if you're just plain bored with the chat rooms that AOL offers, consider creating your own public chat room. Here's what you do:

1. Click the **Chat** button on the America Online toolbar and click **Create a Chat.** America Online displays a dialog box asking if you want to create a member (public) or private room.

2. Click the **Member Chat** button to create a public room. America Online now asks you to pick a category for the room, as shown in Figure 19.3.

Double-click the desired chat room category

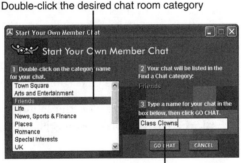

Type a name for your room

Figure 19.3

You can host your own chat room.

3. In the chat category list (on the left), double-click the desired category name.

4. Click in the text box under **3** and type the desired name for your room.

5. Click **GO CHAT** and then sit back and twiddle your thumbs until people start arriving.

Panic Attack
When the last person leaves a chat room, America Online automatically closes down the room and deletes it from the service. Talk about cleaning up after the party!

Chatting It Up on the Internet

There's no doubt about it—chat sells. People flock to online chat rooms where they can be anyone they want to be, travel incognito, and carry on in the relative safety of virtual worlds.

Although America Online first popularized chat rooms, many Internet companies have finally figured out that chat sells and have developed their own chat rooms, where anyone with an Internet connection and a web browser can converse. The following sections show you where to find these chat services on the web.

> **CAUTION**
>
> ### Whoa!
>
> The web is a feature of the Internet that allows you to view interactive multimedia pages using a web browser. It's pretty easy to use, and the following sections provide the detailed instructions you need to access Internet chat rooms. However, if you need more details on using a web browser, skip ahead to the next chapter.

Chatting It Up at Yahoo!

Yahoo! has always been considered a premier Internet search site. Now, Yahoo! has injected its power and simplicity into the Internet chat arena. To access Yahoo!'s chat rooms, first run your web browser and use it to register for Yahoo! Chat. The following steps show you how to use Internet Explorer (a web browser installed on most PCs) to connect to Yahoo! and register for its chat rooms:

1. Double-click the **Internet Explorer** icon on the Windows desktop or click the **Launch Internet Explorer Browser** button on the Quick Launch toolbar.

2. Drag over the entry in the **Address** box near the top of the window and type **chat.yahoo.com.**

3. Press **Enter.** Internet Explorer opens and displays Yahoo!'s chat page with a message indicating that you are not currently signed in.

4. Click the link to sign up for Yahoo! Chat. (A *link* is an icon, picture, or highlighted text that points to another web page. When you click the link, your web browser automatically opens the corresponding page.)

5. Follow the onscreen instructions to complete the registration form and enter the desired chat room.

After you pick a chat room, Yahoo! automatically takes you to that room and displays a chat window, where you can view the ongoing conversation and add your own comments, as shown in Figure 19.4.

Messages from all chatters appear here

Yahoo! Chat toolbar

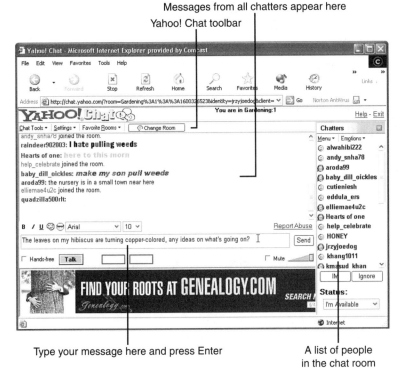

Figure 19.4

Yahoo! brings chat rooms to the web.

Type your message here and press Enter

A list of people in the chat room

After you are in a chat room, you can start chatting. The ongoing discussion is displayed in the large frame in the upper left. To send a message to the other chatters, click in the **Chat** text box just below the ongoing discussion, type your message, and press **Enter.** When you tire of this simple banter, try the following:

- ◆ Click **Emotions** (above the list of chatters) and click an emotion (bow, agree, smile, or some other gesture) to send a text description of it.

- ◆ Click the smiley face icon (below the message area) and click the desired smiley face to send it to the room.

- ◆ Right-click the name of someone in the room. This displays a menu with options that let you find out more about the person, send the person a private message or a file, add the person to a list of friends, or ignore the person (prevent the person's messages from appearing on your screen).

Inside Tip

Although Yahoo! is on the cutting edge of web chat, there are some other web chat services that you can try out. Check out the following sites:

www.flirt.com

www.chatting.com

www.chat-web.com

◆ Just above the message area are several menus. Use the various options on these menus to display your Friends List (see which of your friends are online), turn voice chat on or off, turn webcam on or off, change the chat room settings, or create a list of your favorite chat rooms.

◆ To create or edit your own profile, return to the Yahoo! Chat home page at chat.yahoo.com, and click the **Account Info Link.** Log in, if necessary, and then click the link to edit your profile.

Keeping in Touch with Friends and Family

Relatively recently, developers have come up with an innovative communications feature for the web that allows people to create their own online community centers, family circles, or special-interest groups to keep in touch. For example, if you have a large extended family, you can create a family circle and have all your family members (at least those who have Internet access) join the circle. Members can then post messages, digitized photos, announcements, and calendar dates in a special area where everyone in the family can check them out. Many of these "community" centers also allow you to set up a members-only chat room and exchange electronic greeting cards and virtual gifts.

One of the best online community centers I know of is Yahoo! Groups, which you can find at groups.yahoo.com. If you already registered for Yahoo! Chat, you are registered for Yahoo! Groups, as well. If you did not register, you must register to obtain a member name and password. Use your member name and password to log in. You can then create your own group or join existing groups, invite others to join, create your own online photo albums, enter important dates, post messages, and much more. To create your own group, click the **Start a new Group!** link, as shown in Figure 19.5, and then follow the onscreen instructions.

Inside Tip _____

Although Yahoo! Groups is one of the best places to set up your club or family circle, there are other places on the web. Check out the following:

> clubs.lycos.com
>
> www.faceparty.com
>
> groups.msn.com
>
> www.classmates.com

To send a greeting card or invitation to a friend or relative, check out the online virtual cards. There are hundreds of websites where you can create and send your own greeting cards via e-mail. Just connect to www.yahoo.com and search for virtual greeting cards. Following are a few sites to get you started:

www.bluemountain.com

www.marlo.com

www.regards.com

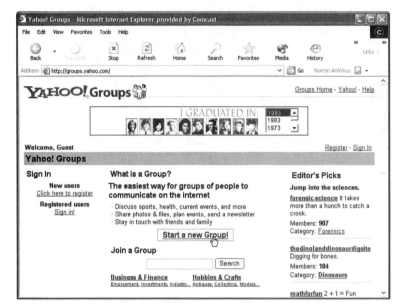

Figure 19.5

At Yahoo! Groups, you can create your own online community to stay in touch with friends and family.

Conversing Privately Outside Chat Rooms

Hanging out with strangers can be interesting, but if you'd like to chat with friends and relatives, spotting them in crowded chat rooms can be a bit difficult. To help track down individuals on the Internet, you can use an instant message program. You simply add the names and tracking information (typically an e-mail address) of each person you might want to contact, and the program lets you know when the person is online. Assuming that your friends and relatives run the same program (and are online), a dialog box pops up on your screen, indicating that the person is available. You can then start your own private chat with that person.

Where do you get such a program? You can pick up America Online's Instant Messenger at www.aol.com, grab a copy of Yahoo!'s Messenger (formerly known as Yahoo! Pager) at messenger.yahoo.com, snatch MSN Messenger Service from Microsoft at messenger.msn.com, or sample ICQ at web.icq.com. Figure 19.6 shows AOL's Instant Messenger in action.

Figure 19.6

With AOL's Instant Messenger, you can keep in touch with your friends, colleagues, and relatives online.

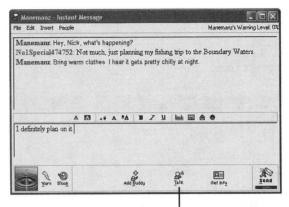

If you and your buddy have a sound card, speakers, and a microphone, click here to establish voice contact

Whoa!

Some developers, including Microsoft and Yahoo!, have attempted to make their instant messaging programs work with each other so that a person using MSN Instant Messaging can chat with another person using Yahoo! Instant Messaging. However, during the writing of this book, the most popular instant messaging program, AOL's Instant Messenger, refused to play along. So if all your friends and relatives use AOL Instant Messenger, you should use it, too.

What About Audio and Video?

You probably have heard about Internet phone programs that let you place toll-free long-distance calls over the Internet using your sound card and speakers. These programs typically use a special server to allow two computers to exchange audio signals.

I could tell you how to set up and use Microsoft NetMeeting (included with Windows) to place a call over the Internet, but there are easier ways to converse over the Internet without dealing with the complexities of Internet phone programs:

◆ Use your instant messaging program, as explained in the preceding section. Most instant messaging programs feature voice support. However, be sure you trust the person you're calling, because a voice call establishes a direct connection between your computer and the computer on the other end of the line. This direct connection is not very secure.

♦ Get your friends or relatives to join Yahoo! Groups or a similar online community. When you choose the option for chatting, you are given the choice of text or voice chat. Choose voice chat to carry on an audio discussion.

For you to experience a high-quality audio connection over the Internet, your computer must be equipped with a full-duplex sound card (which can play and record at the same time), a fairly decent microphone, and a pair of speakers.

Videoconferencing requires additional equipment and a dedicated Internet phone program, such as Microsoft NetMeeting or CUSeeMe (www.cuworld.com). Your computer must be equipped with a video capture card (some display cards support video input) and a digital camera. Even if your computer is properly equipped, don't get your hopes up. Over a 56Kbps connection, the video is typically fuzzy and jerky and might even slow down the audio portion of your conversation.

If you want to be able to use your computer to place free long-distance phone calls to real phones (instead of to other computers), you need special software and a special service, such as Net2Phone. (Of course, you still need a sound card, speakers, and a microphone on your end, but the person on the other end can talk to you on his or her phone.) For more information, check out Net2Phone at www.net2phone.com.

The Least You Need to Know

♦ America Online and Yahoo! are two of the many places to find hordes of eager chatters.

♦ To chat on America Online, click the **People** button, click **Find a Chat,** pick a chat room, and start typing.

♦ To "talk" in a chat room, type your message in the message text box and press **Enter** or click the **Send** button.

♦ To send another America Online member a private message, press **Ctrl+I** to send an instant message.

♦ You can send private messages to your friends and family members over the Internet using a special message program.

20

Poking Around on the Web

In This Chapter

- ◆ Launching your web browser on its virgin voyage
- ◆ Opening specific web pages by entering addresses
- ◆ Skipping from one web page to another with links
- ◆ Finding stuff on the web
- ◆ Bookmarking web pages for quick return trips
- ◆ Understanding cookies (pros and cons)

The single most exciting part of the Internet is the World Wide Web (or web for short), a loose collection of interconnected documents stored on computers all over the world. What makes these documents unique is that each page contains a link to one or more other documents stored on the same computer or on a different computer (down the block, across the country, or overseas). You can hop around from document to document, from continent to continent, by clicking these links.

When I say *documents*, I'm not talking about dusty old scrolls or text-heavy pages torn from books. Web documents contain pictures, sounds, video clips, animations, and even interactive programs. When you click a multi-media link, your modem pulls the file into your computer, where the web browser or another program plays the file. As you'll see in this chapter, the web has plenty to offer, no matter what your interests—music, movies, finance, science, literature, travel, astrology, body piercing, shopping—you name it.

First, You Need a Web Browser

To navigate the web, you need a special program called a *web browser*, which works through your service provider to pull documents up on your screen. You can choose from any of several web browsers, including the two most popular browsers, Netscape Navigator and Internet Explorer. In addition to opening web pages, these browsers contain advanced tools for navigating the web, finding pages that interest you, and marking the pages you might want to revisit.

> **CAUTION**
>
> **Whoa!**
>
> Your ISP might offer you its own custom web browser, which is typically a waste of programming code. These custom browsers are usually customized to feed you more advertising from the ISP and are typically more difficult to navigate than popular browsers, such as Internet Explorer and Netscape Navigator. Stick with the popular browsers for now.

Windows comes with Internet Explorer, which should already be installed on your computer. To keep things simple, we'll use Internet Explorer in our examples. However, if you're using a different browser supplied by your service provider, don't fret. Most browsers offer the same basic features and similar navigation tools. Be flexible, and you'll be surfing the web in no time.

Steering Your Browser in the Right Direction

To run your web browser, click or double-click its icon on the desktop or choose it from the **Start, Programs** or **Start, All Programs** menu. If you're using Internet Explorer, click the icon named **The Internet** or **Internet Explorer** on the Windows desktop or click the big "e" icon in the Quick Launch toolbar.

When your browser starts, it immediately opens a page that's set up as its starting page. For example, Internet Explorer opens Microsoft's or MSN's (Microsoft Network's) home page. You can start to wander the web simply by clicking links (typically, blue, underlined text; buttons; or graphic site maps). You can tell when the mouse pointer is over a link, because it changes from an arrow into a pointing hand. Click the **Back** button (on the button bar just above the page display area) to flip to a previous page, or click the **Forward** button (the button with the right-pointing arrow) to skip ahead to a page that you've visited but backed up from (see Figure 20.1).

Click the Back button to display the previous page

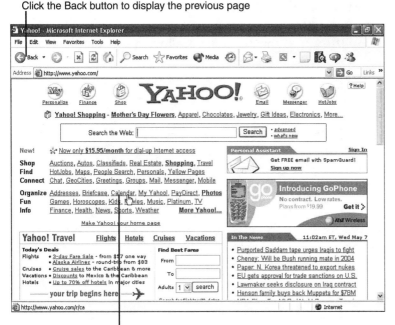

Figure 20.1

A web browser displays and helps you navigate web pages.

Click a link to flip to a page

If you click a link and your browser displays a message that it can't find the page or that access has been denied, don't freak out. Just click the **Back** button and then try the link again. If that doesn't open the page, try again later. In some cases, the web page creator (*webmaster*) might have mistyped the page address that the link points to or might have moved or deleted the page. On the ever-changing web, this happens quite often. Be patient, be flexible, and don't be alarmed.

> **Panic Attack**
>
> If you're not connected to the Internet when you start your browser, it might display a message indicating that it cannot find or load the page. If you have a standard modem connection, re-establish your connection using the Dial-Up Networking icon you created in Chapter 17.

A Word About Web Page Addresses

Every page on the web has an address that defines its location, such as www.si.edu for the Smithsonian Institution or www.walmart.com for Wal-Mart. The next time you watch TV or flip through a magazine, listen and keep your eyes peeled for web page addresses. Not only do these addresses look funny in print, but they sound funny, too; for instance, www.walmart.com is pronounced "dubbayou-dubbayou-dubbayou-dot-walmart-dot-kahm."

Web page addresses are formally called *URLs* (*Uniform Resource Locators*). They allow you to open specific pages. You enter the address in your web browser, usually in a text box called **Go to** or **Address,** near the top of the window, and your web browser pulls up the page.

Tech Term

Every web page **URL** starts with http://. Newsgroup sites start with news://. FTP sites (where you can get files) start with ftp://. You get the idea. HTTP (short for Hypertext Transfer Protocol) is the coding system used to format web pages. The rest of the address reads from right to left (from general to specific). For example, in the URL http://www.mitsubishi.co.jp, .jp stands for Japan, co stands for corporation (a company in Japan), mitsubishi stands for Mitsubishi (a specific company), and www stands for World Wide Web (or Mitsubishi's web server, as opposed to its FTP server or mail server). Addresses that end in .edu are for pages at educational institutions. Addresses that end in .com are for commercial institutions. You can omit the http:// when entering web page addresses, but omitting ftp:// or news:// causes the browser to attempt to connect to a website.

All you really have to know about a URL is that if you want to use one, type the URL exactly as you see it. Type the periods as shown, use forward slashes, and follow the capitalization of the URL. If you make any typos, the browser either loads the wrong page or displays a message indicating that the page doesn't exist or that the browser cannot locate the specified page.

Finding Stuff with Popular Search Tools

The web has loads of information and billions of pages, and this vast amount of information can make it difficult to track down anything specific. The web often seems like a big library that gave up on the Dewey decimal system and piled all its books and magazines in the center of the library. How do you sift through this mass of information to find what you need?

The answer: Use an Internet search tool. You simply connect to a site that has a search tool, type a couple of words that specify what you're looking for, and click the **Search** button (or its equivalent). The following are the addresses of some popular search sites on the web:

www.ask.com

www.yahoo.com

www.google.com

www.lycos.com

www.go.com

www.altavista.com

www.excite.com

Most web browsers have a **Search** button that connects you to various Internet search tools. For example, if you click **Search** in Internet Explorer, Internet Explorer displays a form that you can use to enter your search query. Simply type a couple of key words that describe what you're looking for and click the **Search** button, as shown in Figure 20.2.

The Search bar The Search button

The search returns links to
pages that match your query

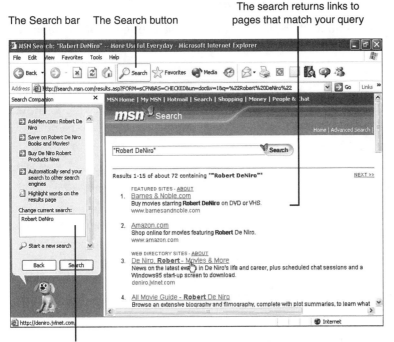

Figure 20.2

Use the Search bar to find the desired web content.

Type your search query here

You can also use special search tools to find long-lost relatives and friends on the Internet. These search tools are electronic telephone directories that can help you find mailing addresses, phone numbers, and even e-mail addresses. To search for people, check out the following sites:

people.yahoo.com

www.bigfoot.com

www.whowhere.lycos.com

www.infospace.com

Opening Multiple Browser Windows

You're hot on the trail of a fabulous website when you encounter a site that catches your eye. Do you stop and explore the site, forsaking the path to your original destination, or do you forge ahead and take the risk of never being able to return to the site?

Neither. Your browser offers some better options:

◆ Bookmark the page and quickly return to it later by selecting it from a menu (see "Marking Your Favorite Web Pages for Quick Return Trips" later in this chapter).

◆ Complete your journey to your original destination and then, later, use the history list to return to the site that caught your eye (see the next section).

◆ Open a new browser window, use it to complete your journey to your original destination, and then return to the other window when you have time. To open a new browser window in Internet Explorer, open the **File** menu, point to **New,** and click **Window** (or press **Ctrl+N**), or right-click the desired link and click **Open in New Window.**

> **Whoa!**
> Every program window you open consumes valuable system resources. When resources run low, your computer gets slow. If your computer seems to be slowing down, close some windows.

Going Back in Time with History Lists

Although the **Back** and **Forward** buttons will eventually take you back to where you were, they don't get you there in a hurry or keep track of pages you visited yesterday or last week. For faster return trips and a more comprehensive log of your web journeys, check out the history list:

◆ In Internet Explorer, click the **History** button to display the History bar on the left side of the window. Click the day or week during which you visited the website, and then click the website's name to see a list of pages you viewed at that site. To open a page, click its name, as shown in Figure 20.3.

◆ In Netscape Navigator, open the **Go** menu and click **History** or press **Ctrl+H** to view the history list. Double-click the name of the page you want to revisit.

Click the day or week icon

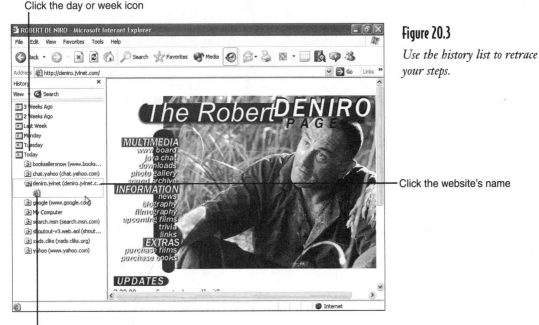

Figure 20.3

Use the history list to retrace your steps.

Click the website's name

Click the page you want to revisit

CAUTION

Whoa!

If you share your computer with someone, you might not want that person to know where you've been on the web. To cover your tracks, clear the history list. In Internet Explorer, choose **Tools, Internet Options** or **View, Internet Options** (in earlier versions of Internet Explorer) and then click the **Clear History** button. In Netscape Navigator, choose **Edit, Preferences,** click **History** (under Navigator), and click the **Clear History** button.

Marking Your Favorite Web Pages for Quick Return Trips

As you wander the web, you pull up pages that you know you want to return to in the future. When you happen upon such a page, flag it by creating a *bookmark* or marking the page as a *favorite*. This adds the page's name to the **Bookmarks** menu (in Netscape Navigator) or the **Favorites** menu (in Internet Explorer). The next time you want to pull up the page, you simply select it from your customized menu.

To mark a page, simply right-click a blank area of the page and select **Bookmark This Page** (in Netscape Navigator) or **Add to Favorites** (in Internet Explorer).

In Internet Explorer, when you choose to add a page to the **Favorites** menu, the Add Favorite dialog box appears, asking if you only want to add the page to your **Favorites** menu or have Internet Explorer make the page available offline (when you're not connected). If you choose the option for making the page available offline, you can click the Customize button and enter settings to have Internet Explorer automatically download updates at a scheduled time (typically when Internet traffic is light) or you can download updates at any time by opening the **Tools** menu and selecting **Synchronize.** When you choose to open the page, Internet Explorer quickly loads it from the cache (a temporary storage area on your computer's hard drive) rather than from the web.

> **Computer Cheat**
>
> Right-click a blank area of the page and click **Create Shortcut.** This places a shortcut icon for the page on your desktop.

After you have added a page to the **Bookmarks** or **Favorites** menu, you can quickly open the page by opening the menu and clicking the name of the page.

Changing the Starting Web Page

Whenever you fire up your browser, it opens with the same page every time. If you have your own favorite page you'd like your browser to load on startup, just let your browser know:

♦ In Internet Explorer, open the page you want to view on startup. Choose **Tools, Internet Options** or **View, Internet Options.** On the **General** tab, under **Home page,** click **Use Current,** and then click **OK.**

♦ In Netscape Navigator, open the page you want to view on startup. Choose **Edit, Preferences.** Under **When Navigator starts up, display,** be sure **Home page** is selected. Under **Home page,** click **Use Current Page,** and then click **OK.**

Can Cookies Hurt Me?

When you visit some websites, they automatically send an electronic passport, called a *cookie*, to your computer. As you browse the site, use its tools, or order products, the site "stamps" your passport to keep track of your interests, passwords, and any products you ordered. Whenever you revisit the site, the site can grab the cookie and immediately identify you. Think of it as living in a small town where everyone knows your business.

Because cookies are used to track your web habits, they give many people the heebie-jeebies and inspire allusions to the "futuristic" novel *1984*. Admittedly, cookies work behind the scenes to spy on you, but most cookies are designed to enhance your web browsing experience and allow companies to target advertisements to your tastes (rather than pitching products you probably wouldn't be interested in anyway).

In short, cookies are either good or bad, depending on how they're used and how you view them. If you love to shop on the Internet, cookies are a necessary evil, because they act as your shopping basket, keeping track of the items you ordered. On the other hand, if you're the kind of person who gets nervous around security cameras, cookies might bother you.

So can you refuse a cookie when a site tries to send you one? Of course—you have the option of blocking all cookies or having your browser prompt for your okay before accepting a cookie. Here's what you do:

♦ In Internet Explorer, choose **Tools, Internet Options.** Click the **Privacy** tab, click the **Advanced** button, and enter your preferences. (In earlier versions of Internet Explorer, you can access the cookies options by clicking the Security tab and then clicking the **Custom Level** button.)

♦ In Netscape Navigator, choose **Edit, Preferences.** Double-click **Privacy & Security** and click **Cookies.** Click **Disable cookies** or **Enable cookies based on privacy settings,** and then click **OK.**

If you've done plenty of web surfing with the cookies feature enabled, you probably have several cookies on your computer. To get rid of cookies in Internet Explorer, open the **Tools** menu, click **Internet Options,** click the **General** tab, and click the **Delete Cookies** button. To delete Netscape Navigator cookies, choose **Edit, Preferences.** Double-click **Privacy & Security** and click **Cookies.** Click the **Managed Stored Cookies** button and then click the **Remove All Cookies** button.

Inside Tip

For additional details about cookies, check out www. cookiecentral.com.

The Least You Need to Know

♦ To start Internet Explorer or Netscape Navigator, double-click its icon on the Windows desktop or select it from the **Start, Programs** or **Start, All Programs** menu.

♦ Links typically appear as buttons, icons, or specially highlighted text (typically blue and underlined).

♦ Click a link to open the page that the link points to.

♦ If you know a web page's address, type it in your browser's **Address** or **Go to** text box and press **Enter.**

♦ To search for a topic or site on the web, use a search engine, such as www.ask. com, www.yahoo.com, www.google.com, www.lycos.com, www.go.com, or www.hotbot.com, and enter a few words to describe what you're looking for.

♦ To bookmark a page, right-click a blank area of the page and select **Add Bookmark** (in Netscape Navigator) or **Add to Favorites** (in Internet Explorer).

Chapter 21

Shopping, Investing, Traveling, and Other Cool Web Stuff

In This Chapter

- Getting up-to-the-minute news, weather, and sports online
- Going shopping at the biggest mall on the planet
- Buying and selling stocks through an online broker
- Checking out some cool vacation spots
- Boning up on your movie trivia
- Downloading and playing your favorite audio clips

Although the Internet hasn't changed anything we humans do, it has completely revolutionized the *way* we do everything. People still watch the news and read magazines and newspapers, but more and more folks are getting their news, weather, and sports on the web. Investors still win and lose millions of dollars on their stocks and bonds, but now they can do it faster online. People still have affairs, but now they can ignite their passions in online chat rooms.

In short, the web offers features that let you perform the same tasks you performed in the past, only more conveniently and (typically) at less expense. This chapter shows you how to take advantage of some of the web's more practical real-life applications.

Keeping Up on News, Weather, and Current Events

TV stations can broadcast the news as it happens. You can watch live speeches, trials, and debates; view late-breaking reports from Washington; and watch Doppler radar track a storm as it moves through your town. The only trouble is that you're at the mercy of what the broadcasters want to show you. You need to wait for the news to come on and then wait for the reporters to get around to relating the information you want.

On the web, news is slightly delayed. It takes a while for someone to format a story and place it on the web. Even "live" video clips on the web are delayed by the time it takes your modem to receive the data. However, the web provides a self-directed approach to the news, so you don't have to sit through commercial breaks or wait for the story to air. You view only the information that interests you when you want it. In addition, web news sites typically cover a story more thoroughly than on TV. Think of web news as the ideal cross between a newspaper and TV news—it's fast and can provide audio and video coverage like TV, but it's thorough and scannable like a newspaper.

The following sections tell you where to find the best news, weather, and sports "channels" on the web.

Checking Out Web Newsstands

Virtually every TV station and news publication has a website where you can find not only the major news stories, but also biographical information, health alerts, book and movie reviews, political analysis, travel information, and much more. Check out the following popular news sites:

- ◆ **CNN at www.cnn.com.** Even if you don't have cable TV, you can check out this award-winning news service online (see Figure 21.1).

- ◆ **ABC News at www.abcnews.go.com.** If you missed the evening news, check out the ABC News site to view the latest stories. You'll also find links to the other ABC news shows, including *20/20* and *Nightline*.

- ◆ **CBS News at cbsnews.com.** This address takes you to the CBS News home page, where you'll find today's headline news plus links to CBS news specials, including *60 Minutes, 48 Hours, Face the Nation, CBS Sportsline,* and *Market-Watch.*

- ◆ **Fox News at www.foxnews.com.** If you're looking for "fair and balanced" reporting, check out this Fox News site. Fox News presents a more conservative slant, featuring reports and opinions from Oliver North, Bill O'Reilly, and Tony Snow.

- ◆ **MSNBC News at www.msnbc.com/news/.** Although this site displays the standard "top stories" you find at most news sites, it's laid out a little differently, displaying a list of features from every NBC news show: *The Today Show, NBC Nightly News, Dateline NBC,* and *Meet the Press.*

- ◆ **Associated Press at www.ap.org.** Go to the source and get the news from the place where the press gets its news: the Associated Press. When you get to the AP home site, click the **AP News** link and then click your state to select a local news site.

- ◆ **Yahoo!'s Daily News at dailynews.yahoo.com.** Although Yahoo! is a little light on news, it does provide an excellent starting point for your search. Here, you find plenty of links to other news sites that offer more thorough coverage.

Figure 21.1

CNN features thorough news coverage on the web.

Computer Cheat

If you're ever unsure of where an organization's website is located (or if the organization even has a website), try guessing its address. For example, for *USA Today*, you might enter www.usatoday.com. You'll probably hit the right site more than 50 percent of the time.

Inside Tip

Go to Weather by E-mail at www.weather-email.com/ or AccuWeather at direct. accuweather.com to have your weather forecast e-mailed to you daily.

If you've poked around at the news sites but you can't find the information you're looking for, use your favorite Internet search tool to search for the topic by name. If you're just browsing, go to Yahoo! (www.yahoo.com), scroll down the page, and click the **News & Media** link. You'll find links to thousands of news sites on the web.

Getting the Latest Weather Reports

Sure, you can get a weather report at any of the sites mentioned in the preceding section, but why settle for second-rate weather forecasts when the best weather station in the world is on the web? Check out the Weather Channel at www.weather.com.

The Weather Channel's opening page displays snippets from the big weather stories, along with any national weather alerts. For a specific local forecast, enter the name of the city or town or a ZIP code for the area in the **Local Weather** text box and press **Enter.** The local forecast appears, as shown in Figure 21.2.

Figure 21.2

The Weather Channel can display local forecasts for any area in the world.

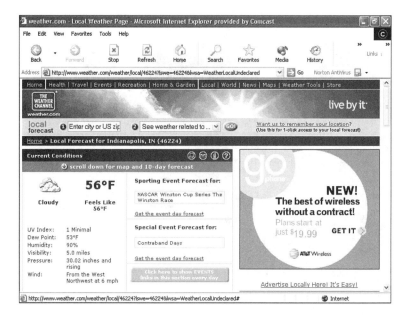

You can find hundreds of weather sites on the web, including the National Weather Service (www.nws.noaa.gov) and EarthWatch Weather on Command (www.earthwatch.com). To find a more complete listing of sites, use any Internet search tool to search for sites.

For Sports Fans Only

If you have cable TV, you can always find some sporting event to keep you entertained. But if you're flipping through stations and all you can find is the national Ping-Pong championships, you might want to take a break and check out a site for your favorite sport.

Given the current popularity of sports, you would expect to find plenty of sports sites on the web, and the web does not disappoint. Every sport you can think of, from archery to wrestling and everything in between, has at least one website devoted exclusively to it. In addition, all the major sports organizations and broadcasters have their own websites. Here are a few of my favorites:

- **ESPN at espn.go.com.** This site is a great place to go for a rundown of scores, as well as in-depth coverage of sporting events and behind-the-scenes interviews with your favorite players and coaches.

- **CNN/SI at sportsillustrated.cnn.com.** This site is the web home of *Sports Illustrated*. Although some of the articles at this site are mere teasers for the printed magazine, this site is packed with scores, team rankings, player statistics, and game analyses. You can even play fantasy sports and see how your teams stack up against those of fellow sports enthusiasts.

- **NFL at www.nfl.com.** This site is the official home of the National Football League. Do you have a favorite NFL team? Click its insignia at the top of the page to view the official team information, win/loss record, and statistics for your favorite players. (Go to www.nba.com for professional basketball, www.mlb.com for baseball [Major League Baseball], or www.nhl.com for hockey.)

- **CBS Sportsline at www.sportsline.com.** This site is the CBS sports center, where you can find coverage of the major professional and college sports. Sportsline offers a robust collection of photos and the latest point spreads (not that I'm saying gambling is okay).

- **FOX Sports at www.foxsports.com.** This is the FOX sports center, where you can find the latest scores and reports for nearly every professional and college sport. This site provides sports headlines, schedules, interviews, feature stories, and much more.

Mail-Order Paradise: Shopping on the Web

After businesses caught sight of the Internet, they began to realize the incredible opportunities it offered for advertising, marketing, and selling products directly to consumers. As more people purchased computers and started exploring online services and the Internet, businesses rushed to the web to establish a presence, and many individuals created their own storefronts on the web.

And boy, is business booming on the web! Go to nearly any site, and an ad will pop up on your screen. Open any Internet search page, and you'll find thousands of links to retail stores, mail-order companies, manufacturers, online mega-malls, bookstores, music stores, and even mom-and-pop specialty shops. I'm not about to list all the great places to shop on the web, because I'm sure you can find what you're looking for with your favorite search tool. However, before you do any serious shopping, you should be aware of the following shopping basics:

◆ When you find the desired product, you typically click a link for ordering it or placing it in your shopping basket. You can then click a link to keep shopping or to check out.

◆ Before you enter any personal information or your credit card number, be sure you are at a legitimate site and that the form you are about to fill out is a *secure web form*. Internet Explorer displays a blue or yellow lock icon at the bottom of the window to indicate that a form is secure. If the form's page address starts with https:// instead of http://, it is stored on a secure server.

◆ When you're ready to place your order, you must fill out an order form, such as the form shown in Figure 21.3. You'll be asked to select a payment method and enter billing and shipping data. Just pretend that you're entering information in a dialog box, and you'll do just fine.

Tech Term

When you enter data using a **secure web form,** your browser scrambles the data before sending it. When the web server receives the scrambled data, it decodes it. This significantly reduces the possibility that someone can intercept the data en route to its destination and read it.

◆ After you place your order, the site might display a confirmation page or send you a statement via e-mail. Be sure to print the statement. It typically contains a confirmation or order number that you can use to follow up on your order in case anything goes wrong. You might even receive a tracking number for the shipment, so you can follow your order from the time it leaves the company till it reaches your home!

https:// indicates that the site is secure

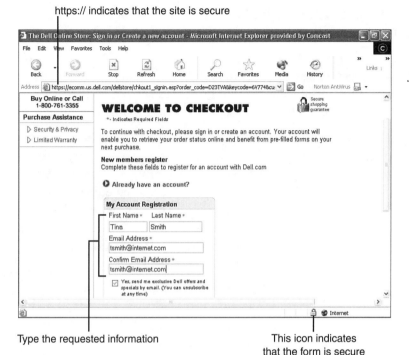

Figure 21.3

Complete the online order form to place your order.

Type the requested information

This icon indicates that the form is secure

Becoming Your Own Stockbroker

Before state lotteries, bingo nights, and local casinos started becoming so popular, the stock market was the only game in town for legalized gambling. But even with the growing availability of lotteries and other betting venues, the stock market remains one of the most popular gambling institutions in the nation. And now, if you have Internet access and a little extra money, you too can place a bet on your favorite corporation.

Several web-based stock trading companies allow you to buy and sell stocks online. You simply set up an account with the company and mail a check to cover your future transactions. After your account is set up, you can buy and sell stocks using the money in your account. These services typically charge a base fee per transaction, which varies from service to service. Most services also provide tools for tracking your investments and researching companies.

To see how this online investing thing works, check out the following online stock brokerages:

◆ **E*TRADE at www.etrade.com.** This site is one of the most popular stock brokerage firms on the web, providing the tools you need to research companies, track your investments, and learn more about investing. You can open an account with a minimum of $1,000. Transactions cost about $20 per 1,000 shares.

◆ **Ameritrade at www.ameritrade.com.** This site is one of the least expensive brokerages, offering a flat fee of about $11 for most transactions. Ameritrade also provides plenty of tools and data for researching and tracking investments.

◆ **Harris Direct at www.harrisdirect.com.** This site is one of my favorite places to check on my stocks and mutual funds. In fact, I set up Harris Direct as my home page, as shown in Figure 21.4. I've never purchased stocks through Harris Direct, but its services are competitive with the two brokerages just mentioned. Harris Direct charges about the same as E*TRADE, but it provides more thorough information than both E*TRADE and Ameritrade.

◆ **Charles Schwab at www.schwab.com.** This site is a more full-service brokerage. As such, it requires a higher minimum balance and charges more than any of the other online brokerages described here, including a quarterly fee of $30 to $45. When you're first learning the ropes, getting professional advice might be worth the extra cost.

Whoa!

To protect myself from lawyers and other whiners, I must say that I don't recommend using any of these online stock brokerages, purchasing stocks online, or even purchasing stocks offline. In short, I'm not responsible for anything you do with your money, your spouse's money, or the money in your kids' piggy banks.

Figure 21.4

Online brokerages provide the information you need to invest wisely.

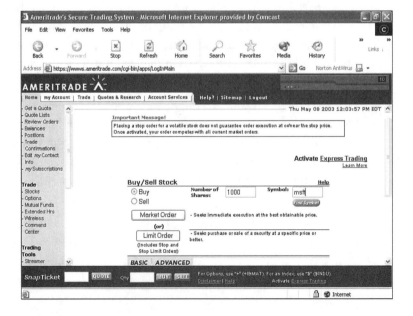

Planning Your Next Vacation

Whether you already have a vacation destination in mind or need a few ideas on where to go, the web has plenty of tools for planning your vacation, buying tickets, and making reservations. If you want to go through a travel agent, you can find several travel agencies online. If you would rather plan the trip yourself, you can find thousands of links for travel bureaus, airlines, motels, campsites, tourist centers, and anything else you can imagine.

One of the best places to start planning your vacation is at Yahoo! (www.yahoo.com). On Yahoo!'s opening page, scroll down to the **Recreation & Sports** category and click the **Travel** link. Scroll down the page to view a list of travel subcategories, as shown in Figure 21.5, and follow the trail of links to obtain the desired travel information.

> **Inside Tip**
>
> Several sites, including Yahoo!, provide free quotes for airline tickets. You simply enter the dates on which you plan to travel and the departure and arrival locations, and the site displays a list of fares, typically from lowest to highest. For plane tickets and other vacation information, check out www. travelocity.com.

Figure 21.5

Yahoo! provides links to all the travel information you could possibly need.

For Movie Buffs Only

Whether you're at a party swapping movie trivia or at home trying to decide which movie to rent, a thorough, up-to-date movie database can come in handy. With a movie database, you can obtain a complete list of movies in which your favorite actor or actress appeared, quickly determine who directed a particular movie, or scan plots to decide which movie you want to rent.

One of the most thorough movie databases on the web is the Internet Movie Database at us.imdb.com. The opening page displays a form that lets you search for movies based on the movie's title or the people involved in its creation (the actors, actresses, director, and so on). Simply type a person's last name or a portion of the movie's title and click the **Go!** button to start your search. Follow the trail of links to narrow your search and find the desired information.

Although the Internet Movie Database is one of the best places to go to answer trivia questions and research the careers of your favorite stars and directors, the Internet offers much more for film buffs. Most major movie studios have their own websites (for instance, Paramount at www.paramount.com) where they typically showcase new and future releases. Video rental stores (such as Blockbuster at www.blockbuster.com) have their own sites, which typically display a list of upcoming video releases along with any promotional deals. Magazines such as *The New Yorker* and *Time* have movie reviews. Many popular actors and actresses have their own "official" websites. You can even find shrines set up by devoted fans.

Use your favorite search tool to explore movies categories or search for a specific movie, director, actor, actress, movie studio, or other movie-related topic.

Many movie sites, especially sites set up by the film industry, contain links for *trailers* (short video clips that let you preview movies). Ideally, when you click a link to play a video clip, your computer downloads (copies) the video file from the website and starts to play it. If you're running Windows Me or XP, for instance, and you click a link for playing an MPEG or AVI movie clip, Windows Media Player kicks into gear and starts playing the clip.

If your computer doesn't have the program required to play the clip, and you're lucky, your web browser displays a dialog box asking if you want to download and install the player. Give your okay, and then follow the instructions. If you're not so lucky, your

Inside Tip

Twenty-four hours a day, seven days a week, you can find movie chat rooms where fans meet to discuss movie facts and trade trivia questions. If you're looking for some friendly banter about the movies you like best, check out the chat rooms. For more about chat rooms, see Chapter 19.

Inside Tip

You can pick up a QuickTime video player at www.apple.com/quicktime/download/. To download Windows Media Player, go to www.microsoft.com/windows/windowsmedia. You can find additional video players at www.tucows.com.

browser displays a dialog box asking if you want to open the file or save it to disk. Click the **Save to Disk** option, click **OK,** and then select the drive and folder in which you want the file saved. Then download the player you need, install it, and use it to open and play the file you saved to disk. After you've installed the appropriate player, your browser should automatically download and play clips without prompting you to open or save video files.

Creating Your Own Music Library

If you thought that the transition from LPs to CDs was revolutionary, the effect that the Internet has had on the music industry will make your head spin. As you would guess, every major label (and most minor labels) has its own website, where you can find out about your favorite recording artists, view video clips, and listen to sample audio clips. You can even find websites for lesser-known, independent artists who use the web to distribute their music directly to fans. Check out the following sites:

- **Internet Underground Music Archive at www.iuma.com.** This site is just what its name describes—a music library where you can listen to bands you won't hear on the radio or see on MTV. If you're a musician yourself, you can create your own website and use it to chase your dream of signing that big record deal—or just have someone other than the neighbors listen to your tunes.

- **VH1 at www.vh1.com.** This site is an online music network where you can get the latest news, music charts, reviews, and lists of events. VH1 features in-depth coverage of the music industry and allows you to search for individual artists by name.

- **Kazaa at www.kazaa.com.** This site features a program you can download and install on your computer to swap music clips with other users all over the world. I agree with the music industry that sharing music clips without paying for them is less than ethical, but millions of people continue to swap music, royalty free. You can obtain another, similar program at www.morpheus.com.

- **RollingStone.com at www.rollingstone.com.** This site is the electronic version of the popular *Rolling Stone* magazine. Here you'll find plenty of reviews, industry news, and interviews. And if you have your own *MP3* clip, you can submit it to the editors for inclusion in their Top 10 list.

Most music sites have audio clips you can download and play. You simply click the link to play the clip, and your computer downloads (copies) the audio file from the website and starts to play it. If your computer doesn't have the program required to play the clip, your web browser might display a dialog box asking if you want to

Tech Term

MP is short for MPEG, which is short for Moving Picture Experts Group, an organization that develops standards for compressing audio and video files. The **MP3** standard improves file compression by stripping data in audio signals that humans cannot hear anyway. This makes audio and video files much smaller so that they take up less storage space and download more quickly.

download and install the player. Simply give your okay and follow the instructions.

If your browser doesn't offer to fetch the player for you, save the file to disk and then poke around on the web to find a player. Windows Media Player, a part of Windows Me and XP, can play MP3 clips as well as other types of audio and video files; you can download the latest version at www.microsoft.com/windows/windowsmedia. Another popular audio player is RealPlayer, which you can pick up at www.realaudio.com. For a wider selection of audio and video players, go to www.tucows.com.

For more information on downloading and playing digitized music clips, copying clips to an MP3 player, and burning your own CDs, see Chapter 24.

Auctioning Stuff on eBay

eBay (at www.ebay.com) is the biggest flea market/auction in the world, enabling you to market your goods to millions of people all over the planet. You can sell everything from your collection of LPs to your used car on eBay simply by listing your item and waiting a few days for the top bid. And best of all, you call the shots. You can specify the starting bid price, the lowest bid you will accept, and the method of payment. You can even specify whether you or the buyer will pay the shipping costs! If you're not interested in selling stuff, you might be interested in buying goods at eBay—you can find a real bargain, assuming you know what you're looking for and what it's worth.

To start selling or buying on eBay, all you need to do is set up an account by entering some personal information, including your name, contact information, credit card number, and a few additional details. Complete online help is available, including tips on how to market your items, avoid scams, and purchase items without getting ripped off. After selling or purchasing the first few items, many users become hooked on eBay. Some people even make a good living on eBay, purchasing goods and then reselling them at higher prices.

The Least You Need to Know

- Thousands of websites are devoted to covering news, weather, and sports.

- Before you hand your credit card number to a company, be sure the company is legitimate and that the site is secure.

- You can research investments and buy and sell stocks on the web for a fraction of the cost you would pay a stockbroker.

- One of the best places to start planning for your next vacation is on Yahoo!'s Travel page.

- Want to know the name of every movie in which Robert De Niro has appeared? Check out the Internet Movie Database at us.imdb.com.

- Most music websites are packed with links for downloading and playing audio and video clips.

Publishing Your Own Web Page or Blog in Ten Minutes or Fewer

In This Chapter

- ◆ Understanding how the web works
- ◆ Sneaking a peek at the codes behind web pages
- ◆ Slapping together your own cool web page
- ◆ Using the web to make money
- ◆ Finding free enhancements for your web page
- ◆ Publishing your thoughts and insights through a blog

You wandered the web. Perhaps you sent out a few electronic greeting cards, played some audio and video clips, and even ordered products online. You can use search tools to track down information about the most obscure topics, and you can monitor the progress of all your stocks and mutual funds.

Tech Term

A **blog** (short for "web log") is a publicly accessible personal journal that enables an individual to voice his or her opinions and insights or just keep an online record of experiences. People also use blogs to share photos with friends and family and function as online clubs.

But now you want more. You want to establish a presence on the web, publish your own stories or poems, place pictures of yourself or your family online, show off your creativity, and communicate your ideas to the world.

Where do you start? How do you create a web page or *blog* from scratch? How do you insert photos and links? How do you add a background? And after you've created the page, what steps must you take to place the page on the web for all to see?

This chapter shows you a quick and easy way to whip up your first web page or blog right online, without having to learn a special program or deal with any cryptic web page formatting codes. And because you create the page online, you don't have to worry about publishing your web page when you're done.

What Makes a Web Page So Special?

Behind every web page is a text document that includes codes for formatting the text, inserting pictures and other media files, and displaying links that point to other pages. This system of codes (*tags*) is called *HTML* (*Hypertext Markup Language*).

Most codes are paired. The first code in the pair turns on the formatting, and the second code turns it off. For example, to type a heading such as "Apple Dumplin's Home Page," you would use the heading codes like this:

```
<h1>Apple Dumplin's Home Page</h1>
```

Inside Tip

Even if a browser is set up to display all level-one headings in a particular way, HTML codes can override the browser's setting and give the heading a different look. For example, they might make the heading appear in a different color or font.

The <h1> code tells the web browser to display any text that follows the code as a level-one heading. The </h1> code tells the web browser to turn off the level-one heading format and return to displaying text as normal. Unpaired codes act as commands; for instance, the <p> code inserts a line break or starts a new paragraph.

Web browsers use HTML codes to determine how to display text, graphics, links, and other objects on a page. Because the browser is in charge of interpreting the codes, different browsers might display the same page slightly differently. For example, one browser might display links as blue, underlined text, whereas another browser might display links as green and bold.

Forget About HTML

A basic introduction to HTML is helpful in understanding how the web works, troubleshooting web page formatting problems, and customizing web pages with fancy enhancements, but you don't need a doctorate in HTML to create your first web page. Many companies have developed specialized programs that make the process of creating a web page as easy as designing and printing a greeting card.

You can use programs such as Web Studio, FrontPage, Netscape Composer, and HotDog to create and format web pages on your computer and then upload (copy) the pages from your computer to a web server (typically your ISP's web server). Or you can create and format your web pages right on the web simply by specifying your preferences and using forms to enter your text. The next section shows you just how easy it is to create and publish your own web page online at Yahoo! GeoCities.

Making a Personal Web Page Right on the Web

When it comes to publishing your own web page, you have simple needs—a single web page that lets you share your interests with others and express yourself to the world. For someone with such simple needs, the web offers free *hosting* services, such as Yahoo! GeoCities. These services offer tools for building your web page online, along with access to a web server where you can publish your page.

> **Tech Term** _____
>
> A web **host** is a server on which you can store your web page and all files related to it, such as photos and other graphics. Think of it as a neighborhood in which you can build your home. Your ISP might provide free hosting services (typically with a limit of 5 megabytes), but in most cases you must create the web page yourself and then upload it to the web server.

So let's get on with it and publish a simple web page at Yahoo! GeoCities:

1. Run your web browser and go to geocities.yahoo.com.

2. Unless you registered with Yahoo! earlier (for example, for Yahoo! Chat), follow the series of links required to sign up as a new user. (Because websites are notorious for changing steps and commands, specific instructions would only confuse you. You have to wing it—trust me.)

3. Fill out the required form, read the legal agreement(s), and jump through what-ever hoops you need to jump through to get your free membership. This gives you an ID (member name) and password so that you can sign in.

4. Use your ID and password to sign in to Yahoo! GeoCities. Your browser loads the Yahoo! GeoCities welcome page, as shown in Figure 22.1.

Figure 22.1

Yahoo! GeoCities welcomes you.

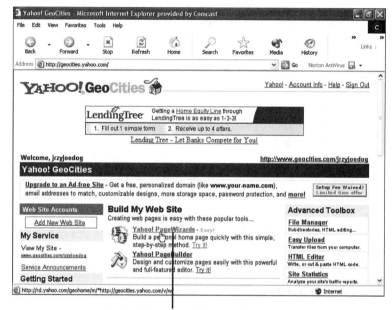

Click the Yahoo! PageWizards link

5. Click the **Yahoo! PageWizards** link. Yahoo! GeoCities displays a list of pre-designed web page templates you can use to get started.

6. Click one of the Page Wizard designs. Yahoo! GeoCities displays a brief intro-duction to the wizard, as shown in Figure 22.2. (If you change your mind and decide to use a different template, click the **Cancel** button and choose another.)

7. Click **Launch Yahoo! PageWizard** to start the wizard with the selected design, or click one of the alternative color schemes or designs near the bottom of the page. The first PageWizard dialog box appears, welcoming you to the wizard.

8. Click the **Begin** button. The wizard prompts you to select a color scheme.

9. Click the desired color scheme, and then click **Next >.** The wizard prompts you to enter your name and e-mail address, as shown in Figure 22.3.

Click here to start the wizard

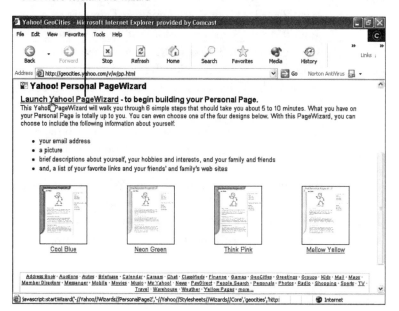

Figure 22.2

Yahoo! GeoCities provides a brief introduction to the selected wizard.

Type your name here

Figure 22.3

The Yahoo! Personal Page Wizard prompts you to type your name and e-mail address.

Type your e-mail address here   Click Next >

10. Follow the wizard's instructions to complete your web page and save it to the Yahoo! GeoCities web server. (The steps vary, depending on which wizard you're running.)

You can change your page at any time. Just go to Yahoo! GeoCities at geocities. yahoo.com, sign in, and run the PageWizard. When the PageWizard appears this time, it displays an option for editing an existing page. Click **Edit Existing Page,** and then open the drop-down menu and click the name of the page you want to edit. Click **Next >** and follow the onscreen instructions to enter your changes.

For more options and control over your web page design and layout, use Yahoo! PageBuilder. This is a full-featured web page creation and editing tool. To run PageBuilder, simply open the Yahoo! GeoCities home page and click **Yahoo! PageBuilder**. This displays an introduction to PageBuilder. Click the **Launch PageBuilder** link to run the program.

Placing Your Business on the Web

Of course, you didn't build that web page to make money or pitch a pyramid scheme to your friends or relatives, but you can use your web page to generate income and set up your own business or online storefront.

One of the easiest ways to generate income from your web page is to form a partnership with an online retail store. You peddle the store's products on your website, and if someone purchases the product from your partner, you receive a commission. Amazon.com, one of the largest online retailers, offers an associates program in which you can earn between 2.5 percent and 15 percent for every referral. To learn more about this program, go to Amazon.com at www.amazon.com, scroll down near the bottom of the opening page, and click the **Join Associates** link. If you're more interested in selling music, check out www.gamemusic.com/associates/. If you want to sell clothing, check out www.graffitionline.com/affiliate_faq.html. For a directory of various merchants that feature affiliate programs, go to AffiliateFirst at www. affiliatefirst.com. If you have more complex business needs (if you manufacture or ship your own product or provide a service), you might need more sophisticated web-based business tools than those that Yahoo! GeoCities offers. You will need access to a secure web server, a form for customers to use to place orders, and an online database that can receive and organize orders and track shipping information. In short, you need a more business-oriented web hosting service. Check out the following sites:

- **Netopia at www.netopia.com.** Netopia features a wide range of products and services for the home and small-business user and makes it easy to set up a business on the Internet. Netopia even provides the tools you need to take credit card orders over the web.

◆ **Yahoo! Small Business at smallbusiness.yahoo.com.** This site costs about $50 per month for your own online store, 10 cents per advertised item per month, plus 3.5 percent revenue share on every sale you make through the Yahoo! Network. Yahoo! Small Business provides the basic tools you need to set up shop on the web.

◆ **PayPal at www.paypal.com.** If you already have a website but have no way for your customers to place orders online and pay you for your products or services, check out PayPal. Your customers can set up accounts at PayPal and then use money in their PayPal accounts to purchase items at your site. PayPal charges a nominal fee to act as the middleman, and you don't need to worry about managing your own credit card orders. PayPal can even help you manage your shipping department.

You can find hundreds of website hosting services on the web that vary greatly in price and service. Use your favorite web search tool to look for "web hosting" or "free web page." (Most services have trial offers that they advertise as "free." These sites typically are free only for 10 to 30 days and might include hidden costs for "special" business features, such as order forms and credit card processing.)

Inside Tip

When shopping for a web host, compare costs and features carefully. Check the amount of disk space you get and whether the service charges you extra every time someone visits your site. Also ask if any sales commissions are involved.

Finding Cool Stuff to Put on Your Page

You can decorate your web page with everything from floral-print backgrounds to cartoon clip art. You can even add clocks, counters that mark the number of times people have visited your page, video clips, audio clips, and even small programs that allow visitors to perform calculations or play games.

Where do you find all this stuff? On the web, of course. Check out the following websites for some cool free stuff you can use to enhance and enliven your website:

◆ **#1 Free Clip Art at www.1clipart.com.** This site features 10,000 free clip art images organized in more than a dozen categories, including Animals, Cartoons, Games, Sports, and Transportation, to name a few. Follow the trail of categories and subcategories until you find the desired image, and then right-click the image and choose **Save Picture As** to save it to your computer, as shown in Figure 22.4.

Right-click the image

Figure 22.4

#1 Free Clip Art features thousands of free clip art images.

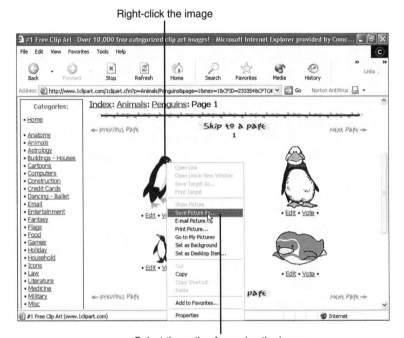

Select the option for saving the image

◆ **CLIPART.COM at www.clipart.com.** This site is one of the best places to go for web graphics, photos, and animations. Here you can find thousands of clip art images and other graphics for nearly every category you can imagine.

◆ **ArtToday at www.arttoday.com.** This site provides access to several graphics sites, with access to more than 40,000 web photos, 2.5 million clip art images, hundreds of Flash (animated) components, and hundreds of other graphics resources. Charges vary from site to site.

◆ **c|net at download.cnet.com.** This site provides plenty of free programs, ActiveX controls and Java *applets* (small programs you can place on your page), clip art, and audio and video clips. You'll need to poke around a little to find what you're looking for.

◆ **Free-Backgrounds.com at www.free-backgrounds.com.** This site specializes in custom background designs. New backgrounds are added every day. However, this is also a great place to pick up free clip art and animated graphics.

Computer Cheat

If you see something you like on a web page, write to the web page author via e-mail (if the person has his or her e-mail address on the page) and ask for permission to use the object. You can drag most clip art images, icons, and other objects right off a page displayed in your browser and drop them onto your page displayed in your web page editor.

Building a Blog and Speaking Out on the Internet

In the not-so-distant past, publishing your insights and words of wisdom was nearly impossible. Unless you won a few poetry contests or tirelessly submitted high-quality articles to magazines or manuscripts to book publishers, your hopes of being published were slim to none. With the advent of electronic publishing, via the web, anyone with a little technical expertise can publish their own writings, but creating and managing a website and keeping it up to date is both challenging and time-consuming. Relatively recently (sometime in the late 1990s), self-publishing on the web became easier with the introduction of *web logs* (or *blogs* for short). These relatively simple web pages are primarily text-based, and you can create and update them by filling out a form. You type a message, comment, or other text and then *post it* to the blog. The most recent posting appears at the top of your blog followed by prior postings. As your list of posted messages grows, old messages are pushed off the main blog and are archived.

The first blogs focused on news and commentary. Bloggers would read an article online and then post a link to the article along with their comments, insights, questions, and sometimes corrections or additional facts concerning the article. Over the years, the scope of blogs has broadened considerably. Now, people commonly use blogs to publish their own poetry and fiction; broadcast news stories that are overlooked by the mainstream media; communicate with family members, friends, and colleagues; promote grassroots movements; keep an online journal; and much more.

Slapping Together a Blog at Blogger

The easiest way to create your own blog is to build it on a site that specializes in blogs, such as Blogger. Using your web browser, you register at Blogger and then use its online forms to create your blog and keep it up to date. The following steps show you just how easy it is to create your own blog at Blogger:

1. Open your web browser, click in the **Address** or **Go To** text box, type **www. blogger.com,** and press **Enter.** Blogger's home page appears.

2. Click the **Start Now!** button or (if the button has been renamed) select the option for getting started. Blogger prompts you to enter the information required to register for a new account.

3. Type the requested information and then click the **Sign Up** button. Blogger prompts you to type a title for your blog and a brief description of it, as shown in Figure 22.5.

Figure 22.5

Name your blog and type a brief description of it.

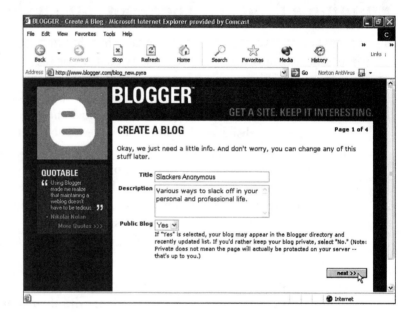

4. Type a title for your blog and a brief description of it in the spaces provided, choose whether you want the blog to be public or private, and then click the **Next** button. Blogger asks where you want your blog stored.

5. To keep this as simple as possible, make sure **Host It at BlogSpot** is selected and then click the **Next** button. (BlogSpot offers free blog hosting, but ads will greet anyone who visits your blog.) Blogger prompts you to type an address for your blog.

6. In the space provided, complete the address for your blog by typing in a one word entry and then click the **Next** button. (Write down the complete web page address, so you can visit your blog when you're done and let your friends, family, and colleagues know where to find it.) Blogger prompts you to select a template for your blog, as shown in Figure 22.6.

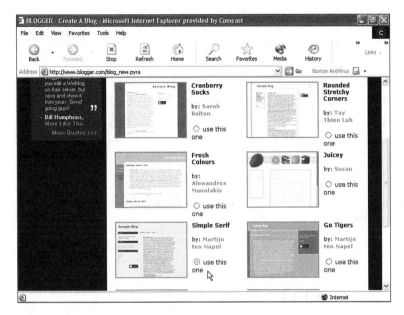

Figure 22.6

Select the desired design for your blog.

7. Scroll down the page and next to the desired template, click **Use This One.** Click the **Finish** button. Blogger displays a message indicating that it is creating your blog. After a few seconds, Blogger displays the screen for editing your blog, as shown in Figure 22.7.

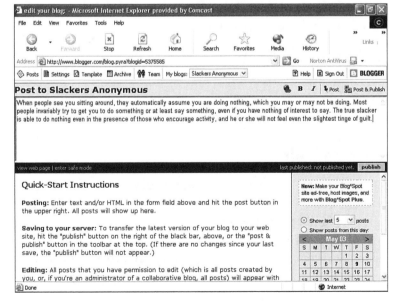

Figure 22.7

Type your thoughts, insights, or other text to have it published to your blog.

8. Type your message to the world in the message area. (If you know how to use HTML codes to format your text, you can type the codes in the message area, as well, but HTML is optional.)

9. To post your message and enter a new message, click the **Post** button. To post your message and publish it to your site, click the **Post & Publish** button. Blogger displays your message in the pane at the bottom. To edit any message in this pane, click the **Edit** link below the message and then type your changes in the message area.

10. To view your blog, click the **View Web Page** link just below the area where you typed your message. Your web browser opens a new window and displays your blog. Close the window when you're done viewing your blog to return to the edit screen.

To view your blog as a visitor will see it, use your web browser to go to the address you entered in Step 6. To edit your blog at any time, display the Blogger home page, log in, and then click the link for editing your blog. To check out some other online blogging sites, try the following addresses:

> www.blogbuilder.com
>
> www.diaryland.com
>
> www.pitas.com
>
> www.blog-city.com
>
> blog.tripod.lycos.com
>
> m-blog.com
>
> www.bloggingnetwork.com

Inside Tip

Blogger's message area features no spelling checker, so consider typing your message in your word processing application and then copy your message, click in the message area, and press **Ctrl+V** to paste it. Remember to click **Post** or **Post & Publish** to save your message and place it on your blog.

Professional Strength Blogging Tools

A simple text-based blog, such as the blog you created in the previous section, is sufficient to get you started in the wonderful world of blogging, but if you would like to jazz up your blog with graphics and other objects to make it act more like a full fledged website, download a copy of BlogWeaver at www.oneseek.com/blogweaver. htm. BlogWeaver is designed to work hand-in-hand with Blogger, providing you with powerful formatting tools to help you enhance your blog with fancy fonts, graphics, and other web page objects. (Blogger also has its own blog-building application that you can access by upgrading your Blogger service to Blogger Pro and paying an annual fee—about $50 at the time this book was being written.)

Most blog building applications function like web page editors, inserting the necessary HTML codes for you behind the scenes. You simply create and format your blog as if you were using a word processor or desktop publishing application. In addition, the blog building application typically posts your updated blog to the host site, so you don't need to use a separate application. Following is a list of popular stand-alone blog-building applications along with website addresses where you can learn more about them and possibly download a shareware version of the software:

- **Greymatter at www.noahgrey.com/greysoft** is a user-friendly blogging application that features powerful search tools, file uploading, image handling, customizable templates, multiple-author support, commenting, and additional features. Best of all, it's free.

- **Moveable Type at www.movabletype.org** is another easy-to-use blogging application that enables you to create, edit, and publish your blog simply by filling out a form on your computer. The opening screen displays a list of your blogs and links for creating new blogs, editing your blogs, deleting a blog, adding or deleting contributing authors, editing your profile, and much more.

- **Radio at radio.userland.com** is a powerful blogging application that enables you to create and edit blogs on your computer and upload updates over a dial-up connection in a matter of minutes. The application costs about $40 and includes a one-year subscription to Userland, a blog-hosting service. Radio also features a tool that can collect posts from several of your favorite blogs and present them on a single page, enabling you to keep up on any current posts. Radio offers a free 30-day trial.

The Least You Need to Know

- HTML (Hypertext Markup Language) is a system of codes used to format web pages.

- You don't need to master HTML in order to create your own attractive web pages.

- The easiest way to create a page at Yahoo! GeoCities is to use one of the Yahoo! PageWizards. To edit your Yahoo! GeoCities web page, sign in at geocities. yahoo.com and click the link for running the PageWizard.

- For a more robust set of web-based business tools, check out Netopia at www.netopia.com.

- For gobs of web page clip art, go to www.clipart.com.

- An easy way to establish a presence on the Internet is to create your own blog.

Chapter 23

Protecting Your Computer and Your Children on the Internet

In This Chapter

- Being sure your child understands the rules
- Spying on … er … supervising your kids
- Blocking undesirable web content with a censoring program
- Avoiding deviants in chat rooms and via e-mail
- Scanning incoming files for viruses
- Blocking unauthorized access to your computer

The Internet is a virtual city packed with shopping malls, libraries, community centers, museums, newsstands, meeting rooms, and other valuable offerings. But like any city, the Internet has its dark side—a section of town ruled by pornography, violence, bigotry, vandalism, and theft. If you have children, you want to provide them access to all the positive material the Internet offers, but you're responsible for preventing them from accessing offensive material. In addition, you need to protect your computer from viruses and from unauthorized access, to prevent your files from being damaged or stolen. This chapter shows you how to protect your children and your computer from the various threats posed by the Internet.

Protecting Children on the Internet

As a society, we want our children to have the freedom to explore the Internet, but we have the responsibility of protecting them from media and individuals who threaten their innocence. We want our children to visit museums online, communicate with students in other parts of the world, take classes, visit political institutions, and research topics of interest. We don't want our kids or students pulling up porno pages, reading racist propaganda, hacking the Pentagon's computer system, or sitting in the Hot Tub chat room conversing with a bunch of old guys and gals who should know better. And we sure don't want our 11-year-olds corresponding via e-mail with deviants twice or three times their age.

The following sections serve as a parent/teacher guide to the Internet. These sections show you how to make your kids more street smart, so they won't fall prey to con artists, how to supervise their Internet use, and how to block access to offensive material by using various censoring tools. Along the way, you will become a little more savvy yourself and begin to understand the various threats posed by connecting to the Internet.

Explaining the Rules of the Road

Most kids aren't rotten. They're confused, frustrated, careless, and selfish, but not intentionally bad. A child usually makes a wrong choice or breaks a rule either because he doesn't understand the rule, he's overly curious, or he faces no consequence for misbehaving. So before you let your child or student fire up the web browser, lay down the rules and explain the consequences. Here are a few rules to pass along to your kids:

- **Keep passwords secret.** Anyone who knows your user name and password can use your account, racking up connect time charges, placing orders, and performing illegal activities in your name.

- **Don't enter any personal information online without permission from a parent or guardian.** Using your real name, address, or phone number in your profile gives stalkers the information they want. Registering for contests and "free" stuff can make your private information public. Never tell someone your real name, address, or phone number in a chat room, where anyone can see it.

◆ **Don't use a credit card.** Leaving your teenager alone on the web with your credit card can be a disaster. The web is the biggest shop-at-home network in the world.

◆ **Don't run or install any programs without permission.** Downloading and running programs from unreliable sources can introduce computer viruses. You and your kids should also be careful with any program files you receive via e-mail.

◆ **Don't view sites that you wouldn't view with parents or guardians next to you.** Later in this chapter, I show you how to block undesirable content, but censoring programs do not block everything that's offensive. Be sure your kids know that you expect them to use good judgment.

◆ **Don't chat or correspond with creeps.** Some creepy adults use the Internet to prey on kids. Have your kids notify you immediately of any suspicious individuals or messages. Tell your kids not to send photos of themselves to strangers or post their photos on their web pages. Let your kids know that people on the Internet can pretend to be anybody; the 14-year-old girl your daughter thinks she is chatting with actually could be a 35-year-old guy.

◆ **Don't meet anyone in person known only from online contact.** If your child wants to meet a friend from the Internet, have your child schedule a meeting in a public place and take you along.

In addition to laying down the rules, specify limits on Internet use, just as you would limit TV viewing. Specify the time of day your child can access the Internet and the amount of time he or she can spend at the keyboard. Although the computer and the Internet can be great tools for education and entertainment, they can also interfere with a child's education and social and physical development.

> **Inside Tip**
>
> Use computer time as a reward for proper behavior. If your child fails to follow the rules, reduce or eliminate the time your child spends on the computer. Your kid might claim that the punishment is harming his education. Don't buy it.

A Little Personal Supervision Goes a Long Way

When my kids started watching TV, I was pretty naive. I told my children to watch only those shows that they would feel comfortable watching with me or their mom.

A couple days later, I walked into the den and caught my 13- and 10-year-old watching MTV's *Celebrity Death Match*. Of course, they saw nothing wrong with it.

> **Whoa!** _____
>
> To be sure your kids can't surf the Internet without your permission, keep the password you use to connect to your ISP secret. Also, remove the check mark from the **Save password** check box in the Connect to dialog box. If you have a cable connection (which is connected all the time), this trick isn't an option.

As a parent, it's your obligation not to be stupid. Don't stick a computer in your kid's bedroom and then celebrate because you now have more quality time to spend with your spouse. The reason your son isn't pestering you or picking on his kid sister is probably because he has found something much more sinister to do on the Internet.

Place the computer in a room that you can enter without looking like a spy. A room that's open to traffic, such as a living room or family room, is a good choice. If you have young children, spend some time exploring the Internet with them and supervising their activities. Your kids might balk and think you're a control freak, but that's your job.

Censoring the Internet

Over the years, people have debated whether the government should censor the Internet. As society wrestles with this issue, offensive material remains readily available. In the following sections, you learn what you can do on your end to prevent this material from reaching you and your children.

> **Computer Cheat** _____
>
> View the history list to see where your kids have been. In Internet Explorer, click the **History** button to display the History bar. Click the folder for the week or day you want to check. The History bar displays a list of sites visited during the selected week or day. Click the site folder to view a list of pages that were opened at the site, and then click the page name to view the page. If your kids are wise to history lists, they might know how to clear the list, so if it's blank, suspect foul play.

Using America Online's Parental Controls

Without some level of censorship, America Online can be the most dangerous place for kids to hang out. Kids can access chat rooms such as The Flirts Nook and Chance Encounters, where chat topics are definitely adults-only and where chatters are likely to receive instant messages directing them to the latest porno site on the web.

America Online's Parental Controls allow you to block access to the red-light districts on America Online and the Internet. Follow these steps to create a screen name for one of your children and set limits in America Online 8.0:

1. Sign on to America Online using your primary screen name. (You can add users to your account only by signing on with your primary screen name, the screen name you used when you first set up your America Online account.)

2. In the button bar (just below the menu bar), click **Settings,** and then click **Screen Names.** The AOL Screen Names dialog box appears, displaying a list of screen names for your account.

3. Click **Create a Screen Name.** The Create a Screen Name dialog box appears, asking if you're creating a screen name for a child.

4. Click **Yes.** America Online displays some important information for parents.

5. Read the information, and then click **Continue.** America Online displays a brief introduction to screen names.

6. Click **Create Screen Name.** AOL prompts you to type a screen name. (Try to use something unique. CutiePie, for instance, is no doubt already being used by someone, so you would need something to distinguish it, such as CutiePie1563xy.)

7. Type the name your child wants to use, and then click **Continue.** AOL prompts you to type a password.

8. Type a password for your child to use when logging on (6 to 8 characters), press **Tab,** type the same password again, and click **Continue.** AOL prompts you to select a Parental Controls setting.

9. Click the desired setting, as shown in Figure 23.1, and click **Continue.** AOL prompts you to confirm or customize the settings.

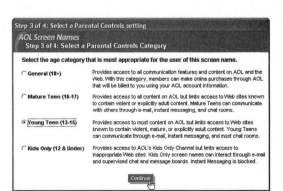

Figure 23.1

Pick the desired age level, and then click Continue.

10. Click **Edit Controls** so that you can check the settings. The Parental Controls dialog box appears, listing the various groups of settings: E-mail control, Chat control, Instant Messaging control, and so on.

11. Click the button next to the control group you want to check or modify. A dialog box pops up, showing your options.

12. Enter your preferences, and then click **Save** or **OK.** For example, if you chose E-Mail control in step 10, you can choose to block all e-mail messages, receive messages only from AOL members, or create a list of people from whom e-mail messages are to be accepted. Whether you click **Save** or **Cancel,** a confirmation message appears.

> ### Panic Attack
>
> If you already created a screen name for your child without specifying restrictions, you can specify restrictions at any time. Click **Settings** on the button bar, and then click **Parental Controls.** Click your child's screen name, and then enter your preferences.

13. Read the confirmation message, and then click **OK.** You are returned to the window for customizing parental controls.

14. Repeat steps 10 through 13 to check or customize any other controls, and then click the close (**X**) button to exit the window.

Censoring the Web with Internet Explorer

If you don't subscribe to America Online or some other commercial online service, you connect to the Internet through an ISP and are responsible for finding your own tools for censoring content. The next section reviews some of the specialized censoring programs currently available. In the meantime, if you use Internet Explorer as your web browser, you can use its built-in Content Advisor to filter undesirable content.

> ### Inside Tip
>
> Unless you change the Content Advisor's settings, it'll block every unrated page on the web—just about every page you try to pull up. To relax the ratings, open the **View** or **Tools** menu, click **Internet Options,** and click the **Content** tab. Click **Settings,** enter your password, and enter your preferences.

To censor sites with Internet Explorer, activate the Ratings feature. Open the **View** or **Tools** menu, click **Internet Options,** and click the **Content** tab. Under **Ratings** or **Content Advisor,** click the **Enable** button, and then click **OK.** The Create Supervisor Password dialog box appears. Type in both text boxes a password that you will remember but that your kids will have a tough time guessing. Click **OK** as many times as needed to save your changes and close the dialog boxes.

Don't set the kiddies in front of the screen just yet. Test your setup first. Try going to www.playboy.com.

If you see hot babes in various stages of undress, the Content Advisor is disabled. Close Internet Explorer, run it again, and then try going to the nudie page. You should see the Content Advisor dialog box, shown in Figure 23.2, displaying a list of reasons why you have been denied access to this site (as if you didn't know). Click **OK**.

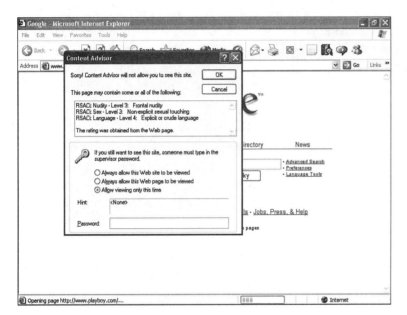

Figure 23.2

The Content Advisor won't let you view the peep show.

Using Censoring Software

If your web browser does not have a built-in censor, or if you want more control over the content and features your children can access, purchase a specialized censoring program. The following is a list of some of the better censoring programs, along with addresses for the web pages where you can find out more about them and download shareware versions:

◆ **Cyber Patrol at www.cyberpatrol.com.** The most popular censoring program on the market, Cyber Patrol uses a list of forbidden words to block access to objectionable material or uses a list of child-friendly words to block access to all web pages except those that contain one of the specified words. Passwords let you set access levels for different users, and Cyber Patrol can keep track of the amount of time each user spends on the Internet and can block or filter chat. The one drawback of Cyber Patrol is that it doesn't keep track of the sites that your kids *try* to visit.

- **CYBERsitter at www.solidoak.com.** Another fine censoring program, CYBERsitter is a little less strict than Cyber Patrol but is easier to use and configure. CYBERsitter has a unique filtering system that judges words in context, so it doesn't block access to inoffensive sites, such as the Anne Sexton home page.

- **Cyber Snoop at www.pearlsw.com.** Not the best content-blocker in the group, Cyber Snoop's claim to fame is that it can create a comprehensive log of a user's Internet activity. The best way to use Cyber Snoop is to install it and tell your kids that Cyber Snoop is recording everything they do on the Internet. You might not even have to buy the program—the threat might be deterrent enough.

- **Net Nanny at www.netnanny.com.** Net Nanny is unique in that it can punish the user for typing URLs of offensive sites or for typing any word on the "no-no" list. If a user types a prohibited word or URL, Net Nanny can shut down the application and record the offense, forcing your child to come up with an excuse. To make the most of Net Nanny, however, you have to spend a bit of time configuring it; it's not the most intuitive program of the bunch.

> **Whoa!**
>
> No censoring program is perfect. Some objectionable content can slip through the cracks, and the program can block access to unobjectionable sites. Use the censoring program only when you personally are unable to supervise your kids.

Adjusting Your Web Browser's Security Settings

Your web browser has its own security guard on duty that checks incoming files for potential threats. If you try to enter information (such as a credit card number) on a form that's not secure, the web browser displays a warning message asking if you want to continue. If a site attempts to install a program on your computer, your browser displays a confirmation dialog box asking for permission to download and install the program. At times, these warnings can become more annoying than useful, but they do provide you with some confidence that your browser is on the lookout for security threats. The following sections show you how to check and optionally adjust the security settings in Internet Explorer and Netscape Navigator.

Zoning In on Security in Internet Explorer

Internet Explorer sets different security levels for different *zones*, enabling you to relax the security settings for sites that you trust and tighten security settings for untested sites or those that you don't trust. Internet Explorer offers the following four security zones:

◆ *Internet* enables you to specify security settings for untested sites. When you wander off to sites that you do not frequent, you might want to tighten security. All sites that are not in one of the other zones in this list fall into the Internet zone.

◆ *Local Intranet* enables you to relax security for sites on your company's intranet or network so you can freely access those sites without being bombarded with warnings. By default, the security level for local intranet sites is set at low.

◆ *Trusted sites* enable you to deactivate the security warnings for sites you trust. This prevents you from being inundated with warning messages at the sites you visit most frequently.

◆ *Restricted sites* enables you to create a list of sites that you do not trust and tighten security for those sites. For example, you might want to prevent a particular site from automatically installing and running programs on your computer.

You can add sites to the Local, Trusted, and Restricted sites lists. To add a site to a list, open the **View** or **Tools** menu, select **Internet Options,** and click the **Security** tab. Click the desired zone at the top of the dialog box, as shown in Figure 23.3, or open the **Zone** drop-down list and choose the desired zone. Click the **Add Sites** or **Sites** button and enter the desired addresses. Click **OK** as needed to save your changes and close the dialog boxes.

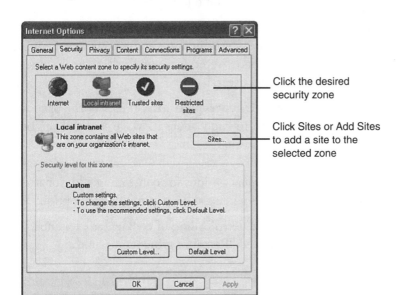

Click the desired security zone

Click Sites or Add Sites to add a site to the selected zone

Figure 23.3

You can add sites to the Local, Trusted Sites, or Restricted Sites lists.

To specify a security level for a zone, open the **View** or **Tools** menu, select **Internet Options,** and click the **Security** tab. Click the desired zone at the top of the dialog box or open the **Zone** drop-down list and select the zone whose security level you want to change. Click the **Custom Level** button and then enter your preferences. You can enter individual settings to specify the type of content you want Internet Explorer to be able to download or you can open the Reset To list and choose the desired security level: High, Medium, Medium-Low, or Low.

Configuring Security Settings in Netscape Navigator

Netscape Navigator stores its security settings in two places. To enter security settings for submitting information securely on the web, open the **Edit** menu, click **Preferences,** double-click **Privacy and Security,** and select **SSL.** You then can select any of the following options to activate or deactivate them, as shown Figure 23.4:

- ◆ **Loading a Page That Supports Encryption.** Displays a warning whenever you view a web page that complies with the latest security standards. Personally, I prefer to have this option turned off. Look to the padlock icon to determine whether you are at a secure site.

- ◆ **Leaving a Page That Supports Encryption.** This is another warning you can deactivate. If you're leaving, why do you care whether it's secure?

- ◆ **Loading a Page That Uses Low-Grade Encryption.** Displays a warning before loading any page that uses a less secure encryption technology than is currently recommended. This option is a good one to check.

- ◆ **Sending Form Data from an Unencrypted Page to an Encrypted Page.** This is the option that makes the security warning pop up on your screen all the time. If you don't trust yourself, leave it activated, but you'll get a warning message every time you perform an Internet search.

- ◆ **Viewing a Page with an Encrypted/Unencrypted Mix.** If part of the page is secure and another part isn't, you want to know about it. Make sure this option is on.

Under Privacy & Security are several additional options for controlling additional security features. The following list provides a general description of each option:

- ◆ **Cookies** lets you disable the automatic downloading of cookies, as explained later in this chapter in the section named "Remaining Incognito on the Internet."

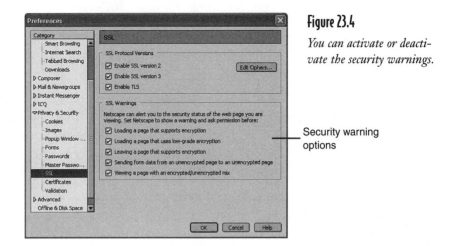

Figure 23.4

You can activate or deactivate the security warnings.

Security warning options

◆ **Images** enables you to turn off automatic downloading of images, which you may wish to do if you have a slow Internet connection and want only the web page text to be displayed. This can significantly increase the speed at which pages load.

◆ **Popup Window** is a very useful tool for preventing most popup advertisements from appearing on your computer.

◆ **Forms** provides a setting that tells Navigator to save information you have entered on forms to your computer's hard disk, so you can fill out forms more quickly next time.

◆ **Passwords** provides settings that enable Navigator to save a password you enter at a site so you do not need to enter the password the next time you visit the site.

◆ **Master Passwords** enables you to password-protect the passwords that Netscape saves so that they cannot be used by unauthorized users. You can specify how often you want Navigator to prompt you to enter the master password.

◆ **Certificates** provides options for managing the site certificates you use to identify yourself to sites and that sites use to identify themselves to you.

◆ **Validation** provides options for enabling Navigator to verify site certificates.

Preventing Viruses from Entering Your System

Picking up a virus on the Internet is like coming home from vacation with some exotic illness. You were having so much fun; how could this happen? And how can you prevent it from happening again? First, follow a few simple rules:

◆ Download programs only from reputable and known sites. If you know the company that created the program, go to its web page or FTP server and download the file from there. Most reputable sites regularly scan their systems to detect and eliminate viruses.

◆ Don't accept copies of a program from another person (for example, by e-mail). Although the program might not have contained a virus when the other person downloaded it, the other person's computer could have a virus that infected the program. Ask the person where he or she got the file and then download the file from its original location yourself.

◆ If your web browser displays a message indicating that a program it is being asked to download is unsigned or from a questionable source, click the button to cancel the download.

◆ If you receive a file attachment from someone you don't know or from a questionable source, delete the attachment. Do *not* open it.

◆ Keep an anti-virus program running at all times. Anti-virus programs scan any incoming program files for viruses and scan your computer on a regular basis to identify viruses before they can damage any files. Two of the best antivirus programs on the market are McAfee VirusScan and Symantec's Norton AntiVirus. You can download a trial version of McAfee VirusScan at www.nai.com. Go to www.symantec.com for details about Norton AntiVirus.

Whoa!

If you receive e-mail you'll eventually receive virus warnings indicating that a nasty new virus is infecting thousands of computers all over the world and wiping out hard drives. Most of these warnings are hoaxes, and you should not forward the message as it instructs you to do. Check the source of the hoax first. If the message says that IBM just discovered the virus, check out IBM's website. Another good place to verify the accuracy of a virus warning is McAfee's Virus Hoax list at vil.mcafee.com/hoax.asp.

Keeping Hackers at Bay with a Firewall

Whenever you are connected to the Internet, you run the risk of having a mischievous hacker break into your system, steal information, and even damage some files.

Hackers rarely break into home PCs that are connected to the Internet by a standard modem, because you typically hang up a modem when you're done working. If you have a DSL or cable modem connection, which keeps your computer connected to the Internet at all times, you should consider installing a *firewall* to prevent unauthorized access to your system.

A *firewall* typically functions in one of two ways: It filters incoming and outgoing data to block anything that seems suspicious or it uses a *proxy server* between you and your Internet service provider to hide your computer, making it much more difficult for a hacker to find it.

Windows XP comes with its own firewall. Windows XP's Internet Connection Firewall (ICF) keeps track of every request for data your computer makes, and then checks incoming traffic to ensure that your computer initiated the transaction. If an outside source attempts to initiate communications, ICF drops the connection. Unlike many firewalls that display warnings of potential security breaches, ICF works in the background, automatically blocking unauthorized access. To turn on ICF, take the following steps:

1. Click the **Start** button and click **My Network Places.** The My Network Places window opens.

2. On the left side of the window, below Network Tasks, click **View network connections.** The My Network Places window displays icons for all of your computer's modem and network connections.

3. Right-click the icon for the network card or modem your computer uses to connect to the Internet, and then click **Properties.** The Properties dialog box for the selected connection opens.

4. Click the **Advanced** tab.

5. Click **Protect my computer or network by limiting or preventing access to this computer from the Internet** to place a check in its check box, as shown in Figure 23.5.

6. Click **OK.**

Panic Attack
If you don't have Windows XP, you can download shareware versions of firewall software at any of the popular Internet add-on sites such as cws.internet.com, www.tucows.com, or download.cnet.com.

Figure 23.5

Enable the Windows XP Internet Connection Firewall.

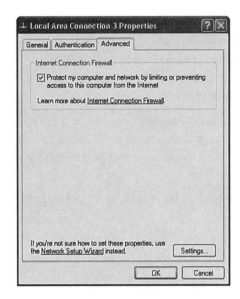

Remaining Incognito on the Internet

When you visit some sites on the Internet, the site automatically pins an identification badge, called a *cookie*, on your computer. This relatively small file can follow you on your journey, keeping track of the pages you visit, the information you enter, the products you order, and any other information it wants to gather concerning your activity on the Internet. Most cookies are designed to make your web browsing experience more productive and enjoyable. Without cookies, you wouldn't be able to shop on the Internet and have the remote web server keep track of your order or remember your password. However, if you are concerned that cookies threaten your privacy, you can choose to disable them in your web browser or have a warning appear whenever a site tries to send you a cookie.

To change your cookie settings in Internet Explorer, open the **View** or **Tools** menu, click **Internet Options,** and click the **Privacy** tab. Click the **Advanced** button, make sure **Override Automatic Cookie Handling** is checked, and then enter your preferences for first-party and third-party cookies, as shown in Figure 23.6: **Accept** (accept all cookies), **Block** (accept no cookies), or **Prompt** (whenever a site tries to send you a cookie).

Inside Tip

For additional details about cookies, search your browser's help system for "cookie" and go to www.cookiecentral.com.

To check and adjust your cookie settings in Netscape Navigator, open the **Edit** menu and click **Preferences.** Double-click **Privacy & Security,** in the pane on the left and then click **Cookies** and select the desired option: **Disable cookies** (accept no cookies), **Enable cookies for the originating web site only** (allow only the website that gave you the cookie to track it), **Enable cookies based on privacy settings** (accept cookies that meet specified guidelines), or **Enable all cookies** (accept all cookies).

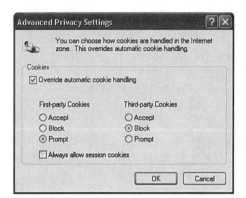

Figure 23.6

Enter your cookie preferences in Internet Explorer.

The Least You Need to Know

◆ Before you unleash your kids on the Internet, lay down the rules you want them to follow.

◆ The most essential rule kids must follow is to never give out any personal or sensitive information, including passwords, phone numbers, addresses, credit card numbers, or even the name of the school they attend.

◆ No censor program can replace the supervision of a loving, caring parent.

◆ If you cannot supervise your kids every minute they're on the Internet (what parent can?), install Cyber Patrol or CYBERsitter and learn how to use it.

◆ To protect your computer against viruses, purchase and install a good anti-virus program and keep it updated with the latest virus definitions.

◆ To prevent unauthorized access to your computer, enable the Windows firewall or install third-party firewall software on your computer.

Part 5

Going Digital with Music, Photos, and Video

Although you may think that your food processor is the most versatile tool in your home, your computer has it beat. With the right software and accessories, your computer can moonlight as a powerful jukebox, photo lab, and video studio.

The chapters in this part introduce you to the most popular home-based computer gadgets. Here, you learn how to download and play music clips from the Internet, burn your own custom music CDs, transfer music to a portable MP3 player, snap and print photos, and edit your home movies. This part takes you from tech weenie to tech wizard in just a few short chapters.

Chapter 24

Playing Digital Music Clips

In This Chapter

+ Playing your favorite audio CD tracks on your computer

+ Finding and installing a free MP3 audio player

+ Copying and playing MP3 audio clips from the web

+ Copying MP3 audio clips to a portable MP3 player

+ Burning your own audio CDs

If you thought the move from LPs to CDs was impressive, you're going to love the latest in audio technology. With your computer and a *CD drive*, a sound card, and a decent set of speakers, you can create your own computerized jukebox that can play hundreds of your favorite songs. Add an Internet connection, and you can download free MP3 music clips to add to your collection. With a portable MP3 player, you can take your favorite tunes wherever you go. And if you have a CD-R or CD-RW drive, you can even "burn" your own custom CDs and play them on any CD player! This chapter steps you through the process of building your own "recording studio" and points out the best places on the web to get free MP3 players and music clips.

Understanding CD and MP3 Audio Basics

To understand CD and MP3 audio basics, you must first know that standard audio CD players and computers differ in how they store and play audio clips. On an audio CD, data is stored in a format called "Red Book," which has been the standard format for more than 20 years. Computers, on the other hand, store audio data in various formats, the most popular of which is MP3, a format that compresses an audio clip to about one twelfth its size with an imperceptible loss of quality. MP3 lets users download audio clips more quickly over the Internet and store them in less space on their computers' hard drives.

The only trouble is that a standard audio CD player cannot play MP3 files, and a computer cannot process audio data stored on an audio CD in the Red Book format (although all newer CD-ROM drives can play audio CDs through an earphone jack or through your computer's sound card). Fortunately, the following specialized programs can handle the required format conversions for you:

- **MP3 player.** An MP3 player lets your computer play MP3 audio clips. You can copy MP3 clips from websites or convert audio clips from your CDs into MP3 files with a CD *ripper*, described next. An MP3 player converts MP3 files into a standard digital audio format (typically a WAV format) that your computer can play through its sound card and speakers.

- **CD ripper.** A CD ripper converts audio clips from a CD into the MP3 format or another format that a computer equipped with the required software can play. A CD ripper is commonly called a *jukebox*, because it stores all the clips you record and lets you play each clip simply by selecting it from a list.

- **CD burner.** A CD burner utility converts MP3 audio clips stored on your computer into the standard Red Book format used to store audio data on CDs and controls the process of recording the audio clips to the recordable CD. You can then play the CD in a standard audio CD player. (Some newer audio CD players can play MP3 files stored on CDs, making it unnecessary to convert MP3 clips into the Red Book format before burning them on a CD. This allows you to store more than 10 times as much music per CD.)

Before you run out and buy a case of CD-R or *CD-RW discs*, you should understand the difference between the two types of discs. CD-R discs let you write to the disc only once; you can't erase the data on a CD-R disc and then record over it. With a CD-RW disc, you can record data to the disc, erase the data, and write new data to the disc. This makes CD-RW discs an excellent storage medium for backing up files. However, CD-RW discs are typically less reflective than CD-R discs, making them a poor choice for recording audio CDs. Some audio CD players have a tough time reading a CD-RW disc. When you're burning audio CDs, stick with CD-R discs.

> **Tech Term**
>
> The surface of a compact disc has smooth, reflective areas and pits or dyed areas that refract rather than reflect light. A **CD drive** or player reads data from a disc by bouncing a laser beam off the surface of the disc and interpreting differences in the intensity of the returning beam. On **CD-RW discs,** the contrast between the reflected areas and the nonreflective dyed areas is less than the contrast found on CD-R discs.

Although MP3 gets all the press, you'll encounter many other audio formats on the web. Some audio formats are designed specifically for *streaming audio;* that is, they are designed to start playing an audio clip as soon as your computer starts receiving it. Streaming audio, such as Real-Audio, is commonly used for online radio stations and "live" broadcasts. Liquid Audio is a newer audio format that's designed to prevent unauthorized copying and distribution of audio clips. If you encounter an audio clip you want to hear in the Liquid Audio format, you might need to download a new audio player.

> **Inside Tip**
>
> Most multimedia compression schemes compress data by stripping redundant data and data that human beings cannot perceive. In the case of graphics, a compression program might strip slight variations in color or reduce the resolution. Audio compression schemes strip audio signals that are outside the range of human hearing.

Using Your Computer as a Jukebox

If you insert an audio CD into your computer's CD-ROM drive, Windows should display the Audio CD dialog box, prompting you to specify which action you want Windows to perform: **Play Audio CD** (with Windows Media Player), **Copy Music from CD** (with Windows Media Player), **Open Folder to View Files** (in Windows Explorer), or perform another action with some other audio program that's installed on your computer. To start listening to the CD, click one of the options for playing it and then click **OK.** (The audio CD might begin to play automatically when you insert the CD, depending on how your system is configured.)

Playing an audio CD makes your computer little more than an overpriced audio CD player. To make your computer a superior overpriced CD player, record your favorite audio clips to your computer's hard drive as MP3 files. This provides you with a virtual jukebox, which you can program to play only the songs you want to hear in the order in which you want to hear them.

Inside Tip

To check out another popular virtual jukebox, go to www. realaudio.com and click the link for downloading the free realONE player. The basic, free version lets you record audio clips from CDs to your hard drive and create custom playlists. With the Plus! version ($19.99), you can record your playlist to a CD—assuming, of course, that you have a CD-R or CD-RW drive.

Media Player, included as part of Windows Me and XP, not only plays audio CDs but also can copy entire CDs or selected tracks to your computer's hard drive to create custom *playlists*. To see if Media Player is installed on your computer, check the Windows **Start, Programs** menu option, the **Start, Programs, Accessories, Entertainment** option, or the **Start, All Programs, Accessories, Entertainment** option. If Media Player is not installed, you can install it from the Windows installation CD or, if you have a version of Windows prior to Windows Me (and you have an Internet connection), pick up a copy of Windows Media Player at www. microsoft.com/windows/windowsmedia/en/ and install it.

Creating a Custom Playlist with Windows Media Player

Using Windows Media Player, take the following steps to record your favorite CD tracks to your computer's hard drive and create a custom playlist:

1. Run the Windows Media Player by selecting **Start, Programs, Windows Media Player** or **Start, Programs, Accessories, Entertainment, Windows Media Player,** or **Start, All Programs, Accessories, Entertainment, Windows Media Player.**

2. Insert a CD that has one or more tracks you want to record into your computer's CD player. (Your computer might have a CD player other than Media Player that runs when you insert an audio CD. At this point, you can either use the player that appears or close the player and proceed with these steps.)

3. In Media Player, click the **CD Audio** or **Copy from CD** button. After some time, Windows displays a list of the tracks stored on the CD, as shown in Figure 24.1.

Click Copy Music to copy the selected tracks to the media library

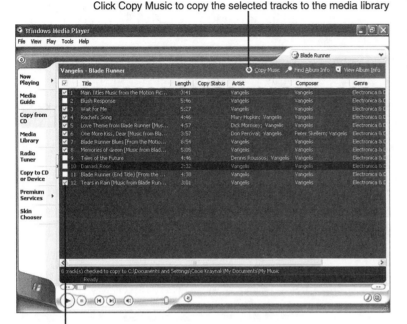

A check mark indicates that the track is selected for recording

Figure 24.1

Windows Media Player makes it easy to copy individual tracks from a CD.

4. If the track names do not appear, and you have an Internet connection, click **Get Names** or **Find Album Info** above the track list to obtain the track names and other information from the web. (Assuming that Media Player finds the information for the right CD, click **Confirm** or **Finish** to copy the information.)

Whoa!

If the track names still do not appear, manually label each track. Click the track title to select it, click it again to highlight the track name, and then type the track name. (If the tracks have no names, identifying the tracks later is nearly impossible.) You can enter artist names for each track as well. To enter the same artist for every track, click the first track, **Shift+click** the last track, right-click **Unknown Artist,** and click **Edit.**

5. Click the check box next to each track you do *not* want to record to remove the check mark from the box.

6. Click the **Copy Music** button. Media Player displays the progress of the copy operation next to each track as it records the track.

7. Repeat steps 2 through 6 for each CD that has one or more tracks you want to record.

8. Click **Media Library** (in the bar on the left) so that you can create a custom playlist. (If a dialog box pops up asking if you want to search for media on your computer, click **No** or **Cancel.**)

9. Click the **New Playlist** button or click **Playlists, New Playlist.** The New Playlist dialog box appears, prompting you to type a name for the playlist.

10. Type a descriptive name for the playlist, such as Exercise Warmup, and click **OK.** A new folder with the name you typed appears below **My Playlists.**

11. If a plus sign appears next to **Album,** click the plus sign to display a list of CDs from which you recorded clips.

12. Click the icon for the CD that has the song you want to add to your playlist. The tracks you recorded from the CD appear in the window on the right.

13. Drag the desired track over the icon for the playlist you created, and then release the mouse button, as shown in Figure 24.2. The track is added to your playlist.

Select the tracks you want to add to your playlist

Figure 24.2

Drag and drop the audio tracks you recorded to your playlist.

Drag the tracks and drop them on the icon for your playlist

14. Repeat steps 12 and 13 for the remaining tracks you want to add to your playlist.

15. To display your playlist, click its icon.

16. To move a song up or down on the playlist, click its name and then drag it up or down in the list to the desired location and release the mouse button.

17. To play your clips, click the clip you want to start playing and then click Media Player's **Play** button (near the bottom of the window). Media Player plays the selected song and then the remaining songs in your playlist.

Changing Media Player's Skin

Many cell phones, handheld computers, and other trendy electronic devices now come with thin, detachable covers called *skins*. Likewise, most onscreen MP3 players come with their own virtual skins. You simply pick the desired skin from a list to personalize the appearance of your player.

To change skins in Media Player, click the **Skin Chooser** button, as shown in Figure 24.3, and then click the name of a skin to preview it. When you find a skin you like, click its name and then click the **Apply Skin** button.

Inside Tip _____

Windows Media Player isn't the only CD player/ripper on the market. Check out these other players on the web: realONE player (www.real. com/jukebox), Audiograbber (www.audiograbber.com-us. net/), and AudioCatalyst (www.xingtech.com/mp3/ audiocatalyst/).

Inside Tip _____

If you don't like the selection of skins, click the **More Skins** button (just to the right of **Apply Skin**). This connects you to Microsoft's website, where you can download additional skins.

Click Apply Skin to "dress" your player

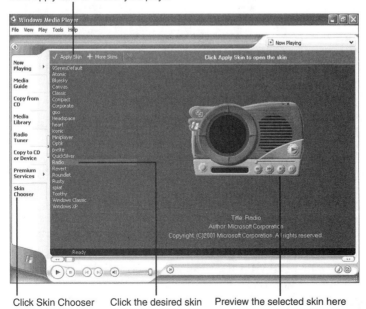

Figure 24.3

Give Media Player a new skin to completely redesign it.

Click Skin Chooser   Click the desired skin   Preview the selected skin here

I Want My MP3: Downloading Music Clips from the Web

You've probably heard of a company called Napster, which allowed users to freely share their MP3 audio recordings over the Internet. You also might have heard that the courts ruled against Napster and slapped some serious restrictions on this free music distribution center. Apparently, a few musicians were upset that they weren't getting paid for their work.

> **Panic Attack**
>
> Although MP3 audio clips are smaller than their audio CD counterparts, they're still fairly large. A 4-minute music clip can be more than 4 megabytes, which can take nearly a half-hour to download over a 28.8Kbps modem connection. If you plan to download MP3s on a regular basis, you should have a 56Kbps modem or faster connection.

At any rate, many legal and illegal MP3 distribution sites remain up and running. Some provide free audio-clip swapping with other users. Some charge a subscription fee to download a certain number of recordings per month. Others charge per recording. And some allow you to download some free tracks or samples of tracks in the hope that you'll purchase a CD online.

The following sections take you on a brief tour of MP3 sites and show you how to download and play MP3 clips using Internet Explorer and Windows Media Player. You also learn how to copy your clips to a portable MP3 player to take them with you wherever you go.

Finding and Downloading Music Clips

Downloading any file is pretty easy. You click a link and follow the onscreen instructions to tell your browser where to save the file. However, before you can download MP3 clips, you have to find some tunes that are worth downloading.

The best way to track down a specific tune is to use an MP3 search tool on the web. Here are some sites to get you started:

- **AudioGalaxy at www.audiogalaxy.com.** This site features an MP3 search tool that scans the Internet for free MP3 clips.

- **Kazaa at www.kazaa.com.** Kazaa is the equivalent of Napster. At this site, you can download the Kazaa Media Desktop, a peer-to-peer file-sharing program that enables you to swap MP3 clips and other files with users around the world. Keep in mind that peer-to-peer MP3 file swapping of copyrighted material is considered illegal in some countries.

- **Morpheus at www.morpheus.com.** Morpheus is another site that provides a peer-to-peer file-sharing program. You can search for your favorite artists and tracks and then copy them to your computer.

- **MP3Board at www.mp3board.com.** MP3 Board features an MP3 search tool that can help you track down MP3 clips by artist or song title. Unfortunately, most of the search results turn up commercial sites that do not offer free MP3 clips.

- **Audiofind at www.audiofind.com.** Audiofind searches newsgroups for posted MP3 clips posted in newsgroups. You need to use a newsgroup reader, such as Outlook Express, to connect to the newsgroup and download the clip.

- **MP3Search at www.mp3search.nu.** MP3 Search features a browse-able, search-able directory of MP3 clips. You can browse by genre or artist or search for a specific artist or track.

If you're just browsing, or you're looking for a more commercial site where you can download clips legally, check out the following MP3 distribution centers on the web:

- **MP3.com at www.mp3.com.** This site has one of the most complete collections of MP3 audio clips on the web, along with links for free MP3 players, rippers, portable players, and other MP3 gear. You can spend days at this site.

- **MusicMatch at www.musicmatch.com.** MusicMatch is one of the most popular online music sites, featuring Internet radio stations. MusicMatch does not offer downloadable MP3 clips that you can burn to CDs or transfer to an MP3 player, but it does offer customizable music stations, so you can listen to the tunes and artists you most enjoy.

- **MusicNow at www.musicnow.com.** Like MusicMatch, MusicNow features on-demand Internet radio and customizable, commercial-free listening for about $5 per month. However, MusicNow also features a Full Access service (for about $10 per month), which allows you to download up to 100 singles per month that can be stored on your computer, burned to CDs, and transferred to your MP3 player.

- **Press*play* at www.pressplay.com.** Backed by most companies in the music industry, press*play* features three services: Unlimited, for $9.95 per month allows you to listen to any and all tracks available at the site, but you cannot burn tracks to CDs or transfer them to an MP3 player; Unlimited Plus, for $17.95 per month allows you to listen to any and all tracks and copy 10 tracks per month for transfer to CDs or MP3 players; and Annual Plus, for $179.40 per year ($14.95 per month) provides the same rights as Unlimited Plus, but you can download 120 clips to transfer to CDs or an MP3 player at any time during the year.

◆ **iTunes Music Store at www.apple.com/music/store/.** This is the home of one of the most popular, legal music stores on the Internet. Here, you can listen to your favorite tunes, preview recent releases, and purchase and download quality clips online. iTunes lets you purchase singles (for about $1 per tune), so you don't need to shell out $15 to $20 for an entire CD if you like only one track on the CD.

◆ **MusicNet on AOL at www.musicnet.com.** MusicNet on AOL is comparable to press*play*, offering unlimited listening for about $9 per month and allowing you to copy 10 clips for CD burning or transfer to an MP3 player. You must be a member of America Online. You can also access a MusicNet service and RealNetworks (www.real.com).

◆ **Amazon at www.amazon.com.** This site is the world's largest online bookstore but also distributes MP3 audio clips. After pulling up Amazon's home page, click the **Music** link, and then click **Free Downloads** in the banner at the top of the Music page.

◆ **Liquid.com at store.liquid.com.** This site features an excellent collection of popular tracks. Each single costs between one and two bucks to download. Complete albums cost about ten bucks.

◆ **EMusic.com at www.emusic.com.** For about $120 per year, EMusic offers unlimited downloads from a collection of more than 250,000 MP3 clips. (The cost is about $15 per month if you opt for the 3-month subscription.) EMusic does not restrict your personal use of the clip; you can listen to it on your computer, copy it to your MP3 player, or burn it to a CD. EMusic does offer a free trial, so it's worth checking out.

Most of these sites feature *tethered downloads*, meaning that you need a special player to play the clips on your computer. The audio clips are not stored in MP3 format or any other format that can be burned to CDs or transferred to a portable MP3 player. The services typically charge extra for *portable* audio clips that can be burned to CDs or copied to an MP3 player. (For more MP3 download sites, use your favorite web search tool to search for "mp3" or "free mp3" or "free mp3 download.")

CAUTION

Whoa!

At this point, you might be wondering if it's legal to copy commercial audio clips. If you're copying tracks from CDs you purchased for your own personal use, you're not breaking any laws. You cannot copy tracks for distribution to your friends and family or to strangers over the Internet. Of course, if the artist gives permission to freely copy and distribute his or her music, you're safe. (Some bands encourage music sharing to increase their fan base.)

Playing Your Clips

As soon as you find a clip you want to download, simply click its link to play it. After your computer is finished downloading the clip, it should run your MP3 player, which typically starts playing the clip. If the clip doesn't start, click the **Play** button.

If your MP3 player does not start automatically, it might not have a *file association* with MP3 files. Here's what you do to check the MP3 file association and change it, if necessary:

1. Run **My Computer.**

2. Open the **Tools** menu and click **Folder Options.**

3. Click the **File Types** tab to view a list of file types and the programs associated with them.

4. Scroll down the **Registered file types** list and click **MP3.** (If MP3 is not in the list, click the **New** button, type mp3, and click **OK.**) The **Details** box near the bottom of the dialog box displays the icon for the program set up to play MP3 files.

5. To associate a different player with MP3 files, click the **Change** button to display a list of programs installed on your system, and continue with step 6. Otherwise, click **OK** and skip the next step; you're done.

6. Click the program you want to use to play MP3 clips, as shown in Figure 24.4, and then click **OK.**

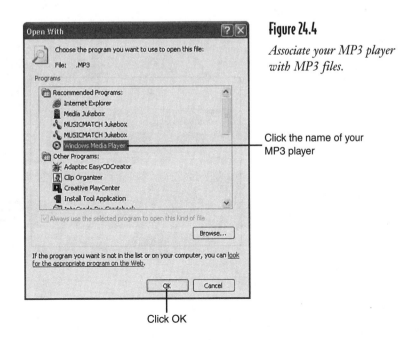

Figure 24.4

Associate your MP3 player with MP3 files.

Click the name of your MP3 player

Click OK

Copying MP3 Clips to a Portable MP3 Player

Building a huge music library on your computer is cool, but a computer is a bit too bulky to replace your Walkman. How do you take your music collection, or at least a portion of it, on the road? The easiest and lightest way is to purchase a portable MP3 player. Portable MP3 players typically come equipped with enough storage to hold one to four CD's worth of music. Typically, you can rip tracks from CDs or download them from various sources on the Internet and then transfer (copy) them to your MP3 player.

If you're lucky, your MP3 player came with its own software for ripping tracks from CDs and copying them to your MP3 player. Unfortunately, many MP3 players come with the software to transfer files to the MP3 player, but they do not include a ripper, so you end up having to use two separate programs to get the job done. I use Music-Match to rip the tracks from CDs and then use my MP3 player's software, MPIO Manager, to copy the MP3 files to my player. As you can see in Figure 24.5, the process of copying MP3 files is similar to the process for copying files in My Computer or Windows Explorer: you select the files you want to copy and then drag them to the window that displays the contents of your MP3 player. (Of course, you must connect your MP3 player to your computer before you can copy files to it.)

Drag the MP3 clips to the window that represents your MP3 player

Figure 24.5

You can copy files from your computer to your portable MP3 player using a Windows Explorer-like window.

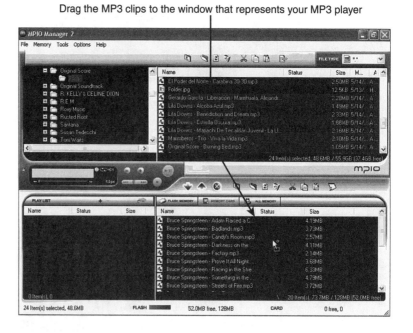

An alternative is to use Media Player to perform both jobs. However, Media Player rips tracks from CDs and stores them in the WMA (Windows Media Audio) format, which many portable MP3 players cannot play. In order to rip tracks from a CD and store them as MP3 files, you must download and install a plug-in that adds this capability to Media Player. For $14.95, you can obtain a Windows Media Player MP3 encoder add-on called Sonic CinePlayer MP3 Creation Pack from www.cineplayer. com. This program enables Media Player to copy and store CD audio tracks as MP3 files. Another problem with Media Player is that it might not support your MP3 player, in which case, you need to check out the website of your MP3 player's manufacturer to determine if the manufacturer offers an add-on for Media Player. In short, it's typically easier to use two programs: a ripper that stores tracks in the MP3 format and a program for transferring ripped tracks to your portable MP3 player.

If you installed an MP3 encoder add-on for Media Player and Media Player supports your MP3 player (or you found and installed the required add-on), take the following steps to use Media Player to copy MP3 clips to your MP3 player:

1. Connect your portable MP3 player to your computer as instructed in the portable MP3 player's documentation and turn it on. (If you connect the device using a USB cable, you need not turn off your computer to make the connection; otherwise, you might need to shut down the computer.)

2. Run the Windows Media Player as explained earlier in this chapter.

3. Click **Copy to CD or Device** (in the bar on the left). Two panes appear to the right of the command bar: the pane on the left displays the contents of the Media Library, and the pane on the right displays any tracks currently on the selected CD or device.

4. Open the drop-down list that's above the pane on the right and select your MP3 player or the drive letter that your MP3 player represents. (If your MP3 player or a drive letter for it does not appear, your MP3 player may not be supported by Windows Media Player.)

5. In the pane on the left, be sure there is a check mark next to each audio clip you want to copy to your portable MP3 player.

6. Click the **Copy Music** or **Copy** button (near the top of the window).

7. Repeat steps 3 through 6 to copy additional audio clips to your portable player.

8. Exit Media Player and disconnect your portable MP3 player as instructed in its documentation.

Burning Your Own Audio CDs

Ever since companies placed the power of recording technology in the hands of the people, people have copied albums, CDs, audiotapes, TV shows, movies, and anything else they can get their hands on. CDs are no exception. As soon as audio CD burners hit the market, people started their own bootleg operations, churning out free CDs for themselves, their friends, and their family.

Some of this copying is acceptable. For instance, if you purchased the entire collection of Beatles CDs and you want to create your own "favorites" CD to play in your car, you won't be prosecuted for copying songs you paid for to another disc for your own use. However, if you copy your entire collection to give as Christmas gifts, you're crossing the line.

Be that as it may, the technology is available for copying CDs and for transferring your collection of MP3s (however you obtained it) to CDs, and I'll show you how to do it. I'll leave the legal and ethical decisions up to you, the courts, and the music industry.

Duplicating CDs

If your computer is equipped with a CD-R or CD-RW drive and a program for copying CDs, you can duplicate your audio CDs. Most computers that come with CD-R or CD-RW drives have a program for copying CDs. If you don't have a CD copy program, check out Roxio's Easy CD Creator at www.roxio.com. At $79.95, it's a little pricey, but Easy CD Creator can help you make the most of your CD-R or CD-RW drive. It includes features for backing up your computer's hard drive to CDs, recording video clips to CDs, transferring MP3 clips to CDs, and much more.

Computer Cheat

Although Windows Media Player features no command for copying directly from an audio CD to a blank CD-R or CD-RW, you can copy all the songs from the CD, save them in a separate playlist, and then copy the playlist to a CD. See the next section for details.

Figure 24.6 shows just how easy it is to duplicate a CD with Easy CD Creator. You simply insert the CD you want to copy, run Easy CD Creator, and click the **Copy** button. Easy CD Creator copies everything on the CD and then displays a dialog box telling you to insert a blank CD-R or CD-RW disc. After you insert the disc, Easy CD Creator transfers everything it copied from the original disc to the blank disc.

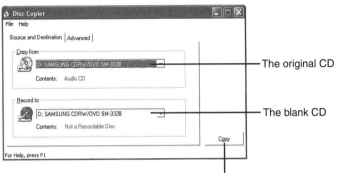

The original CD

The blank CD

Click the Copy button to start the operation

Figure 24.6

Roxio's Easy CD Creator can copy CDs as easily as Windows can copy floppy disks.

Recording a Custom Mix to a CD

Besides the Counting Crows' *August and Everything After* and Tom Waits' *Swordfish Trombones,* I haven't encountered a CD that contains more than three songs I like. Fortunately, with a CD-R or CD-RW drive and the right program, you can pull one or more of your favorite songs off each CD to create and record your own custom mix to a blank CD. You can even add to the mix MP3 clips you downloaded from the Internet.

Again, several programs on the market let you copy tracks from one CD to another and burn MP3 clips to CDs, but Roxio's Easy CD Creator is one of the cleanest tools for the job. As shown in Figure 24.7, Easy CD Creator makes recording tracks as easy as copying files in Windows Explorer.

Click to copy selected track to playlist

Click the CD-ROM drive or the folder in which your MP3 clips are stored

Select the desired destination

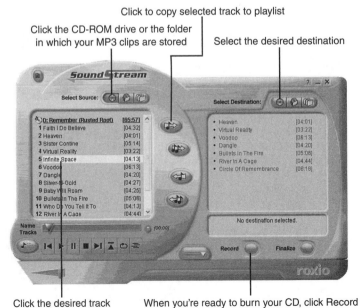

Figure 24.7

Roxio's Easy CD Creator can burn MP3 clips and CD tracks to a blank CD.

Click the desired track

When you're ready to burn your CD, click Record

After you click the button to create your CD, the program displays onscreen instructions telling you which CDs to insert.

> **CAUTION**
>
> ## Whoa! _____
>
> If you insert a CD, and no CD title, artist name, or track names appear, check your CD player program for an option that enables you to download the information from the Internet; Easy CD Creator and Windows Media Player both offer this feature. If the information is unavailable, type it in yourself. Otherwise, you won't know which CD to insert during the copy operation, and you risk overwriting tracks with tracks of the same name.

If you didn't run out and buy Roxio's Easy CD Creator after reading about how wonderful it is, Windows Media Player can do a fine job of transferring tracks to a CD-R or CD-RW disc. First, record the desired tracks and copy them to a separate playlist, as explained earlier in this chapter. Then insert the disc, and click **Copy to CD or Device** (in the bar on the left). This displays a two-paned window, as shown in Figure 24.8. Open the drop-down list that's above the left pane and choose the desired playlist. Insert a recordable CD into your computer's recordable CD drive, and then open the list above the right pane and click the icon for your recordable CD drive. To start copying the playlist to the CD, click the **Copy** button (in the upper right corner of the window).

Figure 24.8

Windows Media Player can write the tracks in a playlist to a disc.

Click the playlist that has the tracks you want to record

Select your recordable CD drive

Click Copy

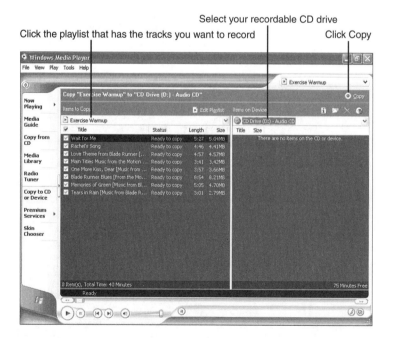

The Least You Need to Know

♦ To play an audio CD, insert it into your computer's CD-ROM drive, and then when a dialog box pops up asking what you want to do, click **Play Audio CD** and click the **OK** button.

♦ To copy tracks from the CD to the Windows Media Library, click **Copy from CD,** be sure a check mark appears next to only the tracks you want recorded, and then click the **Copy Music** button.

♦ To create a new playlist in Media Player, click the **Media Library** button and then click the **New playlist** button or open the **Playlists** menu and click **New Playlist.**

♦ Go to www.mp3.com for a wide selection of MP3 music clips and links to players, rippers, and MP3 gear.

♦ To take your tunes on the road, copy them to a portable MP3 player.

♦ You can use a CD burner program, such as Roxio's Easy CD Creator, to duplicate audio CDs or to copy MP3 clips to a blank CD to create your own mix.

Chapter 25

Buying and Using a Digital Camera

In This Chapter

- ◆ Choosing the right digital camera for your needs and budget
- ◆ Avoiding feature-starved digital cameras
- ◆ Generating your own photo prints for pennies per print
- ◆ Placing photos on your web pages
- ◆ Sending digital photos via e-mail
- ◆ Making your own photo album

Digital cameras are not practical. For $50, you can get a 35mm camera at Wal-Mart that's capable of taking better snapshots than a $300 digital camera. For another $80, you can get a color scanner that reproduces better digital images.

So why are so many people running out and buying digital cameras? I can think of several reasons. First, they're fun; take a digital camera to a party and you automatically become the center of attention. Second, they provide immediate gratification. Right after you take a picture, you can check out the results in the LCD display, plug your camera into a TV set and view the picture, or connect your camera to your computer and print the photo. You don't even have to wait for one-hour service. In addition, digital photography enables you to e-mail photos to your friends and relatives and post them on your website or blog.

In this chapter, you learn the basics of digital photography, including how to shop for a digital camera, take photographs, enhance your photographs with digital imaging software, print and e-mail photos, and even order prints online.

Inside Tip _____

Imagine a very portable, compact, 3-D scanner that looks like a 35mm camera—that's a digital camera. Like a scanner, a digital camera is built around a CCD (charge-coupled device). When you snap a picture, the shudder opens and bombards the CCD with light. The CCD converts the light into electrical impulses, which are then applied to a magnetic storage medium, such as a disk or memory card.

Smart Shopping for Digital Cameras

You can pick up a digital camera for around $100, but after the first few pictures, you'll realize why it was so cheap. Hundred dollar digital cameras produce low-resolution photographs, have no flash, store only a couple pictures, and can take forever to process a single snapshot.

But with all the digital cameras on the market, how can you compare cameras and prices? The following sections explain the most critical features of digital cameras and help you choose the right camera for your budget.

Finding the Right Price Range

Good digital cameras don't come cheap. At the low end, you can expect to pay $150 for the bare-bones basics. At the high end, you might need to consider taking out a second mortgage. In between those two extremes are some more realistic numbers. The following list runs through some price ranges and describes the features you can expect in each range:

- **$200 to $300:** 2.1 megapixel color camera, digital zoom, 8 to 16 megabyte memory card, LCD display may be included.

- **$350 to $600:** 3.1 megapixel color camera with optical and digital zoom, auto-focus, video, 32 megabyte memory card, LCD display, flash, and connectors for outputting to TV.

♦ **$800 to $1,000:** 4.1 megapixel color camera with optical and digital zoom, autofocus, video, 128 megabyte memory card (or a recordable compact disc), LCD display, flash, connectors for outputting to TV, detachable lens.

Of course, these prices are current as of the writing of this book (mid-2003). Expect the prices to dip considerably as the technology improves.

If all this talk of megapixels, digital zoom, LCD, and memory cards seems a little much, the following sections explain these features in greater detail.

Resolution

The most important consideration when purchasing a digital camera is resolution—the higher the resolution the better the image. Don't settle for less than 1600 × 1200 dpi (which is standard for a 2.0 megapixel camera); 1600 × 1200 dpi is optimal for 4 × 6-inch printouts. (Resolutions lower than 2.0 megapixels are acceptable only for e-mail and web pages.) For larger printouts (5 × 7-inch), look for resolutions of 2048 × 1536 dpi or higher—a 3.2 megapixel camera. If you plan on printing many 8 × 10-inch photos or doing professional photography, consider purchasing a 4 or 5 megapixel camera.

You should also determine if the camera uses a CCD or a low-cost, power-saving CMOS (Complementary Metal Oxide Semiconductor) sensor. Although CMOS sensors make the camera less expensive and increase the number of photos you can shoot on a single charge, they're not as light-sensitive as CCDs. A camera that uses a CMOS sensor may support the same resolutions as a camera using a standard CCD, but the image quality will be lower.

Colors

Most digital cameras support at least 24-bit color (more than 16 million colors), but you should check the color depth just to make sure. High-end cameras support 30- or 36-bit color, but if you're printing photos on a color inkjet printer or displaying them onscreen, 24-bit color is sufficient. In addition, the increased color depth increases the size of the files, reducing number of photos the camera can store. (Most high-end cameras enable you to crank down the color depth and resolution to reduce the size of the files.)

Storage Capacity

When you take pictures with a regular camera, you can pop rolls of film in and out as needed. Your digital camera should provide the same convenience or at least enough built-in memory to store 40 high-resolution photos. When considering storage, you have the following options:

◆ **Built-in storage.** Some cameras come with 8 to 16 megabytes of built-in storage, which can store a few high-resolution images if you're in a pinch or several low-resolution images if you're planning on e-mailing them or posting them on your website. Built-in memory is a good feature as long as the camera also has a slot for plugging in additional memory.

◆ **Swappable memory cards.** Most digital cameras store images on high-speed memory cards, ranging from 16MB up to 1GB. When a card is full, you pop it out and pop in a new one. After you download the images from the card to your PC, you can then erase the card and use it again. Memory cards vary considerably; CompactFlash cards are the most popular, but some cameras use Secure Digital/MultiMedia Card (SD/MMC), Sony Memory Sticks, xD-Picture Cards, or other removable storage cards.

◆ **Recordable CDs.** Sony manufactures a model that stores snapshots on miniature, recordable CDs. The CDs are only 6 centimeters across, but each one can store up to 156MB and plays in a standard computer CD-ROM drive. Unfortunately, the camera does not allow you to preview your shots before saving them to the disc, and the discs are not re-writable. Stick with the swappable memory cards.

◆ **Standard floppy disks.** A few cameras, such as Sony's Digital Mavica, can store images on standard 3.5-inch floppy disks, so you can easily share them with others; however, at 1.44MB per disk, you can store only a few high-quality images per disk.

Inside Tip

When considering storage, you should also think about compression, the capability of the camera to compress files and store more photos per megabyte of storage. Make sure the camera can store photos as JPEG files and that it allows you to choose the compression level. As digital camera technology advances, look for cameras that offer improved compression techniques, such as Wavelet compression.

Color photos for e-mailing or posting on websites are relatively small—less than 100 kilobytes. A high-quality image snapped with a 3.2 megapixel camera, on the other hand, is typically 1 megabyte or larger. If you want to store more images on the digital camera and you don't need photo-quality prints, consider lowering the resolution for your snapshots. However, keep in mind that if you shoot photos at low resolutions, you cannot increase the resolution of those photos later.

Focus

Focus options for digital cameras coincide with focus options available with standard 35mm cameras. For general snapshots, look for cameras that feature autofocus or zone focus. With zone focus cameras, you flip a switch to specify the distance your subject is from the camera (for example, 2 to 4 feet or infinity). High-end cameras offer manual focus and may offer manual aperture settings, as well.

Give some serious consideration to digital cameras that have a zoom lens option. If you need a close-up shot and you think you can just take the picture from 4 feet away and then use your imaging software to blow it up, think again. Whenever you enlarge a digital image, it becomes blurry and distorted. With a zoom lens (optical zoom), you can take a close-up photograph of just what you want and not have to worry about cropping and enlarging the image later. Many digital cameras offer two types of zoom: optical (which uses the lens to zoom in) and digital (which uses software to blow up the image). Make sure your camera features 3X or 4X optical zoom. You can probably live without digital zoom; you can always enlarge the photo later using digital imaging software.

Built-In Flash

Contrary to what some digital camera manufacturers seem to think, a built-in flash is not an optional feature. However, there are a few options to consider when comparing cameras that have a built-in flash:

- **Automatic.** The camera automatically senses the amount of light and turns on the flash when it's needed.

- **Always on.** Also called *fill* or *fill-in*, this mode is used for backlit scenes. The flash remains on until you turn it off.

- **Off.** For manual control of lighting (for example, when you're taking pictures in a museum where flash pictures are prohibited), you can turn off the flash so the camera doesn't automatically flash when you're taking pictures.

- **Red-eye correction.** Red-eye correction reduces the red-eye effect commonly seen in flash photos. The flash actually flashes a few times during the shot to reduce or eliminate the red-eye effect.

Battery Life

Several factors determine the number of pictures a digital camera can take with a new set of batteries. If the camera uses a flash or has an LCD viewer, battery life dips considerably. For example, many digital cameras can take up to 100 pictures with the LCD on or nearly 300 pictures with the LCD off. With that in mind, look for the following features to help conserve battery power:

♦ If LCD is included, make sure you can turn it off and use a standard view finder.

♦ Make sure you can turn off the flash. Even autoflash may use additional power.

♦ Look for cameras that have A/C adapters. Although you won't want to plug in the camera when you're taking pictures, the adapter can help conserve power when you're downloading images to your PC.

♦ Automatic power off when not in use. It's tough to remember to turn off your camera when you're taking photos. Make sure the camera can power itself down after 30 seconds or less of inactivity.

Convenient, Logical Controls

Before I went shopping for a digital camera, I read several reviews and settled on a specific model. This model had everything I wanted, 3.2 megapixels, 3X optical zoom, 128MB memory card, color LCD screen, autoflash, autofocus, and it was compact and light enough to carry around in my shirt pocket. I was about to order it online, but then I figured I should probably try using the camera before spending $500, so I took a trip to the local Best Buy store.

When I looked at the model I was about to purchase online, I couldn't figure out where the zoom in and zoom out buttons were or how to change any of the settings. The salesperson couldn't figure it out either. I looked at a few other cameras and found that some cameras had controls that were much more intuitive. I ended up purchasing a different model (a Nikon COOLPIX 3100) that had all the features I wanted, plus much easier controls. The moral of this story is "Try before you buy." A digital camera or other electronic device might look good on paper, but try to use it before you make a final decision.

Additional Features

Although the stock features are the most important, you should be aware of the modern conveniences some cameras offer. If you spend $700 on a camera and later realize that a countdown feature would have been nice, trying to unload that camera a month later when prices have dropped may be impossible. Before you make your final decision, check out the following options:

◆ **LCD viewer.** An LCD viewer can help you frame a picture. However, LCDs use up a lot of battery power. If you do purchase a camera with an LCD, make sure you can turn it off and that the camera has a standard "porthole" viewfinder you can look through.

◆ **Video clips.** Several models of digital cameras are capable of filming brief audio clips, as well as snapshots. Some can record audio along with the video, but most record only the video.

◆ **PC and TV interface.** Nine out of ten digital cameras come with a USB cable attachment for transferring images from the camera to a PC. Some cameras also come with cables for attaching the camera to a TV or VCR, so you can view your photos on TV and record them on tape.

◆ **Automatic timer.** If you want to be in the picture, get a camera with a countdown timer that can automatically snap the picture for you.

◆ **Photo delete.** Most cameras automatically delete images from the internal storage or PC card after you download the images to your PC. However, if you mess up a picture, it's nice to be able to delete it before you snap the next shot to free up storage space on the card.

◆ **TWAIN driver.** Virtually all scanners have TWAIN drivers, which allow you to scan images directly into documents, but few digital cameras offer TWAIN support. Although TWAIN support is not essential, it can come in handy, especially if you decide to use imaging software other than the stock programs that come bundled with the camera.

◆ **Voice annotations.** Several digital cameras allow you to capture short audio clips along with your photographs. If you're using the camera primarily for personal photographs, voice annotations can be a big plus.

Taking Pictures

Because digital cameras are modeled off of standard 35mm cameras, snapping a picture is easy. You just point and shoot. However, before you snap too many pictures, you should check the camera settings.

The procedure for checking the camera settings varies from one digital camera to another. Some cameras have two buttons: one for changing modes (such as flash, image quality, timer, and audio) and another for changing the mode settings. You change to the desired mode (for instance, Flash) and then press the other button to change the setting (for instance, Autoflash or Flash On). Digital cameras that have

LCDs typically use a menu system for changing settings. In addition, many cameras come with preprogrammed settings for specific environments; you simply flip a switch or turn a dial to pick the environment (beach, indoor party, night scene, museum, etc.), and then start snapping pictures—the camera adjusts all the settings for you. You can concentrate on centering your subject in the frame rather than worrying about aperture settings and shutter speeds. As you use your digital camera, always keep the following settings in mind:

◆ **Resolution.** To fit more pictures in storage, crank down the resolution setting. For higher-quality pictures or larger prints, choose a higher setting.

◆ **Flash.** In most cases, leave the flash setting at Auto. If you're taking all your pictures outside, turn off the flash. For backlit scenes, turn on the flash, if this option is available on your camera.

◆ **Audio.** If your camera supports audio input, turn on Audio, if desired. Keep in mind that audio recordings consume quite a bit of storage space.

Whoa!

As you snap pictures, keep track of the amount of storage remaining. Most digital cameras that have LCDs display the remaining space on the LCD or display a warning when you're running out of space. You can then insert a blank memory card or disc or delete photos from the memory card that is currently loaded. If your camera does not have an LCD for framing pictures, it may have a small LCD display that shows the number of pictures you've taken and the available storage.

Copying Pictures to Your PC

Digital cameras typically come with their own software that transfers the image files from the camera to your PC. In addition, the camera should include a cable for connecting to one of the ports on your PC (typically the USB port). Some digital cameras require a PC card reader. Other cameras come with their own docking stations; you simply insert the base of the camera into the docking station to connect it to the computer.

To transfer the images, connect the cable to your camera and to the specified port. Run the photo transfer utility and enter the command to retrieve the images. The program retrieves the images from the camera and displays them on screen (see Figure 25.1). You can then delete the images from the PC card or other storage medium.

Images retrieved from camera

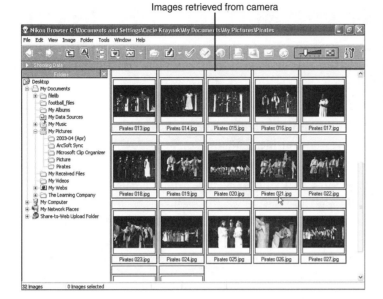

Figure 25.1

The photo transfer utility grabs the photos from the camera and displays them on screen.

Most photo transfer utilities double as photo editing tools. After your retrieve the images from your camera, you can adjust the brightness, color, and contrast of an image, crop it, flip it, resize it, and perform other digital imaging gymnastics. Figure 25.2 shows a sample photo displayed in PhotoImpression, the digital imaging software included with the Nikon COOLPIX 3100. If you purchased a special printer for printing photos, it may include its own digital image enhancing software, as well.

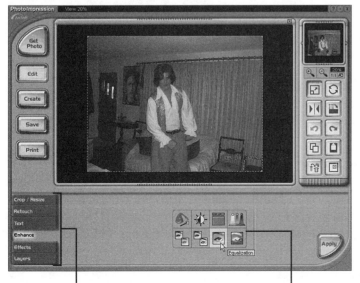

Figure 25.2

With digital image editing software, you can enhance your photos before printing them.

Choose an enhancement option   Use these specific tools to enhance the image

Inserting Digital Images into E-Mail and Web Pages

One of the best features of digital cameras is that they create graphic files that you can immediately use on web pages and in e-mail messages. You don't have to scan the picture after taking it, because it's already in a digital format.

To place a picture on your web page, insert it as you would insert any graphic (see Chapter 12 for more information). In addition, if your e-mail program supports HTML, you can insert images right inside the message area when composing an e-mail message. To insert an image into a message you are composing in Outlook Express, for example, you click in the message area, click the **Insert Picture** button, and then use the resulting dialog box to select the image, as shown in Figure 25.3.

Select the image you want to insert

Figure 25.3

You can insert digital photos right inside your e-mail messages.

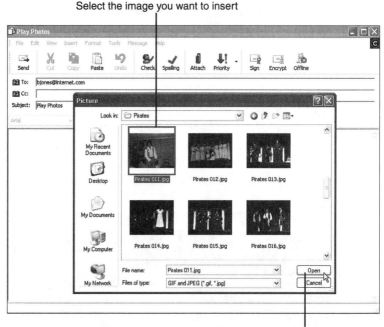

Click Open to the image in your message

The image management software included with many digital cameras features an option that can automatically prepare images for e-mail by reducing the resolution and file size of the image. This makes the image travel across the Internet much faster and take up less space on the recipient's computer. If you have software that offers this feature, use it instead of inserting high-resolution photos. The people on the receiving end sure will appreciate it.

Ordering Photo Prints Online

Many new inkjet printers can generate high-quality photo prints on special photo paper. In addition, manufacturers have developed fairly inexpensive printers designed specifically for printing photos. Hewlett Packard's Photosmart 230, for example, is designed to print exclusively 4 × 7-inch prints. It even has a slot into which you can plug the memory card from your camera, so you can copy pictures directly to the printer without having to connect the camera to your computer.

If you prefer to leave the photo printing up to the professionals, you can order prints online at any of several online film developers, such as Shutterfly (www.shutterfly.com) or Snapfish (www.snapfish.com).

The process is pretty simple. You can either e-mail your photo files to the online photo shop or use the online photo shop's software to upload your photo files to the service. For example, at Shutterfly, you simply drag your photos from your digital camera's program into a special Shutterfly window, as shown in the Figure 25.4. You then complete an order form, specifying the size and number of prints you want and your billing and delivery information. Shutterfly processes your pictures and then mails them to you.

Click Upload

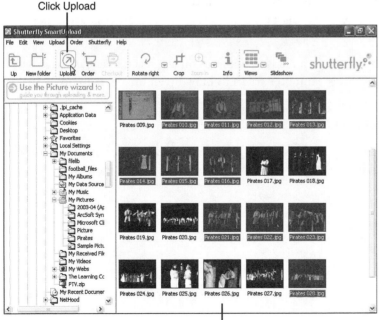

Figure 25.4

At Shutterfly, you drop off your "film" by selecting the photos you want developed and clicking the Upload button.

Select the photos you want printed

If you're in a big hurry and need one-hour processing (or faster), take your digital camera to a professional photo shop. Most photo shops have special printers that can transfer your digital photos into high-quality prints in a matter of minutes.

> **Inside Tip** _____
>
> To make the most of your digitized photos, check out Kodak's PictureCenter online at **picturecenter.kodak.com.** This service allows you to post photos, so your friends and relatives can check them out and order their own prints or special items, such as T-shirts or mugs. In addition, you can e-mail photos directly from the service. Kodak and America Online have set up a similar service called "You've Got Pictures" for AOL members.

The Least You Need to Know

- The single most important feature of a digital camera is the pixel rating. Don't settle for less than 2.1 megapixels.

- Most digital cameras have an LCD screen on the back that can help you frame your picture and preview it to determine if you want to save or delete it.

- The most convenient storage media for digital cameras are compact memory cards, typically capable of storing between 16 and 512 megabytes of data per card.

- Optical zoom uses the camera's lens to zoom in on a subject, resulting in a sharp image. Digital zoom uses computer tricks to blow up an image, commonly making it fuzzy.

- Before you take a snapshot with a digital camera, check the settings.

- Digital imaging software enables you to crop images, zoom in, adjust the color and brightness, add special effects, remove the red-eye effect, and enhance your photos in other ways.

Chapter 26

Playing Film Editor with Digital Video

In This Chapter

- ◆ Transferring video from a camcorder or VCR to your computer
- ◆ Working with digital camcorders
- ◆ Editing your video recordings
- ◆ Adding professional transitions between video clips
- ◆ Recording video clips to CDs or VHS tapes

Back in the 1960s and 1970s, 8mm film was the medium of choice for amateur movie makers. I know people who still have boxes of 8mm film cans in their attics and basements. In the 1980s and 1990s, people traded in their 8mm cameras and projectors for VHS and 8mm camcorders. These relatively compact devices made it easy to record video and play it back on a television set, but the tapes were still bulky, and you had to fast-forward through several minutes of tape to find your favorite clips. The new millennium has introduced a new video technology, *digital video*, allowing us to transfer, edit, and catalog our video clips using a computer. In this chapter, you learn how to take advantage of digital video.

What You Need to Get Started

You can approach digital video from two different directions, depending on how much you have invested in an older camcorder, how many old tapes you have, and how much money you're willing to spend. If you don't have a camcorder or old tapes and you have some cash on hand, purchase a digital camcorder and start filming. Digital camcorders record video in a much higher resolution than analog VHS or 8mm camcorders, and the digital clips won't lose quality when copied to your computer. (The quality of video clips recorded with analog camcorders suffers when they are converted from an analog to a digital format.)

When shopping for a digital camcorder, you need to think about how you will connect the camcorder to your computer. Most digital camcorders have an *IEEE-1394* (*FireWire*) or USB connector. If your computer does not have an IEEE-1394 or USB port, you need to install an expansion board to add the required port.

Tech Term

IEEE-1394 is a standard for transferring data between devices very quickly—at a rate of 400Mbps (megabits per second) or 800Mbps depending on the version. Compare that to the USB standard of 12Mbps and 480Mbps (in USB 2.0), and you can see why IEEE-1394 is the preferred method of transferring video to a computer. IEEE-1394 goes by many names, the most common of which is Apple's **FireWire**. You might also see IEEE-1394 labeled i.link or Lynx.

If you already have an analog camcorder and plenty of old tapes, or if your computer budget is already strained, consider adding a video capture device to your computer. You have several options here. The most convenient way to go is to purchase an external unit that connects to your computer's parallel, USB, or IEEE-1394 port, or into a circuit board that comes with the unit. Figure 26.1 shows Pinnacle Systems' Studio 8 Deluxe, which can capture from digital and analog camcorders and standard VHS tapes. Note that you plug the cables from the camcorder or VCR into the jacks on the front of the unit. To save space on your desk, you can opt for a video capture board, which plugs into an expansion slot inside your computer, but having the jacks right in front of you will make your job much easier.

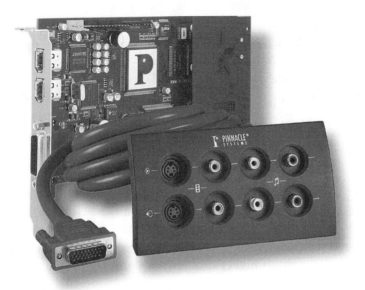

Figure 26.1

An analog-to-digital converter lets you connect a camcorder or VCR to your computer.

(Courtesy of Pinnacle Systems, Inc.)

Video capture boards and external units have special ports that let you connect your camcorder to your computer. They typically capture video at a rate of 15 or more frames per second, and they do a fairly good job of converting your analog clips into a digital format. If you're looking for a way to convert your collection of old camcorder or VHS tapes into a digital format and store them on CDs, this is the way to go.

Setting Up Your Audio/Video Equipment

If you're preparing to record and edit video from a digital camcorder, there's not much to setting up your equipment. You simply connect the USB or IEEE-1394 cable to the USB or IEEE-1394 ports on the camera and your computer, and you're ready to roll.

If you're recording from a VCR or analog camcorder, on the other hand, the setup is a bit more time-consuming. You must first install the video capture device and then connect the VCR or camcorder using several cables. The procedure for installing the video capture card or external device varies. The setup might be as simple as plugging the external device into your computer's USB port, or it might require you to install an expansion board inside the system unit. Read and follow the instructions and safety precautions that came with the card or device.

After the video capture device is installed, you can connect your VCR or camcorder to it. The audio and video connections vary, depending on the video capture card, the cables included with it, and the VCR or camcorder. On an external unit, such as Dazzle's Pinnacle Systems' Studio 8 Deluxe, the jacks are color-coded and match up with the standard A/V (Audio/Video) jacks found on most camcorders and VCRs.

Tech Term

S-video divides the video into two signals—one for color and one for brightness, generating a high-quality image. **Composite video** combines the color and brightness data in a single signal, resulting in a lower quality display.

Video capture cards typically have a single A/V input jack for audio and video input. You need a *four-headed input adapter* to make the necessary connections. This adapter contains a single plug for the A/V input jack on your video capture card and four connectors for the camera: one for left audio, one for right audio, one for *S-video*, and one for *composite video*. You use either the S-video or composite video connector, depending on the camera. (S-video produces higher-quality recordings.) See Figure 26.2.

Figure 26.2

Use the proper cables to connect the video player to the A/V-in port on your video capture card.

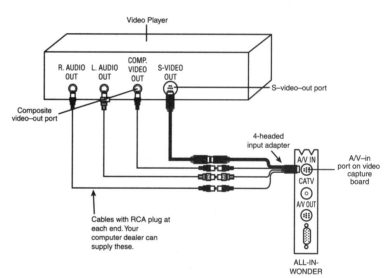

Capturing and Saving Your Clips

Your digital camcorder or video capture device probably came with its own program for recording and editing your video footage. Most of these programs are similar and follow the same overall procedure for recording and editing video. Here's a quick overview of the process:

1. Connect your camcorder or VCR to the video capture device.

2. Run your video recording program and enter the command to start recording.

3. Use your camcorder or VCR controls to play the video you want to record.

4. When you're ready to stop recording, enter the command to stop recording, and then press the **Stop** button on the camcorder or VCR. The video recording program chops the recording into *clips* to make them more manageable. It displays a thumbnail view of each clip.

5. Arrange the clips in the order in which you want them played.

6. Trim the clips. You can trim sections of any clip.

7. Add background music.

8. Add transitions between clips. For example, you can have a clip fade out at the end and fade into the next clip.

9. Save your movie to your hard drive.

10. Record your movie to a CD or tape or e-mail the movie clip.

Windows Me and later versions of Windows include their own video recording and editing software (Windows Movie Maker), so let's use it to run through the basics. If you have Windows Me, open the **Start, Programs, Accessories** menu, and then click **Windows Movie Maker.** In Windows XP, choose **Start, All Programs, Accessories, Windows Movie Maker,** or **Start, All Programs, Accessories, Entertainment, Windows Movie Maker.** Windows Movie Maker appears, as shown in Figure 26.3. You can download a free copy of Movie Maker 2.0 at www.microsoft.com/windowsxp/moviemaker/downloads/moviemaker2.asp.

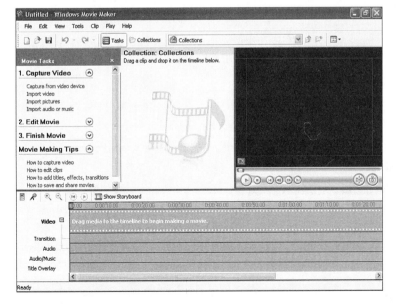

Figure 26.3

Windows Movie Maker.

To start recording clips in Movie Maker from a VCR or analog camcorder, follow these steps:

1. Connect your VCR or camcorder to the video capture device.

2. In Movie Maker, click **Capture from Video Device.** The Video Capture Wizard appears, prompting you to select the video capture device that's connected to your computer.

3. Select the video capture device you plan on using (if more than one such device is connected to your computer), and specify the audio device, video input source, and audio input source. Click **Next.** Video Capture Wizard prompts you to enter a name for the video.

4. Type a descriptive name for the video you are about to record and click **Next.** Video Capture Wizard prompts you to specify the desired video quality.

5. Click the option for the desired video quality. By default, Movie Maker is set to record video for optimal playback on a computer. (Higher quality settings result in larger files.) Click **Next.** Video Capture Wizard displays the controls you need to record the video.

6. To have Movie Maker chop your video footage into manageable clips when you're done recording, make sure **Create Clips When Wizard Finishes** is checked.

7. Use the controls on your VCR or camcorder to locate the beginning of the clip you want to record, and then rewind it slightly. Video Capture Wizard displays a small preview area where you can watch the video, so you can see what you're doing.

8. Press the **Play** button on your VCR or camcorder, and when the video reaches the point at which you want to begin recording, click Video Capture Wizard's **Start Capture** button.

9. When you have reached the end of the clip, click the **Stop Capture** button to stop recording, and press the **Stop** button on your VCR or camcorder.

10. If desired, repeat steps 7 to 9 to capture additional footage from this tape or from another tape.

11. When you are finished capturing video clips for your movie, click Video Capture Wizard's **Finish** button. If you turned on **Create Clips When Wizard Finishes** in Step 6, Movie Maker automatically chops the footage you recorded into smaller clips to make them more manageable and displays a thumbnail view of each clip, as shown in Figure 26.4.

Movie clips   Preview area

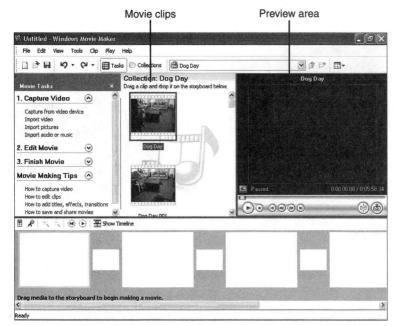

Figure 26.4

Windows Movie Maker chops your film footage into smaller clips.

The procedure for recording from a tape in a digital video (DV) camcorder is a little different, because you can control the camera from Movie Maker. Simply connect the DV camcorder to your computer and set the camcorder mode to play your video. In Movie Maker, click **Capture from Video Device.** The Video Capture Wizard appears, prompting you to select the video capture device that's connected to your computer. Select the DV camcorder from the Available Devices list and click **Next.** Type a filename for the recording and click **Next.** Choose the desired video quality and click **Next.** When prompted to choose a capture method, choose **Capture the Entire Tape Automatically** (to have Movie Maker rewind the tape and record it in its entirety) or choose **Capture Parts of the Tape Manually** (to capture selected portions of the tape). When recording from a DV camcorder, you can use the camcorder's controls or the controls in Video Capture Wizard to control the camcorder during the capture.

Splicing Your Clips into a Full-Length Movie

As soon as you have a few clips to work with, you're ready to start your new career as a professional film editor, cutting undesirable footage, trimming clips, and rearranging clips to create your own feature film. The editing procedure is surprisingly simple. You drag and drop thumbnails of your clips onto the storyboard at the bottom of the Movie Maker window, as shown in Figure 26.5.

Drag a clip from this list to the storyboard.

Figure 26.5

Drag and drop your clips onto the storyboard.

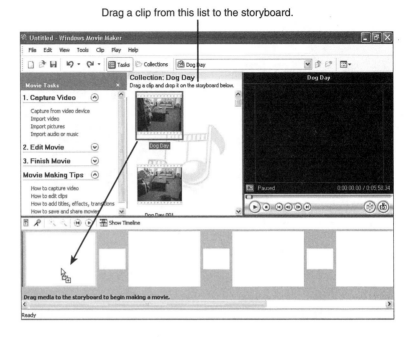

If a portion of a particular clip is out of focus or contains material you do not want to include in your video, you can trim the clip. This process consists of designating a start and end trim point. Movie Player then cuts the beginning and end of the clip, leaving the portion between the two trim points intact. Here's what you do:

1. In the bar above the storyboard, click **Show Timeline,** to view a timeline that shows how the clips are stitched together. (You cannot trim clips in Storyboard view.)

2. Click the clip you want to trim. The play indicator appears at the beginning of the clip as a blue box in the timeline with a vertical line that illustrates where the clip would start playing if you were to click the Play button.

3. Drag the play indicator to the position where you want the beginning of the clip chopped off.

4. Open the **Clip** menu and click **Set Start Trim Point.** Movie Player trims the portion of the clip to the left of the play indicator.

5. Drag the play indicator to the position where you want the end of the clip chopped off.

6. Open the **Clip** menu and click **Set End Trim Point.** Movie Player trims the portion of the clip to the right of the play indicator.

7. Repeat steps 2 to 6 to trim any additional clips in the timeline.

> **Inside Tip** _____
>
> You can add a title frame to your video. Choose **Start, All Programs, Accessories, Paint** to run the Windows graphics program. Open the **Image** menu and click **Attributes**. Type 320 for the width and 240 for the height. Make sure **Pixels** is selected under **Units,** and then click **OK.** Use Paint to draw your title frame, and then save it as a .BMP graphics file. Use the **File, Import** command in Movie Maker to bring the file into Movie Maker, and then drag it to the first frame on the film strip.

Adding an Audio Background

To give your video another dimension, consider recording some background music or narration. To record narration, first change to Timeline view, if it is not already displayed. If Movie Maker is in Storyboard view, click Show Timeline in the bar above the storyboard. Click the Narrate Timeline button (the button with the microphone on it, in the bar above the timeline). Click the **Start Narration** button and start talking into your microphone. When you're finished, click **Stop Narration** and then name and save your narration.

The easiest way to add background music, assuming you have a CD-ROM drive, is to record tracks from your audio CDs or download some MP3 audio clips, as explained in Chapter 24. You can then use Movie Maker's **File, Import** command to import the audio clips into Movie Maker.

After you have imported audio clips into Movie Player, adding them to your video is a snap. First, make sure the timeline is displayed; if the storyboard is displayed, instead, click Show Timeline (in the bar above the storyboard). Next, drag and drop the desired audio clip over the audio bar, as shown in Figure 26.6.

Panic Attack
Movie Maker might have trouble importing audio clips recorded with Windows Media Player. If you receive error messages when trying to import these clips, try recording your audio clips with a different CD ripper.

Drag an audio clip from this list to the audio bar.

Figure 26.6

Drag and drop your audio clips onto the audio bar.

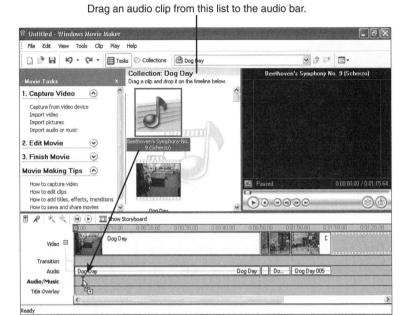

Smoothing Out Your Transitions

When you splice clips and trim sections of clips, some of the transitions might seem a little abrupt and surreal. To reduce the shock, add smooth transitions between clips. With Movie Maker, you can create a transition that makes the end of one clip fade out and the beginning of the next clip fade in.

To create a transition, change to Timeline view, as explained earlier in this chapter. Open the **Tools** menu and click **Video Transitions**. A list of video transition effects appears above the timeline. Scroll down the list to bring the desired transition into view, and then drag the transition from the list and drop it between the two clips where you want the transition to play. To preview the transition, drag the play indicator to a position just before the transition and then click the **Play** button. When Movie Maker reaches the point in the movie clip where you placed the transition, it displays the effect in the preview area.

Inside Tip

To add background music and narration, overlap the narration with the background music. You cannot completely overlap the two audio clips, but you can get pretty close.

Saving Your Movie

When your movie is complete, you can save it to your computer's hard drive, transfer it to a recordable CD (if your computer has a recordable CD drive), e-mail it to a friend or family member, save it to the web, or record it back to your DV camcorder. During the save operation, Movie Maker transforms your collection of clips into a single Movie Maker file. To save your movie, follow these steps:

1. Open the **File** menu and click **Save Movie File.** Movie Maker prompts you to choose what you want to do with the movie file, as shown in Figure 26.7. Save it to your computer's hard drive (using My Computer), transfer it to a recordable CD, e-mail it, save it to a web server, or record it to a tape in a DV camcorder.

Figure 26.7

Specify where you want your movie saved.

2. If you plan on saving your movie clip to a recordable CD, insert a blank CD into your computer's recordable CD drive. To record to a DV camcorder tape, make sure a blank tape is loaded into the camcorder and that the camcorder is connected to the video capture device's video out port.

3. Choose the desired option to specify where you want the file saved and click **Next.** Movie Maker prompts you to enter a name for the file.

4. Type a file name for your movie and select the desired location where you want it saved. Click **Next.** Movie Maker prompts you to specify the desired video quality for the movie. (Low-quality settings are excellent for playing the video on a computer; if you plan on playing the video on a TV set, choose a higher setting.)

5. Choose the desired quality setting and click **Next.** Movie Maker processes the movie, creates a file, and saves it to the specified destination.

Copying Your Movie to a VHS Tape

If you want to copy your movie to a VHS tape to share it with people who don't have computers, good luck. Most video recording devices and programs are much better at pulling video off tapes than recording edited video back to tapes. If your video capture device has an A/V output port, you can connect the device to a VCR to record to tape or a TV set that has RCA jacks. To make the connections, you need an adapter that plugs into the A/V output port on the video capture board and that has the proper connectors for the S-video-in or composite-in jacks on your VCR or TV set. See Figure 26.8.

Figure 26.8

Some video capture cards allow you to output recorded clips to a TV set or VCR.

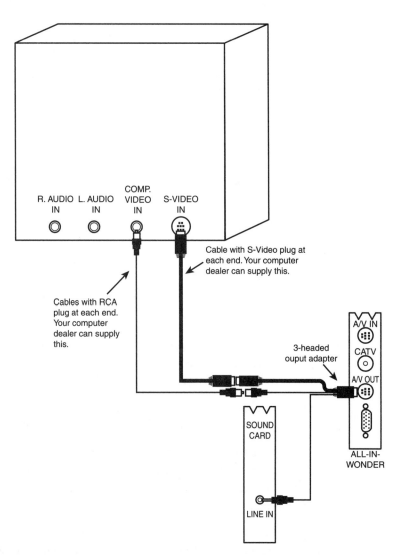

Now that you've made the physical connection between the computer and the VCR or TV, how do you play the video? Movie Maker has no command for sending the video to a VCR or TV. However, if your video card has an option for using a TV as a display device, here's a little trick you can do to record your movie on a tape using your VCR:

1. Connect your VCR to the A/V-out port on your video card, as shown in Figure 26.8.

2. Right-click a blank area of the Windows desktop and click **Properties.**

3. Click the **Settings** tab and then click the **Advanced** button. This displays advanced options for your particular video card.

4. If you see a **Television** option, turn it on. If no **Television** option is available, this feature might not be available for your video card. Check the card's documentation to be sure.

5. Run Windows Media Player, as explained in Chapter 24.

6. Use the **File, Open** command to open the movie file you created.

7. Press the **Record** button on your VCR, and then perform the next two steps as quickly as possible.

8. Click Media Player's **Play** button.

9. Press **Alt+Enter** to change to full-screen mode.

> **Panic Attack**
>
> Some video cards have a very odd configuration. Some cards have a video-out connector that hooks up to the video-in port on a VCR, but the audio-out jack plugs into the sound card on a computer. So you play the video into the VCR and the audio into the computer, making it impossible to record both the audio and video portions to a tape!

The Least You Need to Know

♦ You can connect a digital camcorder directly to your computer via an IEEE-1394 port.

♦ To connect an analog camcorder or VCR to your computer, you must install an internal video capture card or an external video capture device.

♦ To run Windows Movie Maker, open the **Start** menu, point to **Programs,** and then **Accessories,** and then click **Windows Movie Maker.** Or choose **Start, All Programs, Accessories, Entertainment, Windows Movie Maker.**

◆ To start recording video in Movie Maker, use your camcorder to start playing the video and then click the **Start Capture** button.

◆ To create transitions between video clips, display Timeline view, open the **Tools** menu, click **Video Transitions,** and then drag the desired transition between the two video clips where you want the transition to play.

◆ To save your movie as a file, open the **File** menu and click **Save Movie File,** and follow the onscreen instructions.

Part 6

Maintaining Your Investment

You don't need to be a mechanic to use a computer, but you should perform some basic maintenance tasks on a regular basis to keep your computer in tip-top condition.

This part acts as your computer maintenance manual. Here you learn how to clean your monitor, keyboard, mouse, printer, and system unit; give your computer a regular tune-up to keep it running at top speed; troubleshoot common computer problems; find valuable technical support; and optimize the performance of your computer with the most useful upgrades.

Chapter 27

Keeping Your Computer Clean

In This Chapter

- ◆ Sucking the dust from your computer
- ◆ Squeegeeing your monitor
- ◆ Picking hair and other gunk out of your mouse
- ◆ Keeping your printer shiny and new
- ◆ Spin-cleaning your disk drives

One of the best clean-air machines on the market is a computer. The cooling fan constantly sucks in the dusty air and filters out the dust. A monitor acts like a dust magnet, pulling in any airborne particles unfortunate enough to get close to it. And the keyboard and mouse act like vacuum cleaners, sucking crumbs and other debris from your desk. Unfortunately, the dust and smoke that your computer filters out eventually build up on the mechanical and electrical components inside it. When enough dust and debris collect on your computer and accessories, it's time for a thorough cleaning.

Tools of the Trade

Before you start cleaning, turn off your computer and any attached devices, and gather the following cleaning equipment:

- **Screwdriver or wrench.** This is for taking the cover off your system unit. (If you don't feel comfortable going inside the system unit, take your computer to a qualified technician for a thorough annual cleaning. It really does get dusty in there.)

- **Computer vacuum.** Yes, there are vacuum cleaners designed especially for computers.

- **Can of compressed air.** You can get this at a computer or electronics store. Compressed air is great for blowing the dust out of tight spots, such as between keyboard keys.

- **Soft brush** (a clean paintbrush with soft bristles will do). Use the brush to dislodge any stubborn dust that the vacuum won't pick up.

- **Toothpicks.** The only tool you need to clean your mouse.

- **Cotton swabs.** A cotton swab is another good tool for cleaning your mouse, and it's great for swabbing down your keyboard, too.

- **Paper towels.** You need some paper towels for wiping dust off your equipment and for cleaning the monitor.

- **Alcohol.** This is not the drinking kind; save that for when you're done.

- **Distilled water.** You can get special wipes for your monitor, but paper towels and water do the trick.

- **Radio or CD player.** When you're cleaning, you need music …

Don't run out and buy a floppy disk or CD-ROM cleaning kit. If your drive is having trouble reading disks, clean it. If it's running smoothly, let it be.

Vacuuming and Dusting Your Computer

Work from the top down and from the outside in. Start with the monitor. (You can use your regular vacuum cleaner for this part; if you have a brush attachment, use it.) Get your vacuum hose and run it up and down all the slots at the top and sides of the monitor. This is where most of the dust settles. Work down to the tilt-swivel base and vacuum that, too (you might need a narrow hose extension to reach in there). Now, vacuum your printer, speakers, and any other devices. If dust is stuck to a device, wipe it off with a damp (not soaking wet) paper towel.

Now for the system unit. When vacuuming, make sure you vacuum all the ventilation holes, including the floppy disk drive, power button, CD-ROM drive, open drive bays, and so on. If you have a CD-ROM drive, open it and gently vacuum the tray.

Now for the tough part—inside the system unit. Before you poke your vacuum hose in there, you should be aware of the following precautions:

♦ Use only a vacuum designed for computers. Don't use a Dust Buster, your regular vacuum cleaner, or your ShopVac. These can suck components off your circuit boards and can emit enough static electricity to fry a component. A computer vacuum is gentle and grounded. You can use a can of compressed air to blow dust off external peripheral devices, such as your keyboard and speakers, but be careful spraying the air against internal components. Compressed air can be very cold and can cause condensation to form on sensitive electrical components.

♦ Be careful around circuit boards. A strong vacuum can suck components and jumpers right off the boards. Also be careful not to suck up any loose screws.

♦ Touch a metal part of the case to discharge any static electricity from your body, and keep your fingers away from the circuit boards.

Now, take the cover off the system unit and vacuum any dusty areas. Dust likes to collect around the fan, ventilation holes, and disk drives. Try to vacuum the fan blades, too. If you can't get the tip of the vacuum between the blades, gently wipe them off with a cotton swab. Some fans have a filter where the fan is mounted. If you're really ambitious, remove the fan (be careful with the wires) and clean the filter.

Inside Tip _____

Some PCs have a fan that pulls air from the outside and pushes it through the ventilation holes. If the system unit case has openings near the fan, cut a square of sheer hosiery fabric, stretch it over the openings, and tape it in place with duct tape, keeping the tape away from the openings. Check the filter regularly, and replace it whenever dust builds up.

WASH ME: Cleaning Your Monitor

If you can write "WASH ME" on your monitor with your fingertip, the monitor needs cleaning. Check the documentation that came with your computer or monitor to see if

Inside Tip _____

If you don't want to spend money on antistatic wipes, wipe your monitor with a *used* dryer sheet. (A new dryer sheet might smudge the screen with fabric softener.)

it's okay to use window cleaner on it. The monitor might have an antiglare coating that can be damaged by alcohol- or ammonia-based cleaning solutions. (If it's not okay or if you're not sure, use water.) Spray the window cleaner (or water) on a paper towel, just enough to make it damp, wipe the screen, and then wipe with a dry paper towel to remove excess moisture. *Don't* spray window cleaner or any other liquid directly on the monitor; you don't want moisture to seep in. You can purchase special antistatic wipes for your monitor. These not only clean your monitor safely, but they also discharge the static electricity to prevent future dust buildup.

Shaking the Crumbs Out of Your Keyboard

Your keyboard is like a big place mat, catching all the cookie crumbs and other debris that fall off your fingers while you're working. The trouble is that, unlike a place mat, the keyboard isn't flat; it's full of crannies that are impossible to reach. And the suction from a typical vacuum cleaner just isn't strong enough to pull up the dust (although you can try it).

The easiest way I've found to clean a keyboard is to turn it upside down and shake it gently. Repeat two or three times to get any particles that fall behind the backs of the keys when you flip it over. If you don't like that idea, get your handy-dandy can of compressed air and blow between the keys.

For a more thorough cleaning, shut down your computer and disconnect the keyboard. Dampen a cotton swab with rubbing alcohol and gently scrub the keys. Wait for the alcohol to evaporate before reconnecting the keyboard and turning on the power.

Panic Attack

If you spill a drink on your keyboard, try to save your work and shut down the computer fast, but properly. Flip the keyboard over and turn off your computer. If you spilled water, just let the keyboard dry out thoroughly. If you spilled something sticky, give your keyboard a bath or shower with lukewarm water. Take the back off the keyboard, but do not flip the keyboard over with the back off, or parts will scurry across your desktop. Let it dry for a couple of days (don't use a blow-dryer), and put it back together. If some of the keys are still sticky, clean around them with a cotton swab dipped in rubbing alcohol. If you still have problems, buy a new keyboard; they're relatively inexpensive.

Making Your Mouse Cough Up Hairballs

If you can't get your mouse pointer to move where you want it to, you can usually fix the problem by cleaning the mouse. Flip the mouse over and look for hair or other debris on the mouse ball or on your desk or mouse pad. Removing the hair or wiping off your mouse pad fixes the problem 90 percent of the time.

If that doesn't work, remove the mouse ball cover (typically, you press down on the cover and turn counterclockwise). Wipe the ball thoroughly with a moistened paper towel. Now for the fun part. Look inside the mouse (where the ball was). You should see three rollers, each with a tiny ring around its middle. The ring is not supposed to be there. The easiest way I've found to remove these rings is to gently scrape them off with a toothpick. You have to spin the rollers to remove the entire ring. Use a pair of tweezers to extract any dust mats that you can't pull out with a toothpick. You can also try rubbing the rings off with a cotton swab dipped in rubbing alcohol, but these rings are pretty stubborn. When you're done, turn the mouse back over and shake it to remove the loose crumbs. Reassemble the mouse.

Cleaning Your Printer (When It Needs It)

Printer maintenance varies widely from one printer to another. If you have a laser printer, you need to vacuum or wipe up toner dust and clean the little print wires with cotton swabs dipped in rubbing alcohol. For an inkjet printer, you might need to remove the print cartridge and wipe the print heads with a damp cotton swab. If you have a combination scanner/printer, you might have to wipe the glass on which you place your original. Be sure to check the documentation that came with your printer for cleaning and maintenance suggestions.

You also need to be careful about the cleaning solution you use. Most printer manufacturers tell you to use only water on the inside parts—print rollers, print heads, and so on. In other cases, you can use a mild cleaning solution. Some manufacturers recommend rubbing alcohol on some but not all parts.

Even with these variables, there are a few things the average user can do to keep the printer in peak condition and ensure high-quality output:

- When turning off the printer, always use the power button on the printer (don't use the power button on your power strip), or press the **Online** button to take the printer offline. This ensures that the print head is moved to its rest position. On inkjet printers, this prevents the print head from drying out.

Inside Tip _____

Rubbing alcohol is an excellent cleaning solution for most electronic devices, because it cleans well and dries quickly. Use it for your keyboard, plastics, and most glass surfaces (except for some monitors). Avoid using it on rubber (for example, your mouse ball), because it tends to dry out the rubber and make it brittle.

◆ Vacuum inside the printer. Open any doors or covers to get inside.

◆ If the ink starts to streak on your printouts (or you have frequent paper jams in a laser printer), get special printer-cleaner paper from an office supply store and follow the instructions to run the sheet through your printer a few times.

◆ Using a damp cotton cloth, wipe paper dust and any ink off the paper feed rollers. Do not use alcohol. Do not use a paper towel; fibers from the paper towel could stick to the wheels.

What About the Disk Drives?

Don't bother cleaning your floppy, CD-ROM, or DVD-ROM drives unless they're giving you trouble. If your CD-ROM or DVD-ROM drive is having trouble reading a disc, the disc is usually the cause of the problem. Clean the disc and check the bottom of the disc for scratches. If the drive has problems reading every disc you insert, try cleaning the drive using a special drive-cleaning kit. The kit usually consists of a disc with some cleaning solution. You squirt the cleaning solution on the disc, insert it, remove it, and your job is done.

If you have a floppy disk drive that has trouble reading any disk you insert, you can purchase a special cleaning kit that works like the CD-ROM drive-cleaning kit. Although cleaning the disk drive might solve the problem, the problem can also be caused by a poorly aligned read/write head inside the drive, which no cleaning kit can correct.

The Least You Need to Know

◆ Vacuum your system, especially around its ventilation holes.

◆ Wipe the dust off your screen using a paper towel and the cleaning solution recommended by the manufacturer.

◆ Blow the crumbs out of your keyboard with compressed air.

◆ Remove those nasty mouse rings with a toothpick.

◆ Vacuum any ink dust that accumulates inside your printer.

◆ Clean your floppy or CD-ROM drive if it is having trouble reading disks.

Chapter 28

Giving Your Computer a Tune-Up

In This Chapter

- ◆ Clearing useless files from your hard disk
- ◆ Streamlining the Windows startup
- ◆ Repairing hard disk storage problems with ScanDisk
- ◆ Doubling your disk space without installing a new drive
- ◆ Getting more memory without installing more RAM

Over time, you will notice that your computer has slowed down. Windows takes a little longer to start up. Programs that used to snap into action now seem to crawl. Scrolling becomes choppy. Your computer locks up almost every day. You might begin to think that you need a new processor, more RAM, a larger hard disk drive, or even a whole new computer.

Before you take such drastic action, work through this chapter to give your computer a tune-up. By clearing useless files from your disk drive, reorganizing files, and reclaiming some of your computer's memory, you can boost your computer's performance and save a lot of money at the same time.

One-Stop Optimization with the Maintenance Wizard

The Windows Maintenance Wizard (included with Windows 98 and Windows Me) can help you keep your computer in tip-top condition. (Windows XP does not include the Maintenance Wizard, but it does include the tools you need to get the job done, as explained later in this chapter.) Maintenance Wizard automatically performs a series of tests and corrections at a scheduled time to check for problems on your hard disk, defragment files, delete temporary files, remove programs from the **StartUp** menu, and optimize your hard disk. With the Windows Maintenance Wizard, you rarely need to go behind the scenes to perform these tasks manually.

To run the Maintenance Wizard, follow these steps:

1. Click the **Start** button, point to **Programs, Accessories, System Tools,** and click **Maintenance Wizard.**

2. Click **Express,** and then click **Next.** Express tells the wizard to delete temporary files and web files from your hard disk, optimize your hard disk, and check it for errors, but Express does not tell the wizard to remove programs from the **StartUp** menu. The next dialog box prompts you to specify the time of day you want the wizard to run.

3. Click the desired time (a time when you normally have your computer on but are not using it), and then click **Next.** The wizard displays a list of optimization activities it will perform at the scheduled time(s), as shown in Figure 28.1.

Figure 28.1

The Windows Maintenance Wizard optimizes your system on schedule.

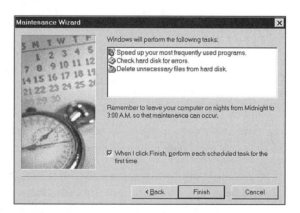

4. To have the wizard perform the selected activities now, choose **When I click Finish, perform each scheduled task for the first time.**

5. Click the **Finish** button. Be sure to leave your computer on at the scheduled time so that Windows can perform the optimization activities at the scheduled time(s).

Clearing Useless Files from Your Hard Disk

Your hard disk probably contains temporary and backup files that your programs create without telling you. These files can quickly clutter your hard disk drive, taking room that you need for new programs or new data files you create. You can easily delete most of these files yourself.

The easiest way to clear useless files from your hard drive in Windows XP is to let the Windows Disk Cleanup utility manage the details. Click the **Start** button, point to **All Programs, Accessories, System Tools,** and then click **Disk Cleanup.** The utility scans your computer's hard drive for useless files and displays a list of various file types you probably will never need. Check the box next to each file

Tech Term _____

Temporary files (files whose name end in .TMP) are files that your programs create but often forget to delete. You can safely delete them.

type you want Disk Cleanup to sweep off your computer's hard drive, and then click **OK.** The More Options tab in the Disk Cleanup dialog box offers additional options for reclaiming disk space, including removing Windows components, programs you don't use, and restore points (files that contain information on how to return your system to the state it was in on a previous date).

You can safely delete all temporary files from your hard drive in any version of Windows by searching for and removing them yourself. In Windows XP, click the Windows **Start** menu, click **Search,** and click **All Files and Folders.** In Windows Me, click the Windows **Start** menu, point to **Search,** and click **For Files or Folders**. In earlier versions of Windows, click the Windows **Start** button, point to **Find,** and click **Files or Folders**. Type *.tmp and press **Enter.** Press **Ctrl+A** to select all the files, and then press **Shift+Delete** and click **OK** to confirm. Gone! You should now have an extra megabyte or more of disk space. (Windows might not be able to delete some .TMP files that it is currently using.)

Inside Tip _____

When you save a file you created, most programs create a backup file that contains the previous version of the file. These files typically have the .BAK extension. If you mess up the original file, you can open the backup file instead. To find backup files, check the folder(s) in which you save your documents; most programs save backup files in the same folder as the original files. Before deleting backup files, make sure

To remove temporary files that your web browser saves, clear the disk cache in your browser. To clear the disk cache in Internet Explorer, open the **View** or **Tools** menu and click **Internet Options.** Under **Temporary Internet Files,** click the **Delete Files** button and then click **OK** to confirm. In Netscape Navigator, open the **Edit** menu, click **Preferences,** double-click **Advanced,** click **Cache,** and click the **Clear Disk Cache** button.

While you're at it, open your e-mail program and delete any e-mail messages you no longer need. When you delete e-mail messages, some e-mail programs, such as Outlook Express, stick the deleted messages in a separate folder (called Deleted Items in Outlook Express). Be sure to delete the messages from that folder as well.

Most of the stuff you deleted is now sitting in the Recycle Bin, where it is still hogging disk space. Open the Recycle Bin, and scroll down the list of deleted files to make sure you will never again need anything in the Bin. If you find a file you might need, drag it onto the Windows desktop for safekeeping, or right-click the file and select **Restore** to restore the file to its original location. Now, open the **File** menu and click **Empty Recycle Bin.**

Checking for and Repairing Damaged Files and Folders

Windows comes with a utility called ScanDisk that can test a disk (hard or floppy), repair most problems on a disk, and refresh the disk if needed. What kind of problems? ScanDisk can find defective storage areas on a disk and block them to prevent your computer from using them. ScanDisk can also find and delete misplaced (usually useless) file fragments that might be causing your computer to crash.

You should run ScanDisk regularly (at least once every month) and whenever your computer seems to be acting up (crashing for no apparent reason). Also, if you have a floppy disk that your computer cannot read, ScanDisk might be able to repair it and recover any data from it.

To run ScanDisk in Windows XP, open My Computer, right-click the icon for the drive you want to scan, click **Properties,** click the **Tools** tab, and (under Error-Checking) click the **Check Now** button. The Check Disk Local Disk dialog box appears, as shown in Figure 28.2. Click the check box next to **Automatically Fix File System Errors** to place a check in the box. To check for bad areas on the disk, click the check box next to **Scan for and Attempt Recovery of Bad Sectors** to place a check in the box. (This option provides a thorough check of your computer's disk drive, and might take several hours; turn on this option only if you don't plan on using your computer for a while.) When you're ready to begin the scan, click **Start.**

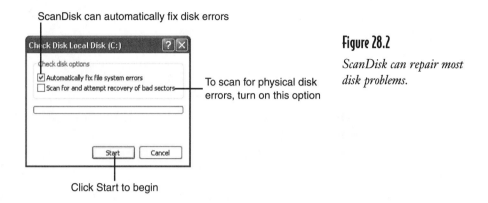

ScanDisk can automatically fix disk errors

To scan for physical disk
errors, turn on this option

Click Start to begin

Figure 28.2

*ScanDisk can repair most
disk problems.*

To run ScanDisk in earlier versions of Windows, follow these steps:

1. Open the **Start** menu, point to **Programs, Accessories, System Tools,** and then click **ScanDisk.** The ScanDisk window appears, prompting you to specify the drive you want to scan and the checks you want to perform.

2. Click the letter of the drive you want ScanDisk to check.

3. To check for and repair only file and folder errors, click the **Standard** option; to check the disk for defects (in addition to file and folder errors), click **Thorough.** (Thorough can take hours; select it only if you're on your way to bed.)

4. If you want ScanDisk to fix any errors without asking for your confirmation, make sure that **Automatically fix errors** is checked. (I always choose this option, and I have never encountered problems with ScanDisk's doing something it was not supposed to do.)

5. Click the **Start** button.

> ### Panic Attack
>
> If Windows shuts down improperly (if you press the power button on your system unit before Windows is ready, if the power goes out, or if Windows locks up), Windows might run Scan-Disk automatically when you restart your computer. It reminds you to shut down properly next time, even though this probably wasn't your fault.

Defragmenting Files on Your Hard Disk

Whenever you delete a file from your hard disk, you leave a space where another file can be stored. When you save a file, your computer stores as much of the file as possible in that empty space and stores the rest of the file in other empty spaces. The file is then said to be *fragmented,* because its parts are stored in different locations on the disk. This slows down your disk drive and makes it more likely that your computer will lose track of a portion of the file or the entire file.

Every month or so, you should run a defragmentation program to determine the fragmentation percent and to defragment your files if necessary. If you ran the Maintenance Wizard as explained earlier in this chapter, Windows Disk Defragmenter automatically performs the operation at the scheduled time. If you did not run the Maintenance Wizard or if you're using Windows XP, you can run Disk Defragmenter yourself.

Before you start Disk Defragmenter, it's a good idea to disable your screen saver and any power management utilities that might interfere with Defragmenter. See "Securing Some Privacy with a Screen Saver" in Chapter 7 to learn how to turn the Windows screen savers on and off. To disable the Windows power management settings in Windows XP, display the Control Panel, click **Performance and Maintenance,** click **Power Options,** and then open the **Power Schemes** list, select **Always on,** and click **OK.** In earlier versions of Windows, open the Windows Control Panel, double-click the **Power Options** icon, open the **Power Schemes** list, select **Always on,** and click **OK.** Save any open documents, and close any programs that are currently running.

Now you're ready to have Disk Defragmenter defragment your files. Follow these steps:

1. Open the **Start** menu, point to **All Programs** (or **Programs**), **Accessories, System Tools,** and click **Disk Defragmenter.** A dialog box appears, asking which disk drive you want to defragment, as shown in Figure 28.3.

Click the disk you want to defragment

Figure 28.3

Defragmenter prompts you to select the drive(s) you want to defragment.

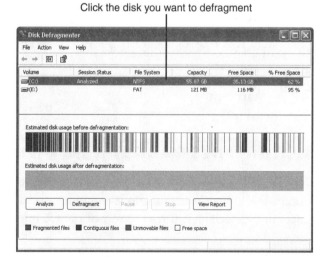

- Fragmented files ■ Contiguous files ■ Unmovable files □ Free space

2. Select the drive you want to defragment. In Windows XP, simply click the icon for the drive. In earlier versions of Windows, open the **Which drive do you want to defragment?** drop-down list, and click the desired drive. If your computer has two or more hard drives, you can defragment all your drives by clicking **All hard drives.** (You don't need to defragment floppy disks.)

3. Click **Analyze** or click **OK.** Defragmenter displays both the percentage of file fragmentation on the disk and whether you need to defragment the disk. (In earlier versions of Windows, Defragmenter may begin defragmenting the disk as soon as you click OK, in which case you can skip to step 5.)

4. When you are ready for Defragmenter to start working, click the **Defragment** or **Start** button. Defragmenter starts defragmenting the files on the disk.

5. Wait until the defragmentation is complete. It's best to leave your computer alone during the process. Otherwise, you might change a file and cause Defragmenter to start over. Don't run any programs or play any computer games.

Making Windows Start Faster

Windows is a slow starter, even on a quick machine. If you have some power-saving features on your computer, you can make Windows start a lot faster. Instead of turning your PC off and on, use the **Power** or **Power Management** icon in the Control Panel to access the options for placing your PC in sleep mode when you're not using it (rather than shutting it down completely). (In Windows XP, display the Control Panel, click **Performance and Maintenance,** and click **Power Options.**) Enter the desired settings to specify which components you want Windows to power down after a specified period of inactivity. When Windows powers down the computer, you can quickly restart by pressing the **Shift** key or rolling the mouse around rather than by turning on the computer and waiting for Windows to restart.

If your computer has advanced power-saving features, you might also be able to shut it down by placing it in Standby or *Hibernation* mode. When you're done for the day, click the **Start** button and click **Shut Down.** In the Shut Down dialog box, click **Stand by** and then click **OK.** To restart your computer, press the **Shift** key.

If you need to turn your computer completely off, try the following to reduce the startup time:

◆ To prevent Windows from running programs that are on the **StartUp** menu, hold down the **Shift** key right after you log on to Windows. If you don't log on to Windows, press and hold down **Shift** when you see the Windows *splash screen* (the screen that appears before you get to the desktop).

◆ To remove programs from the **StartUp** menu in Windows XP, click the **Start** button, point to **Programs, Startup,** and then right-click the program you want to remove and click **Delete.** (Be careful. If you have an antivirus program that runs on startup, you might want to keep it on the **StartUp** menu.) In earlier versions of Windows, right-click the taskbar, click **Properties,** click the **Advanced** or **Start Menu Programs** tab, click the **Remove** button, and click the plus sign next to **StartUp.** Click the program you want to remove, and then click the **Remove** button.

◆ To quickly restart Windows XP without turning your computer off and then on, click **Start, Turn Off Computer, Restart.** In Windows Me or 98, click **Start, Shut Down, Restart.** Hold down the **Shift** key while clicking **Yes** or **OK.**

Tech Term

In addition to Standby mode, some systems support **Hibernation mode.** After a specified period of inactivity, or when you choose to place the computer in Hibernation mode, Windows saves all open files, makes a record of which programs were open, and then completely shuts down the computer. When you press the power button to restart your system, Windows automatically runs the programs that were running when the computer entered Hibernation mode and opens any documents that were open so that you can immediately pick up where you left off.

If you have Internet Explorer on your computer, and you have your Windows desktop displayed as a web page, the active desktop components can add a lot of time to the Windows startup. If you don't use the desktop components, turn them off. The procedure varies depending on which version of Windows you have:

◆ In Windows XP, right-click the desktop and choose **Properties.** Click the **Desktop** tab and then click the **Customize Desktop** button. Click the **Web** tab and remove the check mark next to each desktop component you no longer want to view. Click **OK** to return to the Display Properties dialog box and then click **OK** to save your settings and close the dialog box.

◆ In Windows Me and 98, right-click a blank area of the desktop, point to **Active Desktop,** and choose **Customize My Desktop.** Remove the check mark next to every desktop component you no longer want displayed, and then click **OK.** Also consider turning off **View as Web page.** Right-click the desktop, point to **Active Desktop,** and, if **View as Web page** or **Show Web content** is checked, click the option to remove the check mark.

Inside Tip

Every computer comes with a set of startup instructions called the BIOS (Basic Input/Output System). These instructions include boot settings that can make your computer start faster. For instance, you can enter a setting to have your computer start directly from drive C (instead of checking drive A first). Check the startup screen or your computer's manual for instructions on accessing the BIOS settings, but don't change any settings you are unsure of.

Boosting Performance with Shareware Utilities

Does your 56Kbps modem seem slow? Does Windows frequently lock up or display the "insufficient memory" message, even though your computer has more than 128MB of RAM and plenty of free disk space? Has your computer's performance become so degraded that you just can't stand using your computer for another day? Then it's time to bring out the big guns—utility programs designed to optimize your computer automatically.

The following is a list of shareware programs, along with information on where to find out more about them and where to go to download the latest version:

◆ **MemTurbo** is a memory (RAM) optimizer. When you exit some programs, they fail to free up the memory they were using, reducing the amount of free memory available to other programs. MemTurbo reclaims this memory to make programs run faster and prevent Windows from locking up. You can find out more about MemTurbo and download a trial version at www.memturbo.com.

◆ **WinOptimizer** is designed to pick up where the Windows Maintenance Wizard leaves off. It clears redundant, duplicate files from your system and streamlines the Windows Registry to boost overall system performance. Learn more about WinOptimizer and pick up a shareware version of it at www.ashampoo.com.

◆ **Registry Clean Pro,** shown in Figure 28.4, safely and automatically deletes entries in your Windows registry, an enormous, complex file that Windows uses to control nearly every computer component and program. The Windows registry often becomes cluttered with useless settings and codes that can result in slowing down Windows and making it unstable. You can edit the registry yourself, but it's a risky activity that can cause all sorts of terrible problems. Registry Clean Pro tidies up the registry and can significantly improve the performance of your computer. Download a trial version at www.registry-clean.com.

◆ **TweakDUN** is an Internet connection optimizer for Windows. It automatically adjusts the Windows Dial-Up Networking settings to make Windows transfer data more efficiently over a modem connection. If you're using a 56Kbps modem and you aren't ready to move up to an ISDN, DSL, or cable connection, TweakDUN can improve your current connection speed. Check it out at www.pattersondesigns.com/tweakdun. (You should also check out Download Accelerator at www.speedbit.com.)

Computer Cheat

If you don't have a utility for reclaiming memory, shut down Windows and restart your computer. You might need to do this every day or two to keep your computer running smoothly.

◆ **SiSoft Sandra** is a system information utility that provides a complete inventory of your system's resources. Sandra shows you the processor's type and speed, the amount of memory, the amount of free storage space, the monitor make and model, and descriptions of all installed peripherals. When you want to know more about your computer, check out Sandra at www.sisoftware.demon.co.uk/sandra/.

Figure 28.4

Registry Clean Pro safely and automatically tidies up the Windows registry.

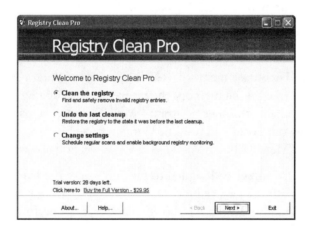

The Least You Need to Know

◆ If you have Windows 98 or Windows Me, use the Windows Maintenance Wizard to schedule regular tune-ups.

◆ Clear temporary files, old e-mail messages, and temporary Internet files from your hard disk, and don't forget to dump the Recycle Bin.

◆ To avoid system crashes and lost files, run ScanDisk and Disk Defragmenter at least once every month.

◆ If you have an older computer that you're not ready to upgrade or replace, obtain a set of utilities for optimizing performance.

◆ Instead of shutting down the power to your computer when you're done working, use Windows' power-management features to place it in Hibernation or Standby mode.

◆ If your computer seems to be running slowly, exit all programs and restart Windows to clear your computer's memory.

29

Troubleshooting Common Computer Problems

In This Chapter

- ◆ Figuring out what to do and not do in a crisis
- ◆ Sniffing out the cause of a problem
- ◆ Recovering safely when your computer locks up
- ◆ Getting your speakers to say something
- ◆ Making your modem dial

Your computer can be quite moody. One day, all the components are running properly and all tasks proceed without a glitch. The next day, your mouse pointer won't budge, your printer refuses to print a document, Windows locks up, or cryptic error messages pop up on your screen. Sometimes, simply installing a program or a new component can bring your computer to a grinding halt. In many instances, the computer provides no clue as to what the problem is, leaving you to troubleshoot on your own.

When problems arise, what should you do? Where do you begin to look for help? How do you track down the root cause of the problem? This chapter is your guide to solving a host of common computer problems. Here you learn common troubleshooting tactics, do-it-yourself repairs, and preventive maintenance. This chapter won't transform you into a professional computer technician, but with a little practice and a lot of patience, by the end of this chapter, you should be able to solve the most common problems and even help your friends with their computer woes.

Troubleshooting Tactics: Pre-Panic Checklist

When you run into a problem that doesn't have an obvious solution, the best course of action is inaction—that is, don't do anything. If you're fidgeting to do something, take a walk or grab a snack. Doing the wrong thing can often make the problem worse. After you've calmed down a little, come back and work through this checklist:

❑ **Are there any onscreen messages?** Look at the monitor for any messages that indicate a problem.

❑ **Is everything plugged in and turned on?** Turn everything off and check the connections. Don't assume that just because something looks connected, that it is; wiggle the plugs.

❑ **When did the problem start?** Did you install a new program? Did you enter a command? Did you add a new device? When my speakers went mute, I realized that the problem started after I installed a new hard drive. I had knocked a tiny jumper off the sound card during the hard drive installation.

❑ **Is the problem limited to one program?** If you have the same problem in every program, the problem is probably caused by your computer or Windows. If the problem occurs in only one program, focus on that program.

❑ **When did you have the file last?** If you lost a file, it probably did not get sucked into a black hole. It is probably somewhere on your disk, in a separate folder. Open the **Start** menu, choose **Find** or **Search,** and start hunting. If you think you accidentally deleted the file, check the Recycle Bin.

❑ **Realize that it's probably not the computer, and it's probably not a virus.** The problem is usually in the software—Windows or one of your programs. Of the problems that people blame on computer viruses or the computer itself, 95 percent are actually bugs in the software or problems with specific device drivers (the instructions that tell your computer and Windows how to use the device).

Whoa!

Write down changes that you make to your system. It takes a little extra time, but it enables you to retrace your steps later.

Preventing and Recovering from Problems with System Restore

Windows Me and later versions of Windows include a nifty utility called System Restore that can help you return your computer's settings to an earlier time when everything was working properly. System Restore monitors your computer, and when you install a program or a new peripheral device or component, it creates a restore point and saves the current settings to your computer's hard drive. System Restore also creates a daily restore point, just in case something goes wrong during the day. If you install a program or change a setting in Windows that causes problems, you can run System Restore and pick the desired restore point. Here's what you do:

1. Click the Windows **Start** button, point to **All Programs** (or **Programs**), **Accessories, System Tools,** and then click **System Restore.** The System Restore window appears.

2. Click **Restore My Computer to an Earlier Time** and click **Next.** System Restore displays a calendar showing the days of the current month. Dates in bold represent days in which a restore point was created, as shown in Figure 29.1.

Select a restore point

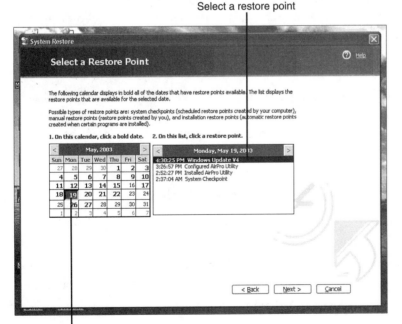

Select the desired date

Figure 29.1

System Restore enables you to return your system to an earlier time.

3. Click the date that has a restore point you want to use to restore your system. A list of restore points created on the selected date appears on the right.

4. Click the desired restore point and click **Next.** System Restore displays a message assuring you that none of your data files or e-mail will be wiped out by the restoration, and informing you that the process is reversible.

Inside Tip

If you plan on changing any system settings in Windows, deleting device drivers, or installing applications, run System Restore and create your own restore point before you begin. If something goes wrong, you can immediately return your computer to its previous condition.

5. Click **Next.**

6. System Restore takes a few seconds to collect the information it needs, and then it restarts Windows and displays the Log on screen. Log on to Windows as you normally do. System Restore runs automatically and displays a window that enables you to undo the restoration.

7. Close or cancel the window.

Identifying Troublesome Background Programs

Don't assume that the programs you run are the only programs running on your computer. Many programs you install or that came already installed on your computer run in the background. You won't see buttons for them on the Windows taskbar or even in the system tray, but they're running just the same and can cause conflicts with Windows and your other programs. They can also consume a great deal of your computer's resources.

Fortunately, Windows features a configuration tool that enables you to disable these programs when Windows starts. You can disable most of the programs to prevent them from running and then enable each program to identify the program that's causing problems. To prevent programs from running in the background, take the following steps:

1. Open the **Start** menu and click **Run.** The Run dialog box appears.

2. Type msconfig and press **Enter** or click **OK.** The System Configuration Utility appears.

3. Click the **Services** tab and click **Hide All Microsoft Services** to place a check in its box, as shown in Figure 29.2. By hiding Microsoft services you avoid accidentally disabling a service that's critical for the operation of Windows.

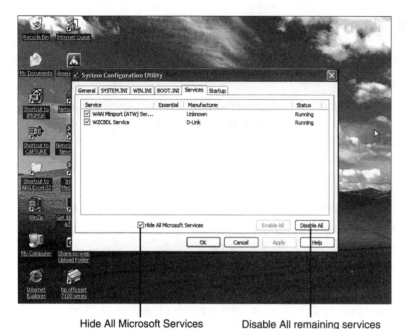

Figure 29.2

The System Configuration Utility enables you to safely disable programs and services that might cause problems.

Hide All Microsoft Services   Disable All remaining services

4. Click the **Disable All** button. This disables all services that are not critical for Windows to function properly.

5. Click the **Startup** tab. A list of all the background programs that run on startup appears.

6. Click the **Disable All** button. This removes the checkmark next to each program.

7. Click **OK.** The System Configuration dialog box appears, prompting you to restart your computer.

8. Exit any programs that are currently running and then click the **Restart** button. Windows restarts and then displays a dialog box indicating that you're running Windows with a selective startup configuration for troubleshooting.

9. Click **OK.** The System Configuration Utility appears.

10. Click **Cancel.**

If Windows and the various applications you use run properly, you know that one of the programs or services that you disabled was causing the problem. Use the System Configuration Utility to re-enable the programs and services one at a time, restarting Windows after each change. If the problem arises, you know that the program or service you just enabled is the cause, and you can focus your troubleshooting efforts on that program or service.

My Computer Won't Start

A computer is a lot like a car; the most frustrating thing that can happen is that you can't even get the engine to turn over. To solve the problem, consider these questions:

♦ **Is the computer on?** Make sure the power switch on the system unit is turned on. Some computers have a power button that you have to press and hold for a couple of seconds.

♦ **Is the surge strip on?** If your PC is plugged into a surge suppressor or UPC, make sure the power is turned on.

♦ **Is the screen completely blank?** If you heard the computer beep and you saw the drive lights go on and off, the computer probably booted fine. Make sure the monitor is turned on and the brightness controls are turned up. Try moving your mouse or pressing the **Shift** key; your computer may be in sleep mode, and this wakes it up.

♦ **Is there a disk in drive A?** If you see a message onscreen that says "Non-system disk or disk error," you probably left a floppy disk in drive A. Remove the disk and press any key to start from the hard disk.

♦ **Can you start from a floppy disk?** Insert the Windows Startup disk in drive A and press **Ctrl+Alt+Del.** If you can start from a floppy, the problem is on your hard disk. You need some expert help to get out of this mess.

> **Inside Tip**
>
> Windows 98 and Me include a utility that can transform a floppy disk into a Startup disk. Open the Windows Control Panel, double-click the **Add/Remove Programs** icon, and click the **Startup Disk** tab. Click the **Create Disk** button, and then follow the onscreen instructions. Of course, you can't create the disk if your computer won't boot, but after you get your computer started, make a Startup disk. If you have Windows XP, boot the computer from the Windows CD.

My Computer Locked Up

The computer might be too busy to handle your request, so wait a few minutes. If it's still frozen, press **Ctrl+Alt+Del.** A dialog box should appear, showing you the names of the active programs. Next to the program that's causing the problem, you should see "[not responding]." Click that program's name and click **End Task.** Frequently, a second End Task confirmation dialog box appears a few seconds after clicking the End Task button; repeat the command to end the task. (You may lose data when you close a program that is not responding.) You should now be able to continue working.

If you close the errant program and Windows is still locked up, press **Ctrl+Alt+Del** again, and close any other programs that are causing problems. If you still cannot regain control of your computer, you may have to press **Ctrl+Alt+Del** again or use your computer's Reset or Power button. Do this only as a last resort. Shutting down your system without exiting programs properly causes you to lose any work you had not saved before shutting down. (Files saved to your hard disk are safe.)

It Could Be a Program

Many programs, especially web browsers, games, and anti-virus programs typically are buggy. They have programming code that makes the program conflict with Windows, other programs, one of your hardware devices, or even your computer's memory. One common problem is that the program never frees up the memory it uses.

The only permanent solution is to install a *patch* or *bug fix* from the manufacturer, assuming a patch is available. (A patch is a set of program instructions designed to fix a programming bug or add capabilities to a program.) Contact the manufacturer's tech support department to determine whether they have a fix for the problem, as explained in Chapter 30. For a temporary solution, use the program in spurts. Use the program for awhile, save your work, exit, and restart before your computer locks up. If your computer seems to be getting sluggish, try restarting Windows to free up memory.

Check Your Mouse Driver

Windows might be having a problem with the mouse driver (the instructions that tell Windows how to use your mouse). Check to make sure that you don't have two conflicting mouse drivers installed. **Alt+click My Computer** and take one of the following steps: in Windows XP, click the **Hardware** tab and then click the **Device Manager** button; in earlier versions of Windows, click the **Device Manager** tab. Click the plus sign next to **Mouse.** If you have more than one mouse listed, you have more than one mouse driver installed. To disable one of the mouse drivers, double-click the mouse that doesn't match the type of mouse you have, click **Disable in This Hardware Profile,** and click **OK.** Click **OK** again and restart your computer.

> **CAUTION**
>
> **Whoa!**
>
> If you pick the wrong mouse driver, you won't have a mouse pointer in Windows, making it tough to navigate. If you pick the wrong driver, start your computer in Safe mode by tapping the **F8** key during startup (right after the computer beeps) and choosing the option to start in Safe mode. Then pick a different driver. See "Dealing with Windows in Safe Mode," later in this chapter, for details.

If that doesn't fix the problem, call the tech support department for the mouse manufacturer and ask if they have an updated driver (they send it to you via e-mail or on a floppy disk). In most cases, the updated driver contains the fix for the problem. (See "Updating the Software for Your Hardware," later in this chapter to learn how to install an updated driver.)

If you cannot obtain an updated mouse driver, try reinstalling the mouse driver. Right-click **My Computer** and click **Properties** and then take one of the following steps: in Windows XP, click the **Hardware** tab and then click the **Device Manager** button; in earlier versions of Windows, click the **Device Manager** tab. Click the plus sign next to **Mice and Other Pointing Devices** and then right-click the icon for your mouse and click **Uninstall.** Press **Alt+F4** repeatedly to shut down all programs and display the Windows Shut Down window, and then choose the option for restarting Windows. When Windows starts, it will install the required mouse driver.

Check the Windows Graphics Acceleration Setting

Windows is initially set up to exploit the full potential of your computer. Unfortunately, sometimes Windows is too aggressive, especially when it comes to your system's video acceleration. Windows cranks up the video acceleration rate to the maximum, which can sometimes cause your system to crash without displaying an error message. Try slowing it down:

1. Right-click a blank area of the Windows desktop and select **Properties.**

2. Click the **Settings** tab and click the **Advanced** button.

3. Click the **Troubleshoot** tab.

4. Drag the **Hardware Acceleration** slider to the second or third hash mark, and click **OK.**

5. Click **Close.**

6. If Windows asks whether you want to reboot your system, close any programs that may be running, and click **Yes.**

Obtain an Updated Video Driver

Hiding behind the scenes of every video card and monitor is a video driver that tells your operating system (Windows) how to use the card and monitor to display pretty pictures. Occasionally, the driver contains a bug that can lock up your system. More frequently, the driver becomes outdated, causing problems with newer programs. In either case, you should obtain an updated driver from the manufacturer of the video card. You can call the manufacturer's tech support line and have them send the driver to you on a floppy disk, or obtain the driver from the company's website. (See "Updating the Software for Your Hardware," later in this chapter to learn how to install an updated driver.)

> **Inside Tip** _____
>
> Some programs have trouble dealing with a large number of colors. Right-click the Windows desktop, choose **Properties,** and click the **Settings** tab. Choose **256 Colors** from the **Colors** drop-down list. Don't go lower than 256; some programs do not work with a lower setting.

Dealing with Windows in Safe Mode

Windows typically starts in Safe mode if you install a wrong device driver (especially a wrong video or mouse driver). In Safe mode, "Safe mode" appears at each corner of the desktop. In most cases, you can simply restart Windows to have it load the previous driver. If on restarting, the Windows desktop is not visible or you cannot use the mouse, restart your computer, wait for it to beep, tap the **F8** key several times, and then choose the option for starting Windows in Safe mode. (You have to be quick with the F8 key—press it before you see the Windows screen.)

Windows loads a standard mouse and video driver in Safe mode, so you can see what you're doing and use the mouse to point and click. This allows you to install a different or updated driver or change settings back to what they were before you encountered problems.

I Can't Get the Program to Run

If you try to run a program using a shortcut icon, the icon might be pointing to the wrong program. Right-click the shortcut, choose **Properties,** and check the entry in the **Target** text box. This shows the path to the program's folder followed by the name of the program file that launches the program. If the text box is blank or points to the wrong file, click the **Find Target** button and use the resulting dialog box to change to the program's folder and choose the right program file.

If the program starts and immediately closes, your computer not have sufficient memory or disk space to run the program. Right-click **My Computer,** select **Properties,** and then take one of the following steps: in Windows XP, click the **Advanced** tab, click the Performance **Settings** button, click the Advanced tab, and under Virtual Memory, click the **Change** button; in earlier versions of Windows, click the **Performance** tab and click the **Virtual Memory** button. Make sure that you have at least 30 megabytes of free space on the disk that Windows is using for virtual memory. Any less, and you have to clear some files from your hard disk.

If the program still won't run, try reinstalling it. If that doesn't work, contact the program manufacturer's tech support department to determine the problem and the required fix. The program may require special hardware or additional software that is not available on your system.

I Have a Mouse, but I Can't Find the Pointer

After you get your mouse working, you will probably never need to mess with it again (except for cleaning it, which we talked about back in Chapter 27). The hard part is getting the mouse to work in the first place. If you connected a mouse to your computer and you don't see the mouse pointer onscreen, there are a few possibilities that you should investigate:

♦ **Is the mouse pointer hidden?** Mouse pointers like to hide in the corners or edges of your screen. Roll the mouse on your desktop to see whether you can bring the pointer into view. (If you have a notebook computer, the mouse pointer might disappear when you move the mouse quickly.)

♦ **When you connected the mouse, did you install a mouse driver?** Connecting a mouse to your computer is not enough. You must install a program (called a *mouse driver*) that tells the computer how to use the mouse. Follow the instructions that came with the mouse to figure out how to install the driver.

I Can't Hear My Speakers!

Several things can cause your speakers to go mute. Check the following:

♦ Are your speakers turned on?

♦ Is the speaker volume control turned up?

♦ Are your speakers (or headphones) plugged into the correct jacks on your sound card? Some sound cards have several jacks, and it's easy to plug the speakers into the input jacks instead of the output jacks.

♦ If you're having trouble recording sounds, make sure that your microphone is turned on and plugged into the correct jack.

♦ Does your sound card have a volume control? Crank it all the way up.

♦ Right-click the **Speaker** icon on the Windows taskbar and choose **Open Volume Controls.** Open the **Options** menu, choose **Properties,** and make sure that every volume control in the list at the bottom of the dialog box is checked. Click **OK.** Use the sliders to crank up the overall volume, CD volume, and Microphone volume. Make sure that the **Mute** options are NOT checked.

If you still can't get your speakers to talk, right-click **My Computer,** select **Properties,** and take one of the following steps: in Windows XP, click the **Hardware** tab and then click the **Device Manager** button; in earlier versions of Windows, click the **Device Manager** tab. Scroll down the list and click the plus sign next to the **Sound...** option. If your sound card is not listed, you need to reinstall the sound card driver. If the sound card is listed but has a yellow circle with an exclamation point on it, the sound card is conflicting with another device on your system. Check your sound card's documentation to determine how to resolve hardware conflicts. This can be pretty complicated and may require you to change settings on your sound card (you may need to go inside the system unit).

I Can't Get My Modem to Work

If your modem can't dial, Windows can help you track down the problem with its hardware troubleshooters. To run the modem troubleshooter in Windows XP, display the Control Panel, click **Printers and Other Hardware,** click **Hardware** (under Troubleshooters in the left pane), and then click the option button to the left of **I'm Having a Problem with a Modem,** click **Next,** and follow the onscreen instructions to track down the problem, as shown in Figure 29.3. In earlier versions of Windows, double-click the **Modems** icon in the Control Panel, click the **Diagnostics** tab, and click the **Help** button.

Inside Tip

Windows comes with several hardware troubleshooters that can help you track down problems with your mouse, sound card, monitor, network, and other devices. To view a list of troubleshooters, open the **Start** menu, click **Help,** and search for "troubleshooter."

The Windows Modem Troubleshooter appears. Answer the questions to track down and correct common modem problems.

Click an option button to give your answer

Figure 29.3

Windows comes with a modem troubleshooter.

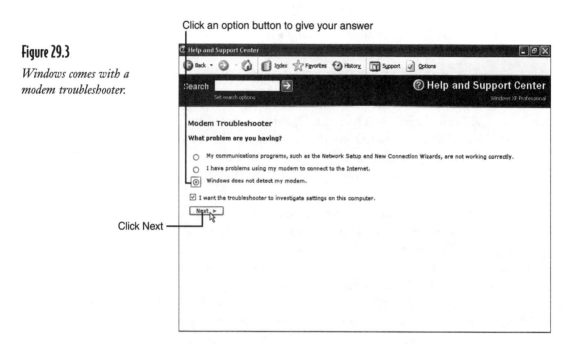

Click Next

My Printer Won't Print

If you run into printer problems, you probably have to do more fiddling than Nero. Look for the following:

◆ **Is your printer plugged in and turned on?**

◆ **Does your printer have paper?** Is the paper tray inserted properly?

◆ **Is the printer's online light on (not blinking)?** If the online light is off or blinking, press the On Line button to turn on the light.

◆ **Is your program set to print to a file?** Many Print dialog boxes have a Print to File option, which sends the document to a file on your disk instead of to the printer. Make sure this option is NOT checked.

◆ **Is the print fading?** If so, your printer may need a new toner or ink cartridge. If your inkjet cartridge has plenty of ink, check your printer manual to determine how to clean the print head. Inkjet cartridges have some sensitive areas that you should never clean, so be careful.

◆ **If you have an inkjet printer, check the print head and the area next to the print head for tape, and remove the tape.** Ink cartridges usually come with two pieces of tape on them. You must remove both pieces before installing the cartridge.

◆ **Is your printer marked as the default printer?** In My Computer, double-click the **Printers** icon. Right-click the icon for your printer and make sure that **Set as Default** is checked. If there is no check mark, select **Set as Default.**

◆ **Is the printer paused?** Double-click the **Printer** icon in the taskbar, open the **Printer** menu, and make sure that **Pause Printing** is not checked. If there is a check mark, click **Pause Printing.**

◆ **Is the correct printer port selected?** In My Computer, double-click the **Printers** icon and double-click the icon for your printer. Click the **Details** tab and make sure that the correct printer port is selected—LPT1 or USB in most cases.

◆ **Did you get only part of a page?** Laser printers are weird; they print an entire page at one time, storing the entire page in memory. If the page has a big complex graphic image or a lot of fonts, the printer may be able to store only a portion of the page. The best fix is to get more memory for your printer. The quickest fix is to use fewer fonts on the page and try using a less complex graphic image.

◆ **Is it a printer problem?** To determine whether the printer has a problem, go to the DOS prompt (choose **Start, Programs, MS-DOS prompt** or **Start, Programs, Accessories, MS-DOS prompt** or **Start, All Programs, Accessories, Command Prompt**), type **dir > lpt1** and press **Enter.** This prints the current directory list. If it prints okay, the problem is in the Windows printer setup. If the directory does not print or prints incorrectly, the problem is probably the printer. (Many printers have a button combination that you can press to have the printer perform a self-test. Check your printer manual.)

◆ If error messages keep popping up on your screen, Windows might be sending print instructions to the printer faster than your printer can handle them. In My Computer, double-click the **Printers** icon, and then right-click your printer's icon and choose **Properties.** Click the **Details** tab and increase the number of seconds in the **Transmission Retry** text box.

Updating the Software for Your Hardware

Computer hardware and software is in constant transition. Whenever Microsoft updates Windows, manufacturers have to ensure that the hardware they're coming out with works with the new operating system, and Microsoft does its best to make sure that the new operating system can handle most hardware devices. In this rush to get their products to market, the computer industry often releases products that contain bugs—imperfections that cause problems.

To help make up for these shortcomings, hardware manufacturers commonly release updated drivers for their devices. The driver works along with the operating system to control the device. You can solve many problems with your display, sound card, printer, joystick, modem, and other devices by installing an updated driver. The best way to get an updated driver is to download it from the Internet, as explained in Chapter 30. If you don't have an Internet connection and you suspect that a device driver is causing problems, call the manufacturer's technical support line and ask whether they have an updated driver. They can send it to you on a floppy disk.

> **Inside Tip**
>
> Windows 98 and more recent versions can check for updated drivers at Microsoft's Internet site and download the updated driver for you. To run it, open the **Start** menu and click **Windows Update** or click **Start, All Programs, Windows Update.**

> **Inside Tip**
>
> Some drivers come with their own installation program. Try changing to the disk and folder in which the driver file is stored and running the installation program.

After you have the updated driver, take the following steps to install it:

1. If you have the updated driver on a floppy disk, insert the disk.

2. Right-click **My Computer** and choose **Properties.**

3. Click the **Hardware** tab and then click the **Device Manager** button or click the **Device Manager** tab (in versions of Windows prior to Windows XP).

4. Click the plus sign next to the type of device that requires a new driver.

5. Double-click the name of the device.

6. Click the **Driver** tab and then click the **Update Driver** button.

7. Choose the option for searching for a better driver and click **Next.** If the driver is on a floppy disk, Windows finds it and prompts you to install it. Follow the onscreen instructions and skip the remaining steps.

8. If you downloaded the driver from the Internet, click the **Other Locations** button, choose the disk and folder where the driver file is stored, and click **OK.**

9. Follow the onscreen instructions to complete the installation.

The Least You Need to Know

◆ Use the **Ctrl+Alt+Del** sequence to thaw your computer when it freezes.

◆ Use System Restore to return your computer to an earlier time when it was working properly.

◆ Use the System Configuration Utility to troubleshoot problems caused by programs that run in the background.

◆ Don't go into shock when Windows starts in Safe mode. Shutting down and restarting your PC usually corrects the problem.

◆ If your printer won't print, check the cables and the online indicator. You can avoid most printer problems by making sure your printer has plenty of paper and is online before you start printing.

◆ Check regularly for Windows and device driver updates and install any updated drivers.

Help! Finding Technical Support

In This Chapter

♦ Prepare for your tech support phone call

♦ Find answers and updates on the web

♦ Have your computer tested online for free at PC Pitstop

In the previous chapter, you learned how to troubleshoot and correct most common computer problems. Unfortunately, not all glitches are so obvious or so easy to fix. A wrong setting in the Windows registry can crash your system whenever you run a certain application. A single typo in your Internet setup can prevent your computer from establishing a connection. A buggy device driver can lock up your system. To make matters worse, you might not be able to identify the cause of the problem at all. When a particularly frustrating problem arises, it's tempting to heave your computer out the window or take a sledge hammer to your monitor.

Before you do that, try one other solution: Contact the technical support (tech support) department for the program or device that's giving you problems. In this chapter, you learn the ins and outs of tech support—what they can and cannot help you with, what to ask, what information you should have ready, and how to find answers to common questions on the Internet.

Phone Support (Feeling Lucky?)

The documentation that came with your program or hardware device usually contains a phone number in the back for contacting technical support. It's usually printed really small to discourage people from calling. Flip through your manuals to find the number you need.

Before you call, be aware that the quality of technical support over the telephone varies widely from one company to another. Most places have a computerized system that asks you to answer a series of questions, usually leading to a dead end. Other places keep you on hold until you eventually give up and call a relative or friend for help. Yet, some tech support departments provide excellent, toll-free service, enabling you to talk with a qualified technician who can walk you through the steps required to solve your problem.

Even if you get to speak with a great tech support person, you need to be prepared. No tech support person can read your mind. You must be able to describe the problem you're having in some detail. Before you call, here's what you need to do:

◆ Write down a detailed description of the problem, explaining what went wrong and what you were doing at the time. If possible, write down the steps required to cause the problem again.

◆ Write down the name, version number, and license (or registration) number of the program with which you are having trouble. You can usually get this information by opening the **Help** menu in the problem program and choosing the **About...** command. Of course, this assumes you can run the program.

◆ Write down any information about your computer, including the computer brand, chip type (CPU) and speed, monitor type, amount of RAM, and the amount of free disk space. In Windows, open the **Start** menu, point to **All Programs** (or **Programs**), **Accessories, System Tools,** and click **System Information.** The opening System Information screen gives you most of the details you need.

◆ Make sure that your computer is turned on. A good tech support person can talk you through most problems if you're sitting at the keyboard.

◆ Make sure you're calling the right company. If you're having trouble with your printer, don't call Microsoft. If you even get through to a Microsoft Windows tech support person, the person will tell you to call the printer manufacturer.

◆ Don't call when you're angry. If you start screaming at the technical support person, the person is going to be less likely to offer quality help.

Finding Tech Support on the Web

Nearly every computer hardware and software company has its own website, where you can purchase products directly and find technical support for products you own. If your printer is not feeding paper properly, you're having trouble installing your sound card, you keep receiving cryptic error messages in your favorite program, or you have some other computer-related problem, you can usually find the solution on the Internet.

In addition, computer and software companies often upgrade their software and post both updates and fixes (called *patches*) on their websites for downloading. If you are having problems with a device, such as a printer or modem, you should check the manufacturer's website for updated drivers. If you run into problems with a program, check the software company's website for a patch—a program file that you install to correct the problem.

The following table provides web page addresses of popular software and hardware manufacturers to help you in your search. Most of the home pages listed have a link for connecting to the support page. If a page does not have a link to the support page, use its search tool to locate the page. You might also see a link labeled FAQs (frequently asked questions), Common Questions, or Top Issues. This link can take you to a page that lists the most common problems other users are having and answers from the company, as shown in Figure 30.1.

Computer Hardware and Software Websites

Company	Web Page Address
Acer	global.acer.com
Adaptec	www.adaptec.com
Adobe	www.adobe.com/support/main.html
ATI Technologies	www.ati.com
Borland	www.borland.com
Broderbund	support.broderbund.com
Brother	www.brother.com

continues

Computer Hardware and Software Websites (continued)

Company	Web Page Address
Canon	www.usa.canon.com
Compaq	www.compaq.com
Corel	www.corel.com
Creative Labs	www.americas.creative.com
Dell	www.dell.com
Epson	www.epson.com
Fujitsu	www.fujitsu.com
Gateway	www.gateway.com
Hewlett-Packard	www.hp.com
Hitachi	www.hitachipc.com
IBM	www.ibm.com/support/us/
Intel	www.intel.com
Intuit	www.intuit.com/support/quicken
Iomega	www.iomega.com
Lotus	www.lotus.com
MPC (Micron PC)	www.buympc.com
Microsoft	www.microsoft.com
Modem Express	www.modemexpress.com
Motorola	www.motorola.com
NEC	www.nec.com
Netscape	help.netscape.com
Packard Bell	www.packardbell.com
Panasonic	www.panasonic.com
Sony	www.sony.com
Texas Instruments	www.ti.com/corp/technical_support.htm
Toshiba	www.toshiba.com
3COM	www.3com.com

Figure 30.1

Check out the FAQs or Top Issues link for answers to common questions.

If the manufacturer you're looking for is not listed in this table, don't give up. Connect to your favorite web search page and search for the manufacturer by name or search for the problem you're having. You should also seek help from online computer magazines. Here are some excellent resources:

- ◆ **CNET Help.com at www.help.com** is a great place if you need technical support for Internet problems as well as hardware and software issues. It's also a great place to check out gaming information and obtain shareware programs.

- ◆ **Protonic at www.protonic.com** is a free online technical support service staffed by qualified volunteers that are eager to help other computer users solve their problems. Post your question and then check the site for answers.

- ◆ **Help2Go.com at www.help2go.com** is maintained by a community of computer users and features free tutorials, a Q&A area, and live support for your computer problems.

> **Inside Tip** _____
>
> Although manufacturers like to keep the tech support phone number a secret, they want you to know their web page address so that you can check out their other products. The website's technical support areas also cut down on calls to tech support.

Troubleshooting Problems with Diagnostic Software

When you purchase a computer, it doesn't come with its own technical support expert, but the manufacturer may include a diagnostic program that can identify common hardware problems. Gateway computers, for example, include a program called PC Doctor that examines the various components and settings, identifies defects, and offers to help you tweak your system to improve performance (check the **Start, All Programs, PC Doctor** menu). Dell computers include a Resource CD that features a diagnostics program for testing the various components that comprise the computer—memory, video card, disk drives, monitor, network card, modem, and so on. Most manufacturers also place an icon on the Windows **Start, All Programs** (or **Programs**) menu for accessing their online help system. Check the Windows menus and desktop for a support icon.

If your computer does not include a diagnostics program, you can purchase such a program or even have your computer examined on the Internet. An industrial strength program, such as PC Doctor Service Center, can be a little pricey (about $500), but if you plan on becoming a service technician or sharing the cost with some friends, it is well worth the investment. You can learn more about this program at www.pcdoctorstore.com. For a more affordable solution, check out TuffTest Pro at www.tufftest.com.

To have your computer examined on the Internet, go to www.pcpitstop.com. PC Pitstop can run a full series of tests on your computer and provide you with a rundown of problem areas and security issues, as shown in Figure 30.2. Best of all the test is free. PC Pitstop also provides links to online technical support (for a fee).

Figure 30.2

Drive your computer into PC Pitstop to have it examined online.

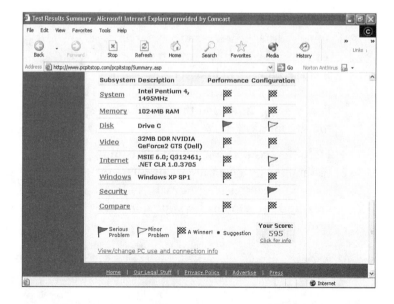

The Least You Need to Know

♦ Prepare for a productive phone conversation with a tech support person by having as much specific information about your PC and the problem before calling.

♦ Check out your computer manufacturer's tech support web page.

♦ Find technical support using computer magazines and support sites on the web.

♦ Use the diagnostics program that came with your computer, if you're fortunate enough to have such a program.

♦ Obtain a computer diagnostics program or have your computer tested online at PC Pitstop.

Speak Like a Geek: The Complete Archive

When you flip through computer documentation, books, and magazines, you might begin to feel as though you just stepped into the tomb of King Tut. How do you interpret the hieroglyphics stamped on your computer? How do you make sense of all the cryptic terms? Where can you get translations for the most common acronyms?

Well, you've come to the right place. Although this limited glossary can't possibly cover all the gobbledygook you'll encounter in the world of computers and the Internet, it does define enough basic terms to get you through your next job interview.

ADSL (asynchronous digital subscriber line) A communications technology that allows fast data transfers over standard copper phone lines. "Asynchronous" indicates that the system uses different data transfer rates for upstream and downstream communications—typically 32Mbps for downstream traffic and 32Kbps to 1Mbps for upstream traffic. ADSL is the most common type of DSL used in North America. *See also* DSL and SDSL.

attachment A file that's tacked on to an e-mail message. Attachments let users exchange files without having to use disks.

BIOS (basic input/output system) The built-in set of instructions that tells the computer how to control the disk drives, keyboard, printer port, and other components that make up your computer. Pronounced *BUY-ose*.

bit The basic unit of data in a computer. A computer's alphabet consists of two characters—1 and 0. 1 stands for on, and 0 stands for off. Bits are combined in sets
of eight to form real characters, such as A, B, C, and D. *See also* byte.

bits per second A unit for measuring the speed of data transmission. Remember that it takes 8 bits to make a byte (the equivalent of a single character). Modems have common bps ratings of 28,800 to 56,600.

boot   To start a computer and load its operating system software (usually Windows).

bps   *See* bits per second.

browser   *See* web browser.

burner   *See* CD burner.

bus   A superhighway that carries information electronically from one part of the computer to another. The wider and faster the bus (speed is measured in MHz), the faster your computer. The old ISA bus could carry 16 bits of data at a time; the newer PCI bus can carry 32 bits or 64 bits.

byte   A group of 8 bits that usually represents a character or a digit. For example, the byte 01000001 represents the letter A.

cable modem   A modem that supports high-speed connections to the Internet via a TV cable connection. (In order to use a cable modem, you must have a cable company that offers Internet service.) *See also* modem.

cache   A temporary storage area in memory or on disk that computer components and various programs use to quickly access data. Pronounced *cash*.

CD burner   A disc drive that lets you copy CDs and record tracks from audio CDs to blank CDs.

CD ripper   A program that reads tracks from an audio CD and converts them into a digital file format that your computer can play. Using a CD ripper, you can create your own music mixes on your computer, transfer them to a portable MP3 player, and (with a CD burner) record your mixes to blank CDs. *See also* MP3 and CD burner.

CD-R (compact disc recordable)   A storage technology in which a CD drive not only reads data from compact discs but also writes data to compact discs (special CD-R discs). A standard CD-ROM drive can only read data from a disc. *See also* CD-ROM and CD-RW.

CD-ROM (compact disk read-only memory)   A storage technology that uses the same kind of discs you play in an audio CD player for mass storage of computer data. A single disk can store more than 600MB of information. Pronounced *see-dee-rahm*. *See also* CD-R and CD-RW.

CD-RW (compact disk rewritable)   A storage technology in which a CD drive reads data from a compact disc, writes data to a disk, and erases data from discs (CD-RW discs) to make them reusable. *See also* CD-R and CD-ROM.

cell   The box formed by the intersection of a row (1,2,3...) and column (A,B,C...) in a spreadsheet. Each cell has an *address* (such as B12) that defines its column and row. A cell might contain text, a numeric value, or a formula.

chat   To talk to another person by typing at your computer. What you type appears on the other person's screen, and what the other person types appears on your screen. You can chat on the Internet or on an online service, such as America Online.

client   Of two computers, the computer that's being served. On the Internet or on a network, your computer is the client, and the computer to which you're connected is the *server*.

Clipboard   A temporary storage area in Windows that holds text and graphics. The **Cut** and **Copy** commands put text or graphics on the Clipboard, replacing the Clipboard's previous contents. The **Paste** command copies Clipboard data to a document.

COM port   Short for communications port. A receptacle, usually at the back of the computer, into which you can plug a serial device such as a modem, mouse, or serial printer.

command   An order that tells the computer what to do. In command-driven programs, you have to press a specific key or type the command to execute it. With menu-driven programs, you select the command from a menu.

computer   *See* PC (personal computer).

context menu   A list of commands or options that pops up on the screen when you right-click a selected object or highlighted text. Context menus contain only commands that pertain to the selected object or text.

cookie   An electronic identification "badge" that many websites store on your computer to help identify you when you return to the site or to record items you buy as you shop online.

CPU (central processing unit)   The computer's brain. *See also* microprocessor.

crash   The failure of a system or program. Usually, you realize that your system has crashed when you can't move the mouse pointer or type anything. The term *crash* is also used to refer to a disk crash (or head crash). A disk crash occurs when the read/write head in the disk drive falls on the disk, possibly destroying data.

cursor   *See* insertion point.

database   A type of computer program used to store, organize, and retrieve information. Popular database programs include Access, Approach, and Paradox.

default   The initial state of a setting or option. Most word processing programs, for example, are set up to print documents in portrait mode rather than in landscape mode. Portrait mode is said to be the default setting.

density   A measure of the amount of data that can be stored per square inch of storage area on a disk.

desktop   The main work area in Windows. The desktop displays several icons for running programs and accessing common Windows tools.

desktop publishing (DTP)   A program that lets you combine text and graphics on the same page and manipulate the text and graphics onscreen. Desktop publishing programs are commonly used to create newsletters, brochures, flyers, resumés, and business cards.

dialog box   An onscreen box that lets you enter your preferences or supply additional information. You use a dialog box to carry on a "conversation" with the program.

directory   A division of a disk or CD that contains a group of related files. Think of your disk as a filing cabinet, and think of each directory as a drawer in the cabinet. Directories are more commonly called *folders*.

disk   A round, flat, magnetic storage medium. A disk works like a cassette tape, storing files permanently so that you can play them back later. The disk itself is typically sealed inside a plastic case, so you rarely see the disk itself. *See* diskette and hard disk.

disk drive   A device that writes data to a magnetic disk and reads data from the disk. Think of a disk drive as a cassette recorder/player for a computer.

diskette   A wafer encased in plastic that stores magnetic data (the facts and figures you enter and save). You insert diskettes (also called *floppy disks*) into your computer's diskette drive (located on the front of the computer).

DOS (disk operating system)   DOS, which rhymes with "boss," is an old program that used to provide the necessary instructions for the computer's parts (keyboard, disk drive, central processing unit, display screen, printer, and so on) to function as a unit. Although Windows makes DOS nearly obsolete, you still see its name floating around in Windows.

DOS prompt   An onscreen prompt that indicates that DOS is ready to accept a command. It provides no clue as to what command you should type. It looks something like c> or c:\.

download   To copy files from another computer to your computer, usually through a modem. *See also* upload.

DSL (digital subscriber line)   Uses standard phone lines to achieve data transfer rates of up to 1.5Mbps (9Mbps if you're within two miles of an ADSL connection center). Phone companies hope that advances in DSL technology and availability will help them compete with cable companies for Internet access and entertainment. *See also* ADSL and SDSL.

DVD (digital versatile disc or digital video disc)   Discs that can store more than seven times as much data as a CD, making them useful for storing full-length movies and complete multimedia encyclopedias. DVD drives are designed to handle the discs of the future and are also designed to play discs of the past (CDs).

DVD-R (digital versatile disc recordable)   A storage technology in which a DVD drive not only reads data from discs but also writes data to discs (special DVD-R discs). A standard DVD drive can only read data from a disc. *See also* DVD and DVD-RW.

DVD-RW (digital versatile disc rewritable)   A storage technology in which a DVD drive reads data from a disc, writes data to a disc, and erases data from discs (DVD-RW discs) to make them reusable. *See also* DVD and DVD-R.

e-mail   Short for electronic mail. E-mail is a system that lets people send messages to and receive messages from other computers. E-mail is available on networks, online information services, and the Internet.

emoticon   A text-only symbol commonly used in e-mail messages and chat rooms to quickly express an emotion or physical gesture. :), for instance, represents a smile.

Ethernet   A common local area network (LAN) protocol developed by Xerox Corporation that allows computers to communicate over network connections. Ethernet supports connection speeds of up to 10Mbps. 100BASE-T Ethernet supports speeds of up to 100Mbps, and Gigabit Ethernet supports speeds of up to 1 gigabit per second. *See also* LAN, Mbps, and Ethernet adapter.

Ethernet adapter   An expansion card that allows a computer to be connected to an Ethernet local area network. *See also* Ethernet, LAN, and expansion board.

executable file   A program file that can run the program. Executable files end in .BAT, .COM, or .EXE.

expansion board   A printed circuit board that plugs into a computer's motherboard and is designed to add a specific capability to a computer. Common expansion boards include modems, sound cards, and video accelerators. *See also* expansion slot and motherboard.

expansion card   *See* expansion board.

expansion slot   An opening on the motherboard (inside the system unit) that lets you add devices to the system unit, such as an internal modem, sound card, video accelerator, or other enhancement. *See also* expansion board.

extension   The portion of a file name that comes after the period. Every file name consists of two parts—the base name (before the period) and the extension (after the period). The file name can have up to eight characters in DOS and Windows 3.x and can have up to 255 characters in Windows 95 and later. The extension (which is optional) almost always consists of three characters.

field   A blank in a database record into which you can enter a piece of information (such as a telephone number, a ZIP code, or a person's last name).

file   A collection of information stored as a single unit on a floppy or hard disk. Files always have a file name to identify them.

file format   An organizational scheme for the data that makes up a file. The simplest file format is text-only, which stores data as typed characters. Program files, graphics, audio-video files, and other file types are more complex and are stored as *binary* files in various formats. You can determine a file's format by looking at its file-name extension. A graphics file, for instance, might be stored as a PCX, GIF, or JPG file.

File Transfer Protocol (FTP)   A set of rules that governs the exchange of files between two computers on the Internet.

fixed disk drive   A disk drive that has an unremovable disk, as opposed to floppy drives, in which you insert and remove disks.

flame war   A war of words between two or more people, typically waged in newsgroups or via e-mail.

floppy disk   *See* diskette.

folder   The Windows name for a directory, a division of a hard disk or CD that stores a group of related files. *See also* directory.

font   Any set of characters of the same *typeface* (design) and *type size* (measured in points). For example, Times New Roman 12-point is a font, Times New Roman is the typeface, and 12-point is the size. (There are 72 points in an inch.)

footer   Text that appears at the bottom of every page of a document. Footers are commonly used to insert the title of the document, the date on which it was composed, and page numbers. *See also* header.

format (disk)   To prepare a disk for storing data. Formatting creates a map on the disk that tells the operating system how the disk is structured. The operating system uses this map to keep track of where files are stored.

format (document)   To establish a document's physical layout, including page size, margins, headers and footers, line spacing, text alignment, graphics placement, and so on.

format (file)   *See* file format.

FTP   *See* File Transfer Protocol.

function keys   The 10 or 12 F keys on the left side of the keyboard, or the 12 F keys at the top of the keyboard (some keyboards have both). F keys are numbered F1, F2, F3, and so on, and you can use them to enter specified commands in a program.

GB   *See* gigabyte.

gigabyte   A thousand megabytes. Often abbreviated as GB. *See also* megabyte.

hard disk   A disk drive that has an unremovable disk. It acts as a giant floppy disk drive and usually sits inside your computer.

Hayes-compatible   A modem that uses the Hayes command set to communicate with other modems over the phone lines. Hayes-compatible modems usually are preferred over other modems because most modems and telecommunications software are designed to be Hayes-compatible.

header   Text that appears at the top of every page of a document. Headers are commonly used to insert the title of the document, the date on which it was composed, and page numbers. *See also* footer.

highlight   To select text in order to cut, copy, delete, move, or format it. When you highlight text, it typically appears white on a black background.

history list   A list of the names and addresses of websites and pages you've accessed with your web browser. Your web browser keeps a history list so that you can quickly return to sites even if you've forgotten a site's address.

HTML (Hypertext Markup Language)   The code used to create documents for the World Wide Web. These codes tell the web browser how to display the text (titles, headings, lists, and so on), insert anchors that link this document to other documents, and control character formatting (by making it bold or italic).

hyperlink   Icons, pictures, or highlighted text commonly used on web pages and in help systems that point to other resources. On web pages, text hyperlinks typically appear blue and underlined.

icon A graphic image onscreen (a tiny picture) that represents another object, such as a file on a disk. Icons can be found almost everywhere in Windows: on the desktop, on toolbars, on menus, and in dialog boxes. Icons commonly represent applications, utilities, disks, folders, and files.

IM (instant message) A private message that reaches the recipient almost immediately after the user sends it. IMs are commonly used in America Online to communicate privately with other users.

insertion point A blinking vertical line used in most Windows word processors to indicate the place where any characters you type are inserted. An insertion point is equivalent to a cursor.

instant message *See* IM (instant message).

interface A link between two objects, such as a computer and a modem. The link between a computer and a person is called a user interface and refers to the way a person communicates with the computer or a program.

Internet A group of computers all over the world that are connected to each other. Using your computer and a modem, you can connect to these other computers and tap their resources. You can view pictures, listen to sounds, watch video clips, play games, chat with other people, and even shop.

Internet service provider (ISP) The company that you pay in order to connect to their computer and get on the Internet.

IRC (Internet Relay Chat) The most popular way to chat with others on the Internet. With an IRC client (chat program), you connect to an IRC server, where you are presented with a list of available chat rooms. You can enter a room and then start exchanging messages with others in the room.

ISDN (Integrated Services Digital Network) A system that allows your computer, using a special ISDN modem, to perform digital data transfers over special phone lines. Non-ISDN modems use analog signals, which are designed to carry voices, not data. ISDN connections can transfer data at a rate of up to 128Kbps, compared to about 56Kbps for the fastest analog modems.

ISP *See* Internet service provider.

Kbps (kilobits per second) A unit used to express data transfer rates, typically for modems. A kilobit is equivalent to 1,000 bits. *See also* bits per second.

keyboard The main input device for most computers. You use the keyboard to type and to enter commands.

kilobyte   A unit for measuring the amount of data. A kilobyte is equivalent to 1,024 bytes (each byte is a character). Kilobyte is commonly abbreviated as K, KB, or Kbyte.

LAN (local area network)   A system of interconnected computers designed to let users share hardware, software, and data and to communicate with each other via e-mail. A LAN is typically confined to a limited area, such as an office, building, or small group of buildings. *See also* WAN.

laptop   A small computer that's light enough to carry. Notebook computers and sub-notebooks are even lighter.

link   *See* hyperlink.

log off   To disconnect from a network or from the Internet.

log on   To enter your user name and password in order to establish a connection to a network or the Internet. *See also* user name.

mail merge   A feature of most word processing programs that allows you to link an address book with a form letter or mailing label document to generate a set of personalized form letters and/or mailing labels.

mail server   A computer on a network whose job it is to receive and store incoming mail and route outgoing mail to the proper e-mail boxes on other mail servers. *See also* e-mail.

Mbps (megabits per second)   A unit used to express data transfer rates for high-speed communications. A megabit is equivalent to 1,000,000 bits. *See also* bits per second.

megabyte   A standard unit used to measure the storage capacity of a disk and the amount of computer memory. A megabyte is 1,048,576 bytes (1,000 kilobytes). This is roughly equivalent to 500 pages of double-spaced text. Megabyte is commonly abbreviated as M, MB, or Mbyte.

memory   An electronic storage area inside the computer used to temporarily store data or program instructions when the computer is using them. Also referred to as RAM.

menu   A vertical listing of commands or instructions displayed onscreen. Menus organize commands and make a program easier to use. Most applications' menus appear on a menu bar, a band near the top of the application's window. To open a menu, you click its name on the menu bar. *See also* context menu.

microprocessor   Sometimes called the central processing unit (CPU) or processor, this chip is the computer's brain; it does all the calculations for the computer.

modem   An acronym for modulator/demodulator. A modem is a piece of hardware that converts incoming signals (from a phone line, cable service, or other source) into signals that a PC can understand and converts outgoing signals from the PC into a form that can be transmitted.

monitor   A televisionlike screen on which the computer displays information.

motherboard   The main printed circuit board inside a computer through which all other devices communicate. The printed circuit board contains the microprocessor and memory chips, expansion slots for plugging in accessories, and connections for the disk drives and other devices. *See also* microprocessor, memory, expansion slot, and expansion board.

mouse   A handheld device that you move across the desktop to move an arrow, called the mouse pointer, across the screen. You can use the mouse to move the insertion point (or cursor), select and move items (such as text and graphics), open menus, execute commands, and perform other tasks.

MP3   Short for *MPEG audio layer 3*. A digital audio format that compresses audio files to one-twelfth their original size with an imperceptible loss of quality.

MPEG   Short for *Moving Pictures Experts Group*. An assembly that sets standards for digital video recording and file formats.

MS-DOS (Microsoft Disk Operating System)   *See* DOS.

network   A system of interconnected computers designed to allow users to share hardware, software, and data. *See also* LAN and WAN.

network protocol   *See* protocol.

newsgroup   An Internet bulletin board for users who share common interests. There are thousands of newsgroups, ranging from body art to pets (to body art with pets). Newsgroups let you post messages and read messages from other users.

notebook   A portable computer that weighs between 4 and 8 pounds.

online service   A network that allows members to obtain information, communicate, and get files via a modem connection. Common online services include America Online, Prodigy, and CompuServe.

option button   A circle next to a setting that indicates whether the setting is on or off. You can select only one option in a group of options. If you select an option other than the option that is currently selected, the option you select is turned on, and the other option is turned off. *See also* check box.

parallel port   A connector used to plug a device, usually a printer, into the computer.

partition   A section of a disk drive that's assigned a letter. A hard disk drive can be divided (partitioned) into one or more drives, which your computer refers to as drive C, drive D, drive E, and so on. The actual hard disk drive is called the physical drive, and each partition is called a logical drive; however, these terms don't matter much—the drives still look like letters to you.

patch   A set of program instructions designed to fix a programming bug or add capabilities to a program. On the Internet, you can often download patches for programs to update the program.

path   The route that the computer travels from the root directory to any subdirectories when locating a file.

PC (personal computer)   A computer designed to help a user perform practical tasks, such as typing documents and performing calculations. PCs are much smaller and less powerful than mainframe computers. The term *PC* is commonly used to refer to computers that run Windows or Linux, as opposed to Apple computers, which run Mac OS.

PC card   An expansion card that's about the size of a credit card, but thicker. It slides into a slot on the side of a notebook computer. PC cards let you quickly install RAM or a hard disk drive, modem, CD-ROM drive, network card, or game port without having to open the notebook computer. *See also* PCMCIA.

PCMCIA (Personal Computer Memory Card International Association)   An organization that sets standards for notebook computer expansion cards. These credit-card-size expansion boards originally were designed to add memory to laptop computers but are now used to add modems, network connections, digital video cameras, USB ports, and other devices. *See also* PC card.

peripheral   A device that's attached to the computer but is not essential for the computer's basic operation. The system unit is the central part of the computer. Any devices attached to the system unit are considered peripheral, including a printer, modem, or joystick. Some manufacturers consider the monitor and keyboard to be peripheral, too.

pixel   A dot of light that appears on the computer screen. A collection of pixels forms characters and images on the screen.

Plug-and-Play   *See* PnP (Plug-and-Play).

PnP (Plug-and-Play)   PnP lets you install expansion cards in your computer without having to set special switches. You plug it in, and it works.

pointer   *See* mouse pointer.

port   A receptacle at the back of the computer. It gets its name from the ports where ships pick up and deliver cargo. In this case, a port allows information to enter and leave the system unit.

PPP (Point-to-Point Protocol)   A language that computers use to talk to one another. What's important is that when you choose an Internet service provider, you get the right connection—SLIP or PPP.

processor   *See* microprocessor.

program   A group of instructions that tells the computer what to do. Typical programs are word processors, spreadsheets, databases, and games.

prompt   A computer's way of asking for more information. The computer basically looks at you and says, "Tell me something." In other words, the computer is prompting you or prodding you for information or a command.

protocol   A group of communications settings that controls the transfer of data between two computers.

pull-down menu   A menu that appears near the top of the screen, on the menu bar, listing various options. A menu's contents are not visible until you click the menu. The menu then drops down, covering a small part of the screen.

random access memory (RAM)   A collection of chips your computer uses to store data and programs temporarily. RAM is measured in kilobytes and megabytes. In general, more RAM means that you can run more powerful programs and more programs at once. Also called memory.

record   Used by databases to denote a unit of related information contained in one or more fields, such as an individual's name, address, and phone number.

Recycle Bin   A virtual trash can into which Windows places files and folders when you choose to delete them. The Recycle Bin is a temporary storage area that acts as a safety net for deleted files. If you delete a file or folder by mistake, you can usually retrieve it from the Recycle Bin.

ripper   *See* CD ripper.

ROM BIOS   *See* BIOS.

scanner   A device that converts images, such as photographs or printed text, into an electronic format that a computer can use. Many stores use a special type of scanner to read bar code labels into the cash register.

screen saver   A program that displays a moving picture on your computer screen when the computer is inactive. Screen savers are typically used as decorative novelties and to prevent passersby from snooping.

Screen Tip *See* tooltip.

scroll To move text up and down or right and left on a computer screen.

scrollbar A band, typically displayed along the bottom and right edge of a window, used to bring the contents of the window into view.

SDSL (synchronous digital subscriber line) A communications technology that allows fast data transfers over standard copper phone lines. "Synchronous" indicates that the system uses the same data transfer rates for both upstream and downstream traffic. In Europe, SDSL (Symmetric DSL) is most common. SDSL lines use the same data transfer rates for both upstream and downstream traffic. *See also* DSL and ADSL.

server Of two computers, the computer that's serving the other computer. On the Internet or on a network, your computer is the *client*, and the computer to which you're connected is the *server*.

shareware Computer programs you can use for free and then pay for if you decide to continue using them. Many programmers start out by marketing their programs as shareware, relying on the honesty and goodwill of computer users for their income. That's why most of these programmers have day jobs.

shortcut A cloned version of an icon that points to a document or program on your computer. Shortcuts let you place programs and documents in more than one convenient location on your computer.

software Any instructions that tell your computer (the hardware) what to do. There are two types of software: operating system software and application software. Operating system software (such as Windows) gets your computer up and running. Application software lets you do something useful, such as type a letter or manage your finances. Other types of software include games and utilities (programs for maintaining and optimizing your computer).

spin box A control in a dialog box that displays an up and down arrow for changing a setting incrementally. In most cases, you can type a specific setting in the spin box or click the arrows to increase or decrease the setting. For example, you might use a spin box to adjust a document's margin settings by tenths of an inch.

spreadsheet A program used for keeping schedules and calculating numeric results. Common spreadsheets include Lotus 1-2-3, Microsoft Excel, and Quattro Pro.

Start button The button in the lower-left corner of the opening Windows screen that provides access to all the programs on your computer.

status bar   The area at the bottom of a program window that shows you what's going on as you work. A status bar might show the page and line number where the insertion point is positioned and indicate whether you are typing in overstrike or insert mode.

style   A collection of specifications for formatting text. A style might include information on the font, size, style, margins, and spacing. Applying a style to text automatically formats the text according to the style's specifications.

surge suppressor   A device that prevents power spikes and dips from damaging a computer and its peripheral devices.

system tray   The area on the right end of the taskbar that displays the current time, as well as icons for programs that are running in the background.

system unit   The central component of any computer, the system unit contains the computer's CPU, memory, disk drives, and other essential components. *See* CPU.

tab stop   A setting commonly used in a word processor that specifies where the insertion point will land when you press the **Tab** key. Tab stops are typically set at a half-inch, unless you change them.

table   A feature in most word processing programs that helps you align text in rows and columns.

taskbar   A fancy name for the button bar at the bottom of the Windows desktop. The taskbar includes the **Start** button (on the left) and the system tray (on the right).

TCP/IP (Transmission Control Protocol/Internet Protocol)   A set of rules that governs the transfer of data over the Internet.

text box   (1) A rectangular area commonly found in dialog boxes and on forms into which you type specific entries. When you choose to save a file, for instance, you type a name for the file in the **File name** text box. (2) A box that can be drawn on a document to hold text that's separate from the document. In desktop publishing programs, you can enter text into various text boxes and then arrange the text boxes on a page.

toolbar   A strip of buttons typically displayed near the top of a program window, below the menu bar. The toolbar contains buttons that you can click to enter common commands, allowing you to bypass the menu system.

tooltip   A small text box that displays the name of a button when you rest the mouse pointer on the button. Tooltips help you figure out what a button does when you can't figure it out from the picture. Also known as a Screen Tip.

undo   A feature in most programs that lets you reverse one or more actions. For example, if you delete a paragraph by mistake, you can choose the **Undo** command to get it back.

uninterruptible power supply (UPS)   A battery-powered device that protects against power spikes and power outages. If the power goes out, the UPS continues supplying power to the computer so that you can continue working or safely turn off your computer without losing data.

upload   To send data to another computer, usually through a modem and a telephone line or over a network connection.

URL (Uniform Resource Locator)   An address for an Internet site.

USB (Universal Serial Bus)   The ultimate in plug-and-play technology, USB lets you install devices without turning off your computer or using a screwdriver. USB lets you connect up to 127 devices to a single port. *See also* hot swappable.

user name   A unique name you choose or have assigned to you by a network administrator, commercial online service, or Internet provider. Your user name gives you access to the network or system and provides you with an identity that other people can use to contact you.

utility   A program designed to optimize, protect, or maintain a computer rather than perform a task for the user. Utilities include backup programs, antivirus software, and memory optimizers.

video capture   The process of transferring video clips to your computer (using a camcorder or VCR) and storing the video as a file on a hard disk or CD.

virtual   Not real. Virtual worlds on the Internet are three-dimensional computer-generated areas that you can navigate but never physically enter—unless, of course, you're Keanu Reeves or Sandra Bullock.

virtual memory   Disk storage used as RAM (memory).

virus   A program that attaches itself to files on a floppy or hard disk, duplicates itself without the user's knowledge, and might cause the computer to do strange and sometimes destructive things, such as reformatting your hard drive.

wallpaper   A graphic design that appears as the background for the Windows desktop.

WAN (wide area network)   A system of interconnected LANs (local area networks) typically set up to let users exchange e-mail and share data over greater distances. *See also* LAN.

web   *See* World Wide Web.

web browser   A program that lets you navigate the World Wide Web (the most popular feature of the Internet). *See also* World Wide Web.

web server   A computer on a network whose job it is to make web pages available upon request. When you use a web browser to open web pages, you connect to a web server.

Wi-fi   A wireless network standard for connecting computers via radio-frequency signals rather than network cables.

windows   A way of displaying information on different parts of the screen. When spelled with an uppercase "W," used as a shortened form of "Microsoft Windows."

wizard   A series of dialog boxes that lead you step by step through the process of performing a task.

word processor   A program that lets you enter, edit, format, and print text.

word wrap   A feature that automatically moves a word to the next line if the word won't fit at the end of the current line.

worksheet   Another common name for a spreadsheet. *See* spreadsheet.

World Wide Web   A part of the Internet that consists of multimedia documents that are interconnected by links. To move from one document to another, you click a link, which might appear as highlighted text or an icon. The web contains text, sound and video clips, pictures, catalogs, and much more. *See also* web browser.

Index

Symbols

#1 Free Clip Art website, 277
2 pages per sheet (margins), 159
3COM website, 386
? button (dialog boxes), 31
;(, ;-((crying), 231
:->, :> (devilish grin), 231
:-|, :| (don't care), 231
:-), :) (happy), 230
%-) (I've been at this too long), 231
:-D, :D (laughing), 230
:-#, :# (my lips are sealed), 231
< > (no comment), 231
:-/, :/ (skeptical, 231
;^) (smirking), 231
:-P, :p (sticking my tongue out, 231
:-(, :((unhappy), 230
;-), ;) (winking), 230

A

A drives, 62
ABC News website, 258
accounts
    .Net passports, 48-49
    administrator, 40-41
    guest, 45
    limited, 41
    user, 10
        adding, 40-42
        deleting, 45
        icons, 43-44
        passwords, 42-43

AccuPoint pointers, 23
AccuWeather, 260
Acer website, 385
active desktop, 88-90
Adaptec website, 385
adapters
    Ethernet, 202
    four-headed input, 336
Add New Hardware dialog box, 11
Add New Hardware Wizard, 11-12
Add/Remove Programs utility, 120-121
adding
    .Net passports, 48-49
    audio
        events, 96
        movies, 341
    clip art, 140
    digitized images, 143-145
    field codes, 169-173
    formulas, 184-185
    guest accounts, 45
    images to e-mail, 228
    passwords, 42-43
    pictures, 330
    text to images, 149-150
    user accounts, 40-42
address book data source, 167-168
Address toolbar, 101
Address.com, 211, 230
addresses
    e-mail, 212, 225
    web pages, 249-250
administrator accounts, 40-41
Adobe website, 385

ADSL (Asynchronous DSL), 200
AFAIK (as far as I know), 231
Align Left (text), 130
Align Right (text), 130
Alt keys, 16
Altavista, 251
Amazon, 312
America Online. See AOL
Ameritrade website, 264
anti-static pads, 7
antivirus protection, 295-296
AOL (America Online), 206
    chat rooms, 236
    Parental Controls, 288-290
applications. See programs
apply to margins, 159
arranging. See moving
ArtToday website, 278
as far as I know (AFAIK), 231
Ask.com, 250
Associated Press website, 259
Asynchronous DSL (ADSL), 200
ATI Technologies website, 385
attachments (e-mail), 228-229
auctions online, 268
audio
    CD/MP3 basics, 304-305
    clips
        downloading, 310
        finding, 310-312
        mixing, 317-318
        MP3s, copying, 314-315
        playing, 313
        portable, 312

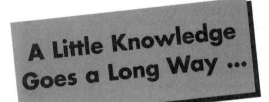
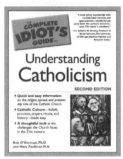

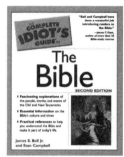